INTENTIONALITY
Past and Future

Edited by
Gábor Forrai and George Kampis

Amsterdam - New York, NY 2005

Cover Design: Studio Pollmann

The paper on which this book is printed meets the requirements of "ISO
9706:1994, Information and documentation - Paper for documents -
Requirements for permanence".

ISBN: 90-420-1817-8
©Editions Rodopi B.V., Amsterdam - New York, NY 2005
Printed in the Netherlands

CONTENTS

Contents

PREFACE

The present volume has grown out of a conference organized jointly by the History of Philosophy Department of the University of Miskolc and the History and Philosophy of Science Department of Eötvös Loránd University (Budapest), which took place in June 2002. The aim of the conference was to explore the various angles from which intentionality can be studied, how it is related to other philosophical issues, and how it figures in the works of major philosophers in the past. It also aimed at facilitating the interaction between the analytic and phenomenological traditions, which both regard intentionality as one of the most important problems for philosophy. Indeed intentionality has sometimes provided inspiration for works bridging the gap between the two traditions, like Roderick Chisholm's in the sixties and Dagfin Føllesdall's and his students' in the early eighties. These objectives were also instrumental in the selection of the papers for this volume. Instead of very specialized papers on narrow issues, we gave preference to papers with a broader focus, which (1) juxtapose different approaches and traditions or (2) link the issues of intentionality with other philosophical concerns.

The organization of the conference and the publication of the present volume were supported by grants from two Hungarian foundations, the National Foundation for Scientific Research (OTKA) and the National Research and Development Program (NKFP). The editors also wish to thank the contributors for their kind cooperation.

Gábor Forrai
George Kampis

LIST OF ABBREVIATIONS

Chapter Two

PES: Brentano, Franz Clemens. (1955) *Psychologie vom Empirischen Standpunkt*. Edited by Oskar Kraus. Also (1995a) *Psychology from an Empirical Standpoint*. Translated by Antos C. Rancurello, D. B. Terrell, and Linda L. McAlister. London: Routledge.

DP: Brentano, Franz Clemens. (1982) *Deskriptive Psychologie*. Edited by Roderick Milton Chisholm and Wilhelm Baumgartner. Hamburg: Felix Meiner. Also (1995b) *Descriptive Psychology*. Translated by Benito Müller. London: Routledge.

Chapter Four

References to John Locke (1975) *An Essay Concerning Human Understanding*. Edited by Peter Harold Nidditch. Oxford: Oxford University Press, 1975, will be expressed in terms of book, chapter, and section, *e.g.*, (Locke, 1975, 1.1.8).

Chapter Five

KW: Refers to the work of Ludwig Wittgenstein as interpreted by Saul Kripke.

Chapter Eight

DT: Disjunctive Theory of Perception
IT: Internalist Thesis
PP: Phenomenal Principle
TT: Transparency Thesis

One

THE NECESSITY AND NATURE
OF MENTAL CONTENT

Laird Addis

1. Introduction

The philosopher of our time who would attempt to understand the nature of mind is, if he or she is a thinker of reasonable sensitivity, inevitably moved by two overarching and, so some may think, contrary constraints, one very old and the other more recent, at least in details. The older one is that consciousness is something unique, something quite different from everything else in the known universe, that a universe with consciousness and one without it are radically different kinds of worlds. Even if the only consciousness in existence were the perceptions of simple insects, there would still be a phenomenon in the world that seems to be quite unlike any in a world altogether without consciousness. The apparent implication of this constraint or, seen positively, this imperative is that any adequate philosophy of mind must reflect, at the basic ontological analysis of consciousness, the uniqueness of mind.

The other constraint, or imperative, is that consciousness is of a piece with nature generally and seems to exist only in intimate conjunction with or, some would say, in identity with highly organized pieces of matter. More generally, any adequate philosophy of mind must be fully consistent with the presuppositions, methods, and findings of empirical science and especially with those of evolutionary biology and the processes of natural selection. I would add, more contentiously, especially in these times of so-called intelligent-design theory, that the best theory of mind must be consistent with a conception of the mind as a product of purely natural processes, that is, of evolution as an unintended, lawfully explainable sequence of events that has taken, and is taking, place on our planet and, possibly, elsewhere. The apparent implication of this constraint is to deny or to disregard the uniqueness of mind and to seek an ontology of mind whose basic categories are no more than those of a world without mind.

Although it is not my main topic here, I state without hesitation or doubt my belief that the best philosophy of mind must reflect the uniqueness of consciousness at the basic ontological level but in a way that is fully consistent with a purely naturalistic worldview backed by the theory and fact of evolution. This sort of strategy guides the remarks that follow. If the phenomenon of consciousness is essential to what it is to have a mind, then the essence of consciousness is, in turn, characterized by its intentionality. Let us see.

2. Intentionality

Let us all imagine that the planet Mars has just exploded. If you have heard and understood what I just said, an event took place "in" you in some sense of "in" that is the event of your imagining that Mars has just exploded. You knew, and still know, that this event took place; and you know, too, that it was only an imagining and not, say, a perceiving of Mars exploding. You knew, and still know, that it was Mars and not, say, Jupiter you were imagining to have exploded.

What is the nature of this event that took place in each of us of imagining that Mars has just exploded; and what significance should we give to the immediate knowledge or, if you prefer, the semblance—genuine or not—of the immediate knowledge that each of us had of the occurrence of that event "in" us? My focus in this paper is on that aspect of the kind of event that took place in each of us that, still pre-analytically speaking, that is its content, that part somehow alluded to by the words "that the planet Mars has just exploded" in the slightly longer expression "imagining that the planet Mars has just exploded." The distinction in a mental state of this kind, between its content on the one hand, and its mode—in this case its being an imagining—on the other, is a familiar one and indeed one of common sense. Yet only a few philosophers, especially among those of the analytic tradition, have attended explicitly to the ontological analysis of both of these features of events like imagining that Mars has just exploded, that is, of intentional states and events.

Let us ignore for the time being those accounts of mentality that treat intentional states as mere states of the brain either directly as in simple identity theory, or more circumspectly as in functionalism or any other forms of causal theories of the mind, or merely as ascribed states to others in order to explain their behavior. I will proceed by stating and defending an ontological account of intentional states and, more narrowly, of mental content, and then later examine some direct competitors to, and some direct criticisms of, theories of mental content like mine. I begin with a specification of just what mental states and events are intentional states and events.

Because when I do philosophy of mind, I speak ontologically and not linguistically, I exclude dispositional mental states as being genuinely intentional states. Persons who are asleep or even unconscious have dispositional mental states, such as the belief that whales are mammals. I treat such mental states as dispositions both to some kinds of behaviors and to some kinds of occurrent mental states. Occurrent mental states figure in the characterization of dispositional mental states in much the same way that the property of dissolving-in-water figures in the property of being soluble: not as constituent (for something can be soluble without dissolving), but as definitional realization. In its inner nature, a dispositional mental state is, in us anyway, just a state of the brain as subject to laws, and as such, is lacking in literal intentionality.

I have argued elsewhere that other occurrent mental states including the having of sensations, moods, and emotions are the only mental entities that have genuine, or literal, or what some call intrinsic intentionality (Addis, 1986). Indeed, a major thesis of this paper is that literal and fundamental intentionality pertains only to those occurrent mental states in us and other conscious beings that constitute what we call "the stream of consciousness." So I affirm the unique intrinsic intentionality of occurrent mental states, not only in contrast with dispositional mental states, but also with the many other kinds of things and events to which we ascribe aboutness—language above all, but also pictures, maps, blueprints, artworks, religious and national symbols, gestures, computer programs, and much more.

My main purpose of the moment is to delimit the class of mental things that are literally intentional; and along these lines, I want to note that we sometimes refer to occurrent mental states as conscious mental states in order to contrast them with dispositional mental states, but that "conscious" is contrasted not only with "dispositional" but also with "unconscious." The notion of unconscious mental states is, in turn, sometimes taken to mean a subset of dispositional mental states, those that are realized in some kinds of abnormal behaviors and occurrent mental states, but sometimes also as a subset of occurrent mental states themselves, those of which the person is not, or perhaps cannot become, consciously aware. We thereby have the awkwardness of unconscious mental states being among the set of conscious mental states when we take the latter as the set of all those events that constitute the "stream of consciousness." Once we are fully aware of this terminological oddity, living with it is easier than attempting to remove it.

Returning to the notion of mental content itself—that feature of occurrent mental states that is or grounds their intentionality—we all know that it has, after a long period of dormancy in the analytic side of the tradition, again become popular in philosophy even if it sometimes takes quite bizarre forms. When we look at the subject historically, until quite recently the notion of mental content has always been that of something in the mind of the person who is aware that correlates uniquely with the object of awareness. So characterized, content may be what is called form by Aristotle and Thomas Aquinas (although the form gets us only to the kind of thing of which we are aware), ideas (*idées*) by René Descartes and many others of the early modern period, *Inhalt* by Alexius Meinong (1899) and others of the Austrian school of the act, matter (*Materie*) by Edmund Husserl (1971), propositions by Gustav Bergmann (1960), or representative content as in John Searle (1983), and so on.

Still speaking only historically, until the twentieth century no philosopher explicitly and probably none even implicitly denied that there is mental content as something in the mind of the person who is aware. Therefore, nearly none of them felt called upon to argue for the existence of mental content so conceived. Meinong is sometimes credited, as I myself have done, with having made the first explicit arguments for mental content in his famous paper of 1899, but probably the honor for this effort should go to Kasimir Twardowski in his rich and unjustly ignored book of 1894 (1977).

Meinong's and Twardowski's arguments for mental content are not good arguments, and I will not rehearse them. I present what I think are good arguments for the existence and specific nature of mental content. First I want to remark on the fact that three of the most important philosophers, Husserl, Bergmann, and Searle, who have explicitly affirmed an analysis of intentional states as consisting of, or involving the exemplification of, two kinds of properties—a mode property (Husserl's *Qualität*, Bergmann's species, Searle's psychological mode) and an intentional property—never made explicit arguments for this analysis.

In Husserl's and Bergmann's cases, they appear to have believed that we are, or can be, directly acquainted with instances of these kinds of properties, and so no argument would be necessary. In Searle's case, whether he is speaking ontologically or only grammatically is unclear. He may be doing no more than merely calling attention to, and reaffirming, the commonsense way of speaking about intentional states, in which case again no argument would be necessary.

This stance is puzzling because there is a widespread and quite natural tendency among philosophers to treat the mode feature of intentional states as a relation between the person and the object of awareness, as indeed grammar strongly and unfortunately suggests, instead of, as all three philosophers maintain, a monadic property of awarenesses. More important for our purposes, this stance is puzzling because two of the most important philosophers of the twentieth century—Bertrand Russell (1956) and Jean-Paul Sartre (1957)—each in his distinctive way denied the existence of mental content. It becomes imperative, even if none of the three did it, to provide arguments for the existence of mental content while at the same time providing a precise and defensible ontological analysis of what they have argued exists.

Here I can only sketch three arguments that I have made in detail elsewhere (Addis, 1989), wanting to have time also to criticize the Russell/Sartre theory and any theory of purely "external" content and to reply to some criticisms of any theory like mine, especially those of Hilary Putnam. I begin by noting a crucial feature of my conception of mental content and introduce an expression to capture that feature. The feature is that of being such that the content by its intrinsic nature and not by habit, convention, causal or other relation to something else, represents whatever it does represent. The expression, taken from William of Occam's *signum naturale* (1957), is that of natural sign. So I will speak of the three arguments for the existence of natural signs. Let us keep in mind that this is not the much more common use of the expression in which, for example, smoke is a natural sign of fire, and of which Ruth Garrett Millikan (1993) makes significant use in her theory of mind. I have labeled my three arguments as the scientific, the phenomenological, and the dialectical; and I will take them up in that order.

The scientific argument for natural signs rests on two fundamental assumptions, widely but not universally held, about the causal explanation of human behavior or, indeed, of the behavior of any macro-objects whatsoever. Restricting ourselves to the human case and putting aside any notions of indeterminism at this level, the assumptions are:

(1) If two persons behave differently in exactly the same external circumstances, there must be some prior difference in them that explains the difference in behavior (the principle of different effects, different causes);

(2) The nature of those differences in the persons, in their role as immediate causes, must be that of being monadic properties of the persons and not of any relations they have to anything else. Such relations may well be mediate causes, but they can affect subsequent behavior only insofar as they result in non-relational properties of their *relata*.

The point I am about to make stands whether or not the objects of awareness are existents, but an example in which those objects are non-existents will be easier to grasp. So let us consider two persons who are alike in all respects except that one is thinking of mermaids and the other is thinking of unicorns. Speaking commonsensically, we would attribute their different responses to the question "What are you thinking about?" to the differences in their thoughts which, again speaking commonsensically, we would take to consist in part of particular properties of them.

The different prior states that seem to explain the differences in behavior—in this case, linguistic behavior—just are the states of mind of the two persons, the one thinking of mermaids, the other of unicorns. In any case—and that is what this example shows most convincingly even though the argument holds also when the objects of awareness are existent and even when they are also the causes of the awarenesses themselves—it cannot be the objects of awareness *per se* that are the causes of the differences in behavior, for they do not exist. Even if the objects of awareness are existent, they cannot be the immediate causes of differences in behavior if only, in some cases, because they are too distant in space or time. The conclusion to be drawn is that if, commonsensically speaking, two persons have qualitatively different thoughts, the thoughts exemplify some different monadic properties. These properties satisfy one of the conditions of natural signs in that they correlate uniquely with the objects of the thoughts.

More generally, for every qualitative difference in what two people might be thinking, there will need to be a difference in their monadic properties in order to account, causally, for subsequent differences in actual or dispositional behavior.

This argument does not show that these monadic properties are, in a strong sense, signs—natural or otherwise—of the objects of awareness. It does establish the minimum condition of so-called content internalism—that there must be monadic properties of the person that are unique correlates of the objects of thought. In this connection—and as a preparation for the phenomenological argument for natural signs—we may consider briefly the views of G. E. Moore, one of the great defenders of the act in the analytic tradition, in his ultimately unsuccessful attempts to understand the nature of consciousness. Moore was convinced, in light of what he called the "diaphonousness" of consciousness, that there are no mental contents; a state of consciousness has no intrinsic feature that indicates its object.

At the same time, considerations of the sort I have just advanced as the scientific argument for natural signs occurred to Moore. Both of these impulses are evident in this brief quote from his still-important paper of 1910, "The Subject Matter of Psychology" where he says:

> it cannot be the different objects which produce the different effects; and therefore there seems to me to be some force in the argument that there must be some internal difference in my consciousness of the one and of the other, although I can discover none (p. 56).

This tension led the usually sober Moore to suggest a view in which the existent and the non-existent combine to explain differences in behavior, a theory he happily never mentioned again.

But what should we make of Moore's inability to find contents in his own states of consciousness? This sort of consideration leads me to the phenomenological argument for natural signs. It does not suffice to declare that Moore and others have not looked carefully enough, that the requisite entities—natural signs—are there for anyone to find in his or her stream of consciousness. That may be true, but to say so is not convincing, nor should it be, to anyone who doubts the existence of natural signs.

The phenomenological argument is instead the assertion that immediate acquaintance with natural signs is the best explanation of the feeling of certainty that each of us has right now that we are imagining Mars having exploded and not some other state of affairs or nothing at all. Yet, some philosophers, in the grip of causal theories of reference, have argued—Putnam, for example, in his brain-in-the-vat fantasy—that a person might be radically mistaken about the objects of his or her thoughts. But skepticism about the objects of your own thoughts is one of those theories that no one believes or could believe. All of us, like it or not, are Cartesians; all philosophizing, indeed all reflective conscious life, begins with the Cartesian assumption of certainty about the objects of thought—which is an excellent reason for rejecting at the outset any causal theory of reference or any other theory that affirms or implies the contrary.

So we all know that Mars exploding is what we are now imagining and not something else. Our certainty attaches only to the fact that we are imagining that Mars has exploded, and not to Mars actually having exploded. The best explanation of that feeling of certainty is, I submit, that each of us is directly acquainted with a monadic property of ourselves that, by its intrinsic nature, "points to" or, as we philosophers like to say, intends, the state of affairs imagined; this property is a natural sign of that state of affairs. To be aware of that state of affairs, Mars having just exploded, is just to exemplify such a property; to be sure that one is aware of that state of affairs is to be aware of exemplifying such a property.

My thesis does not require that you know that you are aware of that property; for here, as in many other kinds of situations, the best explanation of some behavioral or mental phenomenon is that the person had an awareness of a certain character even if the person was not aware of having that awareness, does not remember having had the awareness, and, in extreme cases, denies having such awareness. People with blindsight can see, for that is unquestionably the best explanation of some of their behavior and other mental states, even though some such people vehemently insist that they are blind.

This third argument for natural signs—and this one is most clearly directed to the idea of mental content as consisting of intrinsically intentional entities—rests on the claim that if there is to be any kind of representation in addition to natural representation, that is, if there be either purely conventional representation or what I call quasi-natural representation, then there must be natural representation, a kind of representation that involves entities that by their intrinsic nature represent whatever they do represent. By quasi-natural representation I mean a kind of representation that occurs, or so I have argued (Addis, 1999), in music and possibly also in dreams and religion, due to human nature and the kinds of representing entities involved, that is, lawfully necessary representation. But we may restrict ourselves to the contrast between conventional representation as instanced by language, for example, and natural representation as I specify my argument in more detail.

The word "red," we say, only conventionally represents the color red. There is no resemblance or any other two-term relation that connects the word to the property that the word does not also have to many if not all other properties. How then does the word "red," for one subset of human beings, manage to represent a specified color? The answer at one level is that those human beings just make it so represent, by choice, habit, or otherwise, but by choice in the sense that English speakers could, in principle, simply decide otherwise.

I want to express this situation by saying that conventional representation requires a third term, that is, conventional representation is a minimally three-term relation; a first thing (a word) represents a second thing (a color) because of a third thing (a human being). The third thing cannot be just any kind of thing; it must be a conscious being who is able to be aware of both the first thing and the second thing in order for the first to represent the second. More generally, and as most philosophers would probably agree, without conscious beings, there would be no such phenomenon as representation or intentionality whatsoever; a universe without minds is a universe altogether lacking in that asymmetrical connection of aboutness, whatever resemblances or any other relations its constituents may have to each other.

But then, my argument continues, if a person's awareness of, in our example, the word "red" and the color red required in each, or either, case a third, we would be off on an infinite regress of the vicious variety. For then we would need yet a further explanation of how that third was aware of both the thought and what it represents, and so on. The only way to avoid this regress is to suppose that thoughts, or some constituents of them, are such that they represent by their inherent nature, without the intervention of a third. They are natural signs.

Dale Jacquette, in his book *Philosophy of Mind*, links me with Noam Chomsky and Jerry A. Fodor as a defender of a "language of thought." On the contrary, I must stress that natural signs, as I conceive them, are utterly non-linguistic items. To say of my view, as Jacquette does, that I "explain thought in terms of language, rather than the other way around," is a mistake (1994, p. 105). Indeed, I am one who insists on the primacy of mind to language. At one level, the main opposition to the argument comes from those who, like Wilfrid Sellars and his students, following Ludwig Wittgenstein, who hold that thought in its intentionality can be understood only through the "intentionality" of language.

These philosophers based their line of thought, I surmise, on the false belief that language is a wholly public phenomenon as contrasted with thought, and the further thesis that the "private" becomes philosophically respectable only by way of the public. This belief is false because the essence of language—its aboutness, its semantics—is not a publicly observable feature of it and is only the intentionality of thought itself. What would it be like to observe as a public phenomenon the representation of the color red by the word "red"?

So there you have a theory of mental content, with some brief arguments in its favor. In recent language, some writers would refer to it as a theory of internal content. Alternatively, if there is any philosophical significance in the notion of "broad" content, this theory might be called a theory of "narrow" or "psychological" content.

For the moment, I do not want to consider those many theories that would add something to psychological content in order to arrive at what their proponents would consider more nearly adequate accounts of intentionality. Instead, I will address those more radical theories that we might call either no-content theories or theories of wholly external content. These theories deny that there is anything at all, on the side of the mind, that correlates to, or otherwise indicates, what, or any part of what, a person's object of awareness is. We already saw this view hesitantly expressed by Moore, but we also know that Russell and Sartre defended the theory with more confidence.

Russell expresses the theory by saying, "At first sight, it seems obvious that my mind is in different 'states' when I am thinking of one thing and when I am thinking of another. But the difference of object supplies all the difference required" (1956, pp. 171–172). For Sartre, ascribing any (descriptive, monadic) properties to a state of awareness (he does not express it that way) would make the mind into a "thing" and so make freedom impossible. More recent theories of wholly external content have other motivations, but all such theories, I suggest, are incapable of answering the following two criticisms.

The first objection—what we might call the empirical objection—reiterates what was said in the scientific argument for (internal) mental content. That is, if two persons in the same situation behave differently because, speaking commonsensically, they have different objects of awareness; there must be a difference in the persons themselves to explain the differences of behavior and not merely a difference in the objects of their awarenesses. Unlike Moore, Russell and Sartre never faced up to this obvious difficulty, to my knowledge. Sartre, perhaps, with his radical libertarianism might have welcomed the consequence, but neither Russell nor recent defenders of wholly external content could allow that there just is no any scientific explanation of the differences in behavior. Let them then tell us just what the mechanism is, or could be, for the explanation of the differences. I believe that no coherent answer is possible.

The same is true, I believe, of what we may call the ontological objection. Unlike the empirical objection, it requires us to consider awarenesses whose objects do not exist, cases in which what is, or would be, the external content is non-existent. So let us now all think of mermaids. Now let us all think of unicorns. On the theory of wholly external content, there is nothing in us, in our minds that distinguishes the one thought from the other. But equally, and this is the point, there is nothing outside our minds either such that, in each case, we might be said to stand in some relation to the one but not to the other, nothing in the actual world that distinguishes the one case from the other. On the theory of wholly external content there is nothing that distinguishes one situation from the other.

Or to put the point in the arcane language of "possible worlds": on the theory of wholly external content, a possible world in which a person is thinking of a mermaid is, all other things being the same, qualitatively identical to a possible world in which that person's counterpart is thinking of a unicorn. That, surely, is an absurd consequence, which, I would imagine, no one would deny. Therefore, it remains for the defender of wholly external content to try to show that this is not a consequence of the theory. I believe that any such attempt, as, for example, by invoking Russell's so-called multiple-relation theory according to which to think of a unicorn is to think separately of the exemplified properties that constitute the unexemplified property of being a unicorn, will fail.

Although these arguments are all too brief here, I conclude that the theory of wholly external content is helpless in the face of these objections and, therefore, false. I turn now to a different kind of objection to natural sign theory, one that directly challenges the idea of a natural sign, especially as expressed in the writings of Hilary Putnam.

In a section entitled "The Reasons for Denying Necessary Connections between Representations and Their Referents" from the first chapter of his book, *Reason, Truth and History,* Putnam maintains that the theory of intrinsically intentional entities is, "a survival of magical thinking" (1981, p. 3) and the idea that things have "true" names, knowledge of which gives a person power over those things. I suspect that this piece of historiography, if that is what Putnam intended his claim to be, is false. Regardless, this is completely irrelevant to the plausibility of the theory.

Putnam does make arguments even though the topic of the chapter section shifts mysteriously and apparently unconsciously on Putnam's part from what it is to have an occurrent awareness of something to what it is to understand a sentence. He directs part of his argument against the thesis that images or sense data are intrinsically intentional. I have no disagreement with that. From there he moves, all too hastily, to the conclusion that concepts are the only remaining candidate for intrinsically intentional entities and then argues that concepts are not mental items at all, for to have a concept is only to have a behavioral disposition or capacity that is caused in a particular way.

In this context, Putnam presents his now well-known Twin-Earth example, which is also part of his argument against necessary connections between thought and object. He presents his argument in terms of concepts which he has already denied are mental items; but I assume, with others and probably Putnam himself, that we can take it to apply to any kind of entity or putative entity whatsoever that is claimed to be intrinsically intentional. In my criticism of that argument, I too will use the language of concepts.

Let us orient ourselves a little more precisely. We must surely agree—for this is obvious from considering a simple disjunctive awareness—that the actual truth conditions and, in that sense, the actual referent for a given thought may be different in different possible worlds. I take Tyler Burge's argument for social content (1979) to be but an elaborate variation on this idea along with his implicit assumption of the falsity of a descriptionist theory of reference. If all Burge, Putnam, or anyone else means, in saying that what is in the mind does not wholly determine its referent, is that the referents of qualitatively identical thoughts will vary in different possible worlds, we should reply, yes, that is true and we already knew it. But Putnam purports to describe a situation in which, in the same possible world, exactly similar thoughts have different referents. This, if true, would be quite interesting indeed. Whether Putnam has succeeded is highly questionable, as I will now try to show.

As we all know, Putnam asks us to imagine that each of us has a *Doppelgänger*, or exact twin, on a distant planet whose thoughts are qualitatively identical to our own. But, according to Putnam, if it happened that on that planet what is called water is composed of elements *XYZ* and not of H_2O as water is here, then the referents of absolutely qualitatively identical thoughts of those who are thinking of what each calls water here and on Twin Earth are different because their extensions are different. Putnam expresses this conclusion by saying that "contrary to a doctrine that has been with us since the seventeenth century, *meanings just aren't in the head*" (1981, pp. 18–19, his emphasis).

But, on the assumption that would make the conclusion quite interesting—that Earth and Twin Earth are in the same possible world—the conclusion just does not follow. For, either your and your twin's concepts of water do include its chemical composition or they do not. If they do—yours being that of water as H_2O and your twin's as being *XYZ*—then we obviously do not have exact similarity of concept (content) to begin with.

Suppose instead that the concepts do not include the chemical composition, in which case we might say that water is the concept of "the clear, odorless liquid that quenches my thirst." Ignoring the possible different effects of H_2O and *XYZ*, and, for the moment, any other indexical aspects of the situation, in that case our concepts do have exactly the same extension; namely, all of what is composed of H_2O, all of what is composed of *XYZ*, and all of whatever else there is, if anything, that is a clear, odorless liquid that would quench my thirst. In neither case, therefore, do we have sameness of concepts with difference of extension. That can happen, indexicals aside, only across, but never within, possible worlds.

Putnam's implicit reply to this argument appears in one of his much more extensive discussions of meaning, "The Meaning of 'Meaning'," in which he insists that so-called natural-kind terms like "water" are implicit indexicals. The thesis is that even if a person's concept of water does not include its being composed of H_2O molecules, it does include the notion that all water has the same (or perhaps highly similar) composition. If this liquid in the glass before me is water, and is composed of H_2O, then all water is composed of H_2O. In addition, insofar as I take this liquid to be water, the extension of my concept of water is all and only what is composed of H_2O. Finally, according to this line of thought, even if for me water is only "this clear, odorless liquid that quenches my thirst," any liquid with those properties that is not composed of H_2O is not in the extension of my concept of water.

I can find no reason to agree that my or anyone's concept of water, insofar as it does not include its chemical composition, includes the notion that all water is of the same (or highly similar) chemical composition. Nor can I find any direct argument for the thesis in Putnam's writings. The closest thing I find to an argument are two assumptions that are, ironically, contrary to the spirit, if not the main theses, of the essay and to Putnam's thought as a whole. Those two assumptions are: (1) that there is a neat category of concepts, of which the concept of water is a member, to be called natural-kind concepts; and (2) that the concept of a natural kind is such that the members of a natural kind must all be of the same or highly similar chemical (or other) composition.

If I were to submit that my concept of water does not require that all water be of the same chemical composition, I imagine it would be objected that this is to put dubious phenomenology ahead of more reliable . . . what? Neat categorization and conceptual analysis? But can we discover through conceptual analysis, as Putnam appears to claim to have done, that our concepts of water and relevantly similar notions must, as so-called natural kinds, include the mono-composition feature? I doubt it in the extreme, but must here leave the argument and conclude that we have no reason from Putnam to deny the possibility of natural signs conceived as entities that specify only their possible truth conditions but which, if they are multiply-exemplified, will have the same actual truth conditions within the same possible world.

I find it curious that analytic philosophy is, in its name, committed to the idea of a mode of understanding the world by way of the simples that, in some sense or senses of "simple," make it up while so many of its practitioners resist the suggestion that, in any particular case, one might actually have arrived at that level. Therefore, in many quarters some will continue to consider it impossible that one might have, that one could have, arrived at entities that just, by their nature, represent and are, therefore, the ultimate terms of analysis in the theory of intentionality. It just has to be more complicated than that, these critics will say.

I will not try to argue my case any further in this regard but, in keeping with my title, close by outlining an argument that natural signs are simple not only in being the final terms in the analysis of intentionality but also in the sense of not being complex properties. Even though they are monadic properties that intend complex states of affairs, they are themselves such that they have no properties as simpler constituents. My thesis is, in short, a rejection of the widely-held dogma that the complexity of the object of awareness must be reflected in an ontological complexity of the awareness itself.

The basic idea of my argument, made in greater detail elsewhere (Addis, 2000), is that as soon as one allows a complexity of property in any property that intends, there is no way to account for what is traditionally known as the unity of thought and no way to distinguish qualitatively different thoughts. Let us see.

There are various ways in which a thought might be, or be conceived as being, complex. But all of them, including Russell's "multiple-relation" theory, are unequipped, so I claim, to explain what must be explained in the following example. There is the thought that A is to the left of B, and there is the thought that B is to the left of A, both of which thoughts we all now have. These are clearly qualitatively distinct thoughts, as I will assume, if A and B are, and are thought of, as qualitatively distinct. Also obvious is that not both, and therefore not either, can be analyzed as a complex consisting only of the thought of A, the thought of B, and the thought of to-the-left-of. So the putatively complex intentional property of being-the-thought-that-A-is-to-the-left-of-B, for example, cannot consist only of the putatively simpler intentional properties of each item. But it will be and has been said that something has been left out—a relation that orders the three, putatively component thoughts one way in the thought of A's being to the left of B and the other way in the case of B's being to the left of A. Following Meinong, who speaks of a "similarity of structure" between thought and object, we may call such a relation a structural relation.

I can now reformulate my thesis as the claim that there cannot be any such thing as a structural relation, so conceived. The reason is that both the assumption that the relation is a constituent of the intentional property, and the assumption that the relation is not a constituent of the intentional property, leads, in different ways, to vicious infinite regress, as might perhaps be half-suspected even without thinking it through. Twardowski made an argument for the impossibility of a structural relation's being part of the content itself but failed to see, additionally, that it cannot be something that is there and not part of the content.

So, all too quickly here, I conclude that the natural sign that is the intentional property that-A-is-to-the-left-of-B is, like all natural signs, a simple property that is just different from the natural sign of B's being to the left of A, much as the simple property of phenomenal red is just different from that of phenomenal green. As intentional properties, and unlike red and green, natural signs point to objects that, in my example, clearly do have constituents in common. But the natural signs, as simple monadic properties, themselves have no shared constituents just because they have no constituents and yet are numerically distinct.

3. Conclusion

I have argued that natural signs, conceived as entities that intend by their inherent nature, exist; that they belong to the ontological subcategory of simple, monadic properties; and that every state of awareness has such an entity as a constituent. What I have not done is to discuss the nature of the connection between a natural sign and that of which it is a sign, as a full discussion of the topic would require. In concentrating on mental content as natural signs, I hope, nevertheless, to have contributed to our understanding of that curious and endlessly fascinating phenomenon that is the subject of our conference on intentionality.

Two

READING BRENTANO ON
THE INTENTIONALITY OF THE MENTAL

Philip J. Bartok

Franz Brentano's attempts to develop a new empirical psychology, as presented in works like *Psychology from an Empirical Standpoint* of 1874 (Brentano, 1955/1995a; hereafter in text as "PES") and the later lectures posthumously published in *Descriptive Psychology* (Brentano, 1982; 1995b; hereafter in text as "DP"), stand at the historical point of departure of the two dominant traditions in twentieth-century philosophy, the analytic and phenomenological traditions. Prominent thinkers in both of these camps have identified Brentano's psychological explorations as an inspiration for central aspects of their philosophical views. But thinkers in these two traditions have read Brentano's psychology and his most important discovery, his intentionality thesis, in quite different ways. As a result, they have arrived at different interpretations of the same theoretical elements. This state of affairs raises puzzling questions: How can the work of a single philosopher have given rise to such variant readings? Do relevant texts equally support both these readings? To what extent did the philosophical projects of Brentano's readers color their understanding of his thought? Have his readers in either of these traditions recovered anything like Brentano's understanding of his psychological project and his intentionality thesis?

I will argue that while both of these broad strategies for reading Brentano involve significant misrepresentations of his intentionality thesis, phenomenologists have generally read Brentano in a far more methodologically sensitive fashion than have his analytic interpreters. Because of this, the phenomenological reading corrects some of the more serious interpretive errors made by many of his analytic readers. My strategy will be to examine each of these readings in turn, beginning with the analytic reading. A brief concluding section summarizes the results of these examinations.

1. The Analytic Reading

In introductory texts in the philosophy of mind, or encyclopedia entries entitled "Brentano," or "Intentionality," Brentano is often identified as the nineteenth-century philosopher responsible for having revived the doctrine of intentionality from the relative neglect into which it had fallen after its heyday in

Aristotelian and Scholastic philosophy. This doctrine, "Brentano's thesis," is the claim that all and only mental phenomena are characterized by what Brentano called "intentional (or mental) inexistence of an object . . . reference to a content, direction toward an object, . . . or immanent objectivity" (PES, pp. I.124–125/88). Brentano's revival of the intentionality thesis is widely held by analytic philosophers to have been a significant early contribution to the project of providing an analysis of mental states and properties, an analysis that fulfills the Cartesian task of distinguishing the mental from the physical. To a surprising extent we can trace this way of reading Brentano and his significance for contemporary philosophy of mind to the work of a single interpreter. Roderick Chisholm's pioneering readings of Brentano's psychological works (1957, chap. 11; 1967a; 1967b) have come to represent the "received view" among analytic philosophers of Brentano's philosophy and empirical psychology. The central elements of Chisholm's reading may thus with some justification be said to have defined a distinctively "analytic" reading of Brentano and his thesis.

In calling this reading of Brentano's thesis the "analytic" reading, I do not wish to imply that it is held universally by all who consider themselves to be analytic philosophers. Some historically minded philosophers working within the analytic tradition reject Chisholm's position based on their independent examinations of Brentano's texts (Smith, 1994; Mulligan and Smith, 1984; Crane, 1988). Adherents to the "analytic" reading are primarily those philosophers who, as participants in mainstream contemporary debates in analytic philosophy of mind concerning intentionality, reference, and propositional attitudes, identify Brentano as having anticipated their theoretical concerns. Since these philosophers are in general far less concerned to get Brentano right than to solve the problems that they take him to have raised, they have typically been content to adopt uncritically Chisholm's "analytic" reading of Brentano's thesis (Dennett and Haugeland, 1987; Lycan, 1994).

Central to the analytic reading is the tendency, evident in Chisholm's well-known *Encyclopedia of Philosophy* article, "Intentionality" (Chisholm, 1967a), to read Brentano's thesis as a pair of theses, one psychological and the other ontological. According to the psychological thesis, intentional relatedness to an object serves as a distinctive "mark of the mental," a criterion according to which we can distinguish mental phenomena from physical phenomena. This thesis is a psychological one because it aims to draw attention to a property unique to the mental realm, a property revealed through a first-person psychological study of mental phenomena. By contrast, the ontological thesis is Brentano's purported assertion that the objects intended by mental acts are objects with a special "ontological status" or unique "mode of being," namely, "intentional inexistence" (Chisholm, 1967b, pp. 7–8). According to Chisholm, it was necessary for Brentano to posit this special mode of being in order to account for our apparent ability to think about non-existent objects.

Thus Brentano's "doctrine of intentional inexistence" holds that, "the object of [a] thought about a unicorn is a unicorn, but a unicorn with a mode of being (intentional inexistence, immanent objectivity, or existence in the understanding) that is short of actuality but more than nothingness" (Chisholm, 1967a, p. 201). The doctrine aims to preserve the intentional relatedness of the mental in cases where we cannot find an existing object to serve as a *relatum* by introducing a realm of "merely intentional" objects, objects that exist only in the understanding and presumably only when they are being intended in mental acts.

In the later writings of Chisholm and subsequent thinkers in the analytic tradition, each of these theses has given rise to a veritable research program in its own right. Chisholm read the psychological thesis as an attack upon physicalism, since he took it (or perhaps some improved version of it) to entail the irreducibility of the mental to the physical. Seeking greater conceptual precision, he later recast Brentano's thesis in semantic terms (as a doctrine about the logical properties of the kinds of sentences we must use in talking about the mental) in an attempt to produce a version of it that would entail the failure of physicalism (1963; 1967a). While the attempt to produce an acceptable analysis of intentionality remains an active research project, contemporary analytic philosophers of mind generally reject the anti-reductionist conclusion that Chisholm sought to draw. For a survey of recent work on intentionality in the analytic tradition, see John Haugeland (1990). The contemporary consensus appears to be that we must account for intentionality in physicalistic terms or, failing this, eliminate it.

As for the ontological thesis, concerns about the status of the intentional relation have largely absorbed Chisholm's worries about the special status of intentional objects, their "intentional inexistence." Analytic philosophers tend to be squeamish about talk of special "modes of being," preferring instead a univocal conception of being/existence that would assimilate all such modes to differences in an object's properties. The hope appears to be that a successful analysis of intentionality will show such spooky ontological talk to have been unnecessary.

While the analytic reading has given rise to a rich and active field of research in contemporary philosophy of mind, it rests upon significant misunderstandings of Brentano's thesis and of the distinctive features of his empirical psychological approach. For one, as even some of Brentano's analytic commentators have recently noted, Chisholm and many of his successors misinterpret the crucial Brentanian term "phenomena" (*Phänomene*) (McAlister, 1976; Moran, 1996; Bell, 1990; Crane, 1998). Brentano's use of the term does not apply, as in contemporary "broad" usage, to states or events in general regardless of whether these are "in the mind" or "in the world." Instead, the term is applied in a more restricted sense only to members of the class of what Brentano calls "immediate experiential facts" (*Erfahrungstatsachen*), the immediate data of our conscious experience (DP, pp. 130/139). Brentano draws his fundamental distinction between the mental and the physical entirely within this domain of conscious experience, "The entire domain of our conscious appearances (*Die gesamte Welt unserer Erscheinungen*) is divided into two great classes—the class of physical and the class of mental phenomena" (PES, pp. I.109/77, translation modified). As examples of mental phenomena Brentano cites such things as:

> hearing a sound, seeing a colored object, feeling warmth or cold, . . . similar states of imagination, . . . the thinking of a general concept, . . . every judgment, every recollection, every expectation, every inference, every conviction or opinion, every doubt, . . . [and] every emotion (PES, pp. I.111–112/79).

As examples of physical phenomena Brentano identifies, "a color, a figure, a landscape which I see, a chord which I hear, warmth, cold, odor which I sense, as well as similar images which appear in the imagination" (PES, pp. I.112/79–80). Roughly speaking, then, the class of mental phenomena includes all mental acts or states, while the class of physical phenomena is comprised of what we commonly call "sense data," or "qualitative properties." The mental/physical distinction, as Brentano understands it, cannot be a distinction between consciousness (the mental or "inner" in René Descartes' sense) and the events or states of some external physical realm (the physical or "outer" in Descartes' sense), but is instead a distinction drawn entirely within the realm of conscious experience. As Brentano insists in his lectures on descriptive psychology, "all phenomena are to be called 'inner'" (DP, pp. 129/137).

Beyond its misinterpretation of the crucial Brentanian term "phenomena," and thus of what it takes to be the psychological prong of Brentano's thesis, the analytic reading is also guilty of a misunderstanding of Brentano's doctrine of intentional inexistence (what Chisholm calls the "ontological prong" of his intentionality thesis). Brentano's use of the term "inexistence" (*Inexistenz*) has been a source of much confusion for his analytic interpreters. One mistake that analytic readers often make is to read the term as "nonexistence." Read in this way, the doctrine of intentional inexistence asserts that the objects of intentional acts need not exist in order to serve as objects, as the case of our ability to think about a unicorn purportedly illustrates. For one example of this reading see Daniel Dennett and John Haugeland (1987, p. 384). But as Brentano uses the term, the "in" in "inexistence" refers not to the failure of (some) intentional objects to exist, but to the fact that all intentional objects must be understood as existing, in a sense that remains to be clarified, inside or within consciousness. The "in" is intended not to negate existence, but to modify or specify it.

To his credit, Chisholm does not make this mistake (though many of his followers do). But while his reading of Brentano's thesis, in this respect, is on the right track, it fails to do justice to the kind of claim that Brentano intended his thesis to be. Given the methodological framework of Brentano's empirical psychology, we must understand his intentionality thesis as a descriptive psychological claim. What this means, and what its significance for a proper understanding of this thesis may be are topics best taken up in the context of an examination of phenomenologists' readings of Brentano's psychology.

2. The Phenomenological Reading

Like Chisholm and his followers in the analytic tradition, the phenomenological thinkers Edmund Husserl and Martin Heidegger also found much of interest in Brentano's empirical psychology. But these phenomenological readers of Brentano were far more concerned than their analytic counterparts to understand the distinctive methodological features of his psychological approach. Unlike Chisholm, who took Brentano to be an early analytic philosopher of mind concerned to solve the Cartesian problem of demarcating the mental from the physical, the phenomenologists took seriously his claim to be engaged in the development of a new, empirically based psychology. Accordingly, they assumed many of his central doctrines to be properly understood as psychological rather than metaphysical or philosophical claims. Most importantly, phenomenologists took seriously the claim of the descriptive branch of Brentano's psychology to be a genuinely descriptive (as opposed to theorizing) approach to the study of mental phenomena. This tendency to read Brentano as primarily a descriptive rather than a theorizing thinker is characteristic of what I will call the "phenomenological" reading of his thesis and his psychology as a whole. For two examples of this way of reading Brentano, see the discussions in Husserl (1970, Appendix) and Heidegger (1985, Preliminary Part).

Descriptive psychology is one of two branches into which Brentano divides his empirical psychology. In his lectures on descriptive psychology (DP), he draws the distinction between these branches in terms of the two basic tasks that he sets for his empirical psychology as a whole:

> exhaustively determining (if possible) the elements of human consciousness and the ways in which they are connected, and describing the causal conditions to which the particular phenomena are subjected (DP, pp. 1/3, translation modified).

The first of the tasks identified here is the taxonomic project of distinguishing mental phenomena, sorting them in to appropriate kinds or categories, and specifying the different ways in which they may be composed into wholes or decomposed into parts. The second is the causal-explanatory task of demonstrating how complexes of phenomena arise (in time) and give rise to one another. The former is to be carried out under the heading of "descriptive psychology" while the latter is to be the task of what Brentano calls "genetic (or explanatory) psychology."

Descriptive psychology, as Brentano understands it is "pure" (untainted by physiological or other natural scientific elements) and "exact" (able to achieve certainty in many of its claims). It is able to achieve this purity and exactness because of its grounding in what Brentano took to be the self-evident data of inner perception. As a descriptive enterprise, it eschews all hypotheses and deductions, proceeding instead in strict reliance upon the objects themselves whose classification is sought (*aus dem Studium der zu klassifizierenden Gegenstände*) (PES pp. II.28/194). Significantly, descriptive psychology does involve a crucial analytic component, in that its classificatory task involves it in an attempt to get at the fundamental component parts out of which observed mental wholes are composed. This generates Brentano's tendency on occasion to speak of his method as "analyzing description" (*analysierende Beschreibung*) (DP, pp. 129/137). In order to fulfill this task, Brentano introduces (in DP) the mereological apparatus of part and whole as a logical tool for helping to distinguish the varieties of parts and part-whole relationships uncovered in the realm of mental phenomena.

Crucially for our present study, taking seriously the claim of descriptive psychology to be a purely descriptive study, as the phenomenological reading insists we must, bears significant implications for a proper understanding of Brentano's thesis. After all, Brentano intended this thesis to be a descriptive psychological claim. Indeed, the thesis can hardly have other status within the framework of his empirical psychology. Taking the descriptive psychological status of this claim seriously reveals that he intends it to be merely an application of the mereological apparatus of part and whole to the intentional relation itself. That he intended the thesis to be taken this way is already evident in PES's formulation of the intentionality thesis as the claim, "every mental phenomenon includes something in it as an object" (PES, pp. I.124–125/88). His intention is even more apparent in the context of his discussions in DP of the nature of the intentional relation, "As in every relation, two correlates can be found here. The one correlate is the act of consciousness, the other is that upon which it is directed . . . the two correlates are only distinctionally separable from one another" (DP, pp. 21/23–24). The intentional relation, then, may be characterized as a part-whole relation involving merely distinctional (separable in principle only, not in fact) parts (DP, pp. 80/84–85).

While some analytic commentators have recently begun to acknowledge, in line with the phenomenological reading, that Brentano intended us to take his intentionality thesis as a descriptive psychological claim, the full implications of this fact have gone almost universally unappreciated. On one hand, these commentators concede that Brentano's thesis is not a "theory" or "explanatory account" of intentionality, but is instead merely an attempt to discover and describe a feature common to all mental phenomena. For an example, see Dermot Moran (1996, p. 3; 2000, chap. 1).

On the other hand, these commentators persist in evaluating Brentano's thesis using standards appropriate for the evaluation of philosophical theories rather than descriptive analyses. For example, almost immediately after arguing that PES is, "almost entirely a work of descriptive [psychology]," David Bell chastises Brentano for not having provided, "a theoretical account the nature of [the intentional] relation" (Bell, 1990, pp. 4–9). For Bell, descriptive psychology is much closer to traditional philosophical analysis than the phenomenological reading of Brentano permits. While he is willing to admit that PES is a work of descriptive psychology, he appears to take this to mean that it is a work of philosophical analysis.

Herbert Spiegelberg offers a similar diagnosis, characterizing the investigations of PES as, "philosophical prolegomena to an empirical psychology" (Spiegelberg, 1982, p. 32). Both Bell and Moran charge that Brentano's "theory" of inner perception is ultimately incoherent (Bell, 1990, p. 9; Moran, 1996, p. 20).

Given the metaphysical and epistemological framework in which his descriptive psychology is constrained to operate, it cannot be Brentano's aim to develop anything like a "theory" of intentionality or inner perception in the traditional sense. The descriptive psychological claim that a given mental act is characterized by reference to or directedness upon an object seeks merely to descriptively characterize the act as it is revealed in inner perception. As even Moran acknowledges:

[I]t was never [Brentano's] intention to offer an explanation of intentionality . . . he simply did not see it as the function of his "empirical" or "descriptive psychology" to provide such an explanation . . . . [Instead] [h]e consciously restricted himself to what could be gained by precise description carried out by "inner perception," confident that inner perception could empirically discover fundamental *a priori* truths about the mental. (Moran, 1996, p. 3)

From this, we can conclude that reading intentionality as an "ontological" thesis in Chisholm's sense of the term is incorrect. That is, we should not read it as proposing a metaphysical or ontological theory of intentionality, one that, for instance, attempts to get at or reveal the special "mode of being" of the intended object. Instead, it is merely a matter of the application of the part-whole apparatus to the task of descriptively characterizing and categorizing the contents of inner perception. If this is the case, then what is ultimately at

issue for the descriptive psychologist is not the theoretical viability of the re-
sulting descriptions, but their descriptive adequacy. As Brentano repeatedly
insists, despite his forays into metaphysical speculation and his occasional
tendency to provide argumentative justifications of his descriptive psychological claims, inner perception is "the very foundation upon which the science of
psychology is erected" (PES, pp. I.61/43). Descriptive psychological claims
are justified, in the end, not by virtue of their theoretical adequacy but instead
by virtue of their accuracy as descriptions of "the things themselves."

Brentano's descriptive psychological study of intentionality does raise deep
and significant metaphysical puzzles about the ontological status of the intentional
object and its relationship to the denizens of the extra-phenomenal "external
world." I am not suggesting that Brentano did not appreciate these difficulties and
devote himself to their solution. He did in both PES and DP, and even more so in
his later, more explicitly metaphysical works (Chrudzimski, 2001).

In several places in both PES and DP, Brentano interrupts his descriptive
analyses to reflect upon the ontological implications of the "containment" of the
intentional object within the intending act. An especially notable example is the
following reflection on the status of intentional objects, inserted into the middle
of one of Brentano's descriptive psychological accounts of intentionality in DP:

> [The] correlates [of the intentional relation] display the peculiarity that
> the one alone is real, [whereas] the other is not something real (*nichts
> Reales*). A person who is being thought is as little something real as a
> person who has ceased to be. (DP, pp. 21/24)

The intrusion of such metaphysical theorizing into the middle of a descriptive psychological analysis is evidence of the extent to which Brentano
was actively grappling in the early 1890s with the metaphysical issues raised
by his descriptive psychological studies. As Brentano saw it in 1874, the intentional directedness of mental phenomena can be toward real or "irreal" objects.
See also DP (pp. 21/24). But by the time of the appendix to the 1911 edition of
PES, he had come to adopt the "reist" metaphysical view that only individual
concrete substances exist and can be the objects of intentional acts. On Brentano's reism, see Jan Wolenski (1996).

To follow out these theoretical moves, and the related moves made by
Brentano's students including Alois Höfler, Alexius Meinong, and Kasimir
Twardowski, would take us too far afield. What is crucial for our present study
is to realize that in offering such metaphysical speculations on the ontological
status of the intentional object Brentano was exceeding the bounds of his empirical psychology (Antonelli, 2001, pp. 338–340). For neither the descriptive
psychologist's characterizations of mental phenomena nor the genetic psychologist's investigations of the laws governing their genesis and succession

entail any particular substantive ontology of intentional objects. Indeed, as Arkadiusz Chrudzimski correctly notes, we can meet the descriptive psychological thesis of the intentionality of consciousness with a variety of metaphysical responses, occupying different points on the continuum between positions that aim at strict faithfulness to the descriptive characterization to those that depart quite radically from it (Chrudzimski, 2001, p. 20). A consistent reading of Brentano's empirical psychological works demands that we carefully distinguish such metaphysical speculations from the descriptive psychological claims they so often accompany, and from the meta-scientific claims that serve to establish the epistemological and metaphysical framework of Brentano's psychology. From the point of view of the ostensibly descriptive investigations that Brentano carries out in PES and DP such metaphysical issues simply do not arise. That is, as long as we remain at the level of analyzing description of what inner perception reveals, we cannot even pose questions about the relationship of the entities or ontological categories discovered therein to the "external" or non-phenomenal world or to the metaphysical framework within which the descriptive study itself operates.

Brentano's repeated transgressions of his role as descriptive psychologist and metatheoretician for his new empirical psychology are evidence of the depth and continuing influence of his metaphysical interests. Similarly, it is Chisholm's metaphysical interests that motivate him to read Brentano's thesis in a way that brings these metaphysical reflections to the fore, obscuring the fact that it was Brentano's intention to provide an empirical psychological grounding for metaphysics (Antonelli, 2001, chap. 13). But if Brentano is serious about this project, then his metaphysical reflections on the ontological status of intentional objects must themselves be provided with such a ground. The ungrounded and free-flowing character of these metaphysical reflections reveals them as speculative suggestions rather than the products of careful metaphysical theorizing.

3. Conclusion

I do not intend to suggest that phenomenologists, unlike their analytic counterparts, succeeded in reading Brentano's psychological works entirely on his own terms. Husserl and Heidegger, despite their attentiveness to the methodological aspects of Brentano's psychology, also involved themselves in misreadings of his intentionality thesis. These misreadings resulted from their tendency to read Brentano's psychology as merely a step "on the way" to their phenomenological approach. Reading Brentano in this way involved attributing to him their theoretical motives, motives that were not, or not primarily, his. My more limited aim here has precluded such explorations into the ultimate adequacy of the phenomenological reading. Instead, I have made use of this reading in order to gain leverage for a critical examination of the analytic reading.

In summary, the analytic reading of Brentano's thesis, with its division of this thesis into distinct psychological and ontological theses, embodies a dual misreading. The psychological thesis interprets Brentano's thesis as a theoretical construct intended to provide a criterion for distinguishing the mental (in Descartes' sense) from the physical (also in Descartes' sense). But Brentano's thesis is neither theoretical nor concerned with this Cartesian distinction. The ontological thesis interprets Brentano's thesis as an attempt to specify the special mode of being that supposedly must characterize non-existent objects like unicorns if they are to serve as objects of intentional acts. But while Brentano does indulge in metaphysical speculation about the ontological status of intentional objects, this speculation lies outside of the proper bounds of his empirical psychological science. Within the limits of his empirical psychology *per se*, the term "in-existence" refers to the mereological containment of intended objects within their intending acts, as may be revealed through a descriptive psychological study of those acts. The phenomenological reading, by attending to the distinctive character of Brentano's descriptive psychological method, manages to avoid both of these misreadings. It thereby permits a deeper appreciation of the distinctive nature of descriptive psychology and of its descriptive analyses.

Three

EMOTIONS, MOODS, AND INTENTIONALITY

William Fish

Under the general heading of what we might loosely call emotional states, we can draw a familiar distinction between emotions (strictly so-called) and moods. In order to judge under which of these headings a subject's emotional episode falls, we advance a question of the form: Of, or about what is the subject's emotion? In some cases (for example fear, sadness, and anger) the provision of an answer is straightforward: the subject is afraid of the loose tiger, or sad about England's poor performance in the World Cup, or angry with her errant child. Although the ways we find natural to talk in such situations can alter (afraid of, sad about, angry with, and so on), in each case the emotion has what Ronald de Sousa, following Ludwig Wittgenstein, calls a target—"an actual particular to which that emotion relates" (1987, p. 116).

In the case of other emotional states, we find an answer to this kind of question is not forthcoming. General feelings of elation, anxiety, or depression, for example, may not be targeted in this sense. What is the subject elated/anxious/depressed about? Well, nothing in particular; the subject is just elated/anxious/depressed. Emotions proper are, then, that subset of emotional states that are targeted, and the target-less remainder fall under the general heading of moods.

The distinction between emotions and moods—between targeted and untargeted emotional states—has traditionally been accounted for by an appeal to the intentionality of the respective states: whereas the targeted nature of emotions shows that they are world-directed and intentional, the absence of targets for moods shows that they are non-intentional. John Searle offers an often-cited example of this claim:

> Some, not all, mental states and events have Intentionality. Beliefs, fears, hopes and desires are Intentional; but there are forms of nervousness, elation and undirected anxiety that are not Intentional . . . . My beliefs and desires must always be about something. But my nervousness and undirected anxiety need not in that way be about anything. (1983, p. 1)

But we can find reasons for dissatisfaction with the distinction between intentional emotions and non-intentional moods. One cause for concern is that, pretheoretically, emotions and moods appear to share many similarities, yet this distinction forces us to treat emotions and moods as fundamentally different kinds of mental states. This is especially worrisome as we are not only forced to treat, say, anger and anxiety as dissimilar, but we are also forced to treat two kinds of anxiety—directed and undirected anxiety—as significantly different.

Another concern, raised by Tim Crane, is that if moods are non-intentional, then their characteristic phenomenological feels must be due:

[to] properties which are phenomenologically detectable to the subject, but are non-intentional, involving nothing beyond themselves. These properties must therefore be qualia: non-intentional, subjective properties. (1998, p. 240)

But, argues Crane, once we introduce qualia into the picture, we also let in the familiar specter of qualia inversion. Briefly, the concern with this consequence is that, while we may be able to make sense of qualia inversion where color perception is concerned, it does not obviously make sense in the case of moods. After all, to hold that anxiety has the functional role it does because of the way it feels is eminently plausible—how could a state that felt like elation possibly make us behave as we do when we are anxious?

In the light of these concerns, Crane proposes an intentional account of moods. To explain how moods can be intentional when no answer exists to the question of what they are of or about, Crane begins by pointing out that we can say the same of pain. Even though no obvious answer exists for the question of what a given pain is of or about, pains can be seen to be outwardly directed:

[I]n bodily sensation, something is given to the mind, namely the body, or a body part. Calling this phenomenon "intentionality" classifies it together with the case of outer perception, where the perceived portion of the world is "given" to the mind; and with thought, where some object, property, or state of affairs is "given" to the mind. (1998, p. 238)

What is distinctive about intentional states, Crane suggests, is not that we can provide answers to questions about what the states are of or about, but that when we are in one, something is "given" to our mind.

If we understand intentionality in this way, we can also ask whether something is given to the mind in cases of untargeted moods. The answer to this question appears to be yes: when I am in the different moods, the world is given to me in different ways—if I am anxious, then the world appears disturbing or threatening; if I am irritated then the world is given to me as annoying and provocative; if I am elated then the world just appears to me to be a wonderful place to be. On this conception of intentionality, moods can be seen to be intentional—in each case, "there is the experiencing subject, the world experienced (or the thing in the world experienced) and the particular way of apprehending the world" (Crane, 1998, p. 245).

While I think this move represents a significant step forward in our understanding of the role emotions and moods play in our mental lives, we still have work to do. Still a significant difference between emotions and moods exists—emotions have targets while moods do not—and this requires explanation.

While Crane does not explicitly address this issue, he does appear to indicate where he would locate the difference. In the quote above, he suggests that in all cases of emotional consciousness, "there is the experiencing subject, the world experienced (or the thing in the world experienced) and the particular way of apprehending the world." The key parts of this passage are where he allows for some emotional states to be directed at, "the world experienced," and others to be directed at a particular, "thing in the world experienced." This difference would map quite neatly on to the distinction between moods and emotions: moods are intentionally directed at the world in general, whereas emotions are directed at particular things in the world.

If this is an accurate interpretation of Crane, his position appears to closely resemble that of Robert Solomon:

Moods are generalized emotions: An emotion focuses its attention on more-or-less particular objects and situations, whereas a mood enlarges its grasp to attend to the world as a whole, typically without focusing on any particular object or situation. (1976, pp. 172–173)

On this general account, the difference between moods and emotions is located in the extent of their intentional focus. The suggestion appears to be that, where moods are concerned, the intentional object of the state is the world in general, and the intentionality of moods exhibits a wide focus. In cases of emotions, the intentionality of the emotion focuses narrowly on a particular object.

I suggest that this analysis of the relationship, and in particular the claim that emotions focus narrowly on particular objects or states of affairs, is incompatible with the phenomenology of emotions. When an individual enters a particular mood, it affects the way he or she perceives the world in general—I call this phenomenon "global affectivity"—and because of this, moods are said to have wide focus. But global affectivity is also present in the case of targeted emotions.

I can illustrate this with some examples. If I feel that I have been treated unfairly by my boss and this makes me angry, my anger changes the way I both apprehend and respond to the world in general. For example, because I am angry at my boss, insignificant things may irritate me: I might slam my office door, or shout at my wife, or kick my cat. Although I am angry with my boss, and in a sense, I focus my anger narrowly on him, my anger also has the

wide focus characteristic of moods in as much as it changes the way I apprehend and respond to the world in general.

We can also provide similar examples with respect to other paradigmatic
emotions such as fear and joy. If I am afraid that a loose tiger might attack me,
then in a sense, I focus my fear narrowly on the beast itself. But my fear is
globally affective in one sense—I jump at small noises, I am wary of shadows,
and so on. Similarly with joy; I am happy because England have won the
Ashes—this is the target or focus of my pleasure—but my happiness affects
the way I apprehend and respond to the world in general. When I am happy,
little things make me smile and the world just appears like a great place to be.

But if targeted emotions are narrowly focused on a particular object, and
are in no way directed upon the world in general, then it becomes difficult to
see how we could account for their global affectivity. On the other hand, if
emotions, like moods, are widely focused upon the world in general, then it
becomes equally difficult to see how to explain why emotions, but not moods,
are targeted. In the light of this dilemma, I suggest we need to move to a two-
component theory of emotion of the sort outlined by Laird Addis (1995). On
this general approach, an emotion proper would consist of two components.
Emotions and moods would share the first component and would both explain
global affectivity and underpin our intuition that emotions and moods are importantly similar. The second component would be exclusive to the emotions
and would account for their being targeted.

While I think this proposal is on the right lines, it stands in need of further development, especially where the natures of the two components are concerned. The brief for the remainder of this paper is to make a start on this task
and sketch the structure of what I believe to be a promising approach. Let us
begin, then, by addressing the first question: what is the nature of the first
component—the component common to both moods and emotions? Addis
postulates a sensational common core, but this would appear to fall foul of
Crane's transposition concerns. In light of this, I will develop a proposal more
in tune with Crane and Solomon—that the component common to moods and
emotions is a widely focused, mood-like intentional awareness of the world in
general—and see where this takes us.

First, if we are to endorse the general line that moods are intentional
states, we should note that this proposal is subject to an important and interesting ambiguity. A key aspect of Crane's position is that the different moods and
emotions are different manners or ways in which subjects experience the
world. But this claim is ambiguous. On the standard interpretation, the different emotions and moods are a range of independent intentional states, each
supplying a new kind of intentional engagement with the world. So we could
perceive a horse, or think about a horse, or be afraid of a horse, or be angry
with a horse, and so on.

However, Jean-Paul Sartre, one of the inspirations behind Crane's theory, points out that not only is a given emotion a "specific manner of apprehending the world" (Sartre, 1939, p. 57), but is also, "a transformation of the world" (1939, p. 63). According to Sartre, when we enter a particular mood or emotion, the way we experience the world is transformed.

When I enter a particular mood, for example when I become irritated, I begin to see things differently—I begin to see objects in the world as annoying and malign. If we follow this thought through, it suggests that the kind of intentional engagement we have with the world remains the same: just as I perceived the world before I became irritated, I still perceive the world afterwards. What changes is the way the world is given to me in perception. On this interpretation, moods do not supply a new kind of intentional engagement with the world; instead they modify the way in which our existing (perceptual/conceptual) intentional states make us aware of the world.

Although the standard interpretation appears to favor the first reading and treat emotions and moods as independent kinds of intentional states, I am inclined to favor the second. As Martin Heidegger suggests, in even our most neutral engagements with the world, we perceive the world in a particular way (1927, p. 138). When I perceive my cat Edgar, for example, I perceive him as white, fluffy, and loveable. The way I perceive the cat is naturally captured at the level of perceptual content: I perceive that Edgar is white, fluffy, and loveable. If I then become irritable, I may come to see the same cat to be annoying and bothersome—I come to perceive that Edgar is annoying and bothersome. But what appears to change here is not the kind of engagement with the world I enjoy—I am perceptually related to Edgar in both cases—but the way I perceive Edgar.

In addition to this consideration is the thought that, if moods and emotions were independent modes of intentional engagement with the world, we should be able to conceive of a mental event consisting of just that kind of engagement. For example, we can easily imagine that we might have a mental event that consisted solely of a perception—as when we are thoughtlessly engaged in driving. We can also imagine that a mental event might consist of nothing but thought—thinking in a sensory deprivation tank for example—or perhaps even an isolated pain. But to make sense of the idea that we could be angry, say, in the absence of any perceptions or conceptions is not so easy—what would constitute my being angry in the absence of any angry thoughts for example?

If we cannot make sense of the idea that we could be angry in the absence of any perceptions or conceptions, it suggests once more that anger serves to modify an existing intentional mode of engagement, rather than supplying a new, independent intentional mode of engagement with the object of our anger.

To enter an emotion or a mood is, I suggest, analogous to putting on a pair of tinted spectacles. Putting on a pair of green-tinted glasses has the effect of changing the way I see the world. What is more, the way I see the world changes in a way similar to wearing green glasses—the objects of perception now appear tinged with green, and so on. Similarly, when I become anxious, the way I see the world changes in a characteristic way—the objects I perceive now appear to be threatening and malign.

So my answer to the question as to the nature of the first component—our mood-like awareness of the world—is that, contrary to received wisdom, this component is not a new way of apprehending the world. Instead, I suggest that moods are characteristic modifications of our existing (perceptual/conceptual) modes of intentional engagement. This not only explains why moods and emotions affect our experiences of the world, but also has the parsimonious consequence that we do not need to endorse several additional intentional modes (one new mode per kind of mood) in our taxonomy of intentional states.

But what about the nature of the second component? Do we need to endorse additional intentional modes in order to account for the targeted nature of the emotions? To answer this question, we need to do two things. First, we need to look more closely into what is involved in the claim that emotions, but not moods, have targets. Second, we must investigate whether we can account for the evidence that emotions have targets without recourse to additional intentional modes. My tactics here will be to show that we can account for all the relevant evidence without appealing to any additional kinds of intentionality over and above those already accepted.

The general idea behind the claim that emotions have targets is that we can isolate particulars towards which emotions such as anger, fear, or happiness are directed. Which particulars are these? Well, a common suggestion is that "for O to be an object of an emotion E is commonly for O to be taken by the subject to be the cause of E" (de Sousa, 1987, p. 110). What is critical, on this account, is that the subject takes, or believes, the target object to be the cause of the emotion. But we should be wary of placing too much weight on the idea that the subject has to take the emotion to be the cause of their state. For example, Anthony Kenny points out that we can be in an emotional state, and have beliefs about its etiology, without the (believed) cause thereby being the object of the emotion, as when we say, "I was angry because I was hungry" (1963, pp. 74–75).

Nevertheless, there does appear to be a close link between what the subject believes about the genesis of their emotion and its target. For example, consider another of Kenny's examples in which a subject says, "I was angry because he burst in without knocking" (1963, p. 71). The cause of the anger here appears to be an event—the event of his bursting in—but one would expect the target of the anger to be the man, instead of the event. What these situations appear to show is that what is relevant is not what the subject takes to be the immediate cause of the emotion, but instead what the subject takes to be the reason for the existence of the emotion. Similarly, the questions designed to elicit the target of an emotion (What are you angry about? Why are you sad?) are most naturally read as asking for reason-giving, as opposed to merely causal, explanations. In the light of this, I suggest that, in most cases, the target of an emotion will be what I will call the "perceived ground" of the emotion. "Perceived" because what is crucial is what the subject takes, or believes to be the case, and "ground" to get across the idea that the subject takes the target to be, in some sense, ultimately responsible for the emotion.

When we understand this, we can see how to address J. R. S. Wilson's concern that I may not be angry with the man who burst in, but, "with my secretary who allowed him to burst in without knocking" (1972, p. 59). On my proposal, what is relevant when it comes to specifying the target of the emotion is who or what the subject takes to be responsible for their being in an emotional state. If I had explicitly told my secretary that under no circumstances was I to be disturbed, for example, then I may well take the man's being allowed to burst in to be my secretary's fault. I would take my secretary to be responsible for my being angry. Even in cases where no agent exists, say when I am sad that a friend died naturally, the object of my emotion is the death of my friend, and I take this event to be responsible for my being in the emotional state.

If an emotional state is indeed targeted at the person, object or event the subject takes to be responsible for their emotion, we now need to examine our reasons for thinking that emotions, but not moods, can be targeted in order to see whether these require us to endorse additional intentional modes. I see that two prime motivations for this claim exist—subject testimony and subject behavior. Let us take these in turn.

The rationale behind the first source of evidence is that we know emotions have targets because the subjects of emotion tell us that they are targeted. All we need to do is ask the question: What are you happy/sad/angry about? The subject's response reveals the target of the emotion.

Instead of being revelatory of emotions having a special kind of intentionality, I suggest that all an ability to answer this question shows is that, for some emotional states, the subject believes a particular object (or state of affairs) to be the reason they are in an emotional state. Sometimes we enter an emotional state and we think we know why—it was the tiger's escaping that led to my being afraid, or Brazil's beating England that led to my being sad. Our beliefs about the reasons for, or grounds of, our emotional states supply us with the means necessary to answer questions of the type outlined above, not anything intrinsic to the emotional episode itself. Where moods are concerned, we are in a similar kind of state but, in the absence of appropriate beliefs, we are unable to supply a reason—I may be anxious, but I do not know why. So I suggest that an ability to answer such a question is only revelatory about a subject's beliefs about his or her emotional states (it reveals that the subject believes they are aware of a reason for being in that emotional state) and not revelatory about the intentionality of the emotional states themselves.

In the case of emotions, I suggest the subject is both in an emotional state (understood as a mood-like awareness of the world as described above), and has beliefs about why they are in that state. The subject's beliefs about their reasons for being in this state provide the ammunition to enable the subject to answer questions concerning the objects of their emotion. In the case of moods, the subject has no such beliefs, and is unable to respond to these questions. In as much as we need to turn to intentionality to account for this evidence, we do not need to appeal to any additional kind of intentionality enjoyed by the emotion itself, but merely to the intentionality of the beliefs about the ground of the emotion.

We could argue that this is not all the relevant evidence—subjects do not only tell us that their emotions are directed; their actions bear this out. As Sartre says, the emotional consciousness, "grasps the world differently, under a new aspect, and imposes a new behavior" (1939, pp. 64–65)—a behavior particular to the emotion or mood experienced. What is peculiar to emotions is that these behavioral manifestations can also show signs of being targeted.

Take a case of anger. If I am angry with Clive, then the targeted nature of this anger is manifested by my behavior towards Clive—if I meet Clive I might shout at or hit him; even in his absence I can rail against him in conversation—the existence of this kind of targeted behavior is a feature of emotions, but not of moods, and because of this, needs explaining.

I will investigate the characteristic targeted behavior that accompanies emotion in more detail, but as a first point we should remember that Clive is not the only person towards whom I might behave aggressively. Emotions, like moods, are globally affective; even if I am angry with Clive, I might instead snap at my wife, or kick my cat. But this does not, as it stands, go any way to explain why my apparently being angry with Clive makes me more likely to engage in especially Clive-directed angry behavior.

Imagine, for example, that I face with a group of people, one of whom is Clive. Because I am angry with Clive, my angry behavior will probably be directed towards him more than any of the other people present. So even when we acknowledge the globally affective nature of emotions, we are not thereby enabled to say all we need to about the targeted behavior that can be present when a subject is emotional.

To show how we can explain the existence of such directed behavior without invoking a further kind of intentionality, I will begin by evaluating the claim to the contrary: that I have Clive-directed angry behavior because Clive is the intentional object of an additional anger-mode. I take this claim to imply the following: if Clive were not the object of my anger-mode, then I would not be disposed towards engaging in Clive-directed behavior.

To evaluate this claim we need to engage in a little imaginative reconstruction. Imagine I am angry with Clive because Clive has harmed Edgar. The first question to ask is why this has made me angry—what is it about the harming of Edgar that leads me to become angry?

In his 1988 paper on emotions, Robert Campbell Roberts points out that emotions are "concern-based":

[T]o be angry is not just to see a person as having culpably offended; it requires a concern about some dimension of the offence . . . . To be afraid of heights is not just to see them as a danger to something-or-other; it requires that something I hold dear seem threatened. (p. 191)

What is vital, then, is that Edgar's well-being concerns me—in some way, it must matter to me, or be important to me. Because I have this relationship of concern to Edgar's well-being, I find the state of his being-harmed to be undesirable and abominable. In turn, the existence of this state of affairs leads me to become angry. More, as I see Clive as the agent responsible for this undesirable state of affairs and as the reason for my anger, I am angry with Clive, and my becoming angry with Clive leads me to acquire particular behavioral dispositions that include highly Clive-specific dispositions such as, let us imagine, abusing or physically attacking Clive in public. On the proposal we are considering, this is explained by our entering an anger-mode that has Clive as its intentional object, and our being in this state explains why I acquire the particular Clive-directed behavioral dispositions.

This explanation appears to imply that were it not for my being angry with Clive, I would not have acquired any Clive-directed behavioral dispositions. Is this the case? We can find out by imagining that my anger with Clive is somehow removed, while everything else about my mental make-up is held constant, and then ask whether this would thereby remove any explicitly Clive-directed behavioral dispositions. I suggest not.

What is significant about this imagined anger-free situation is that everything but the anger has been held constant. This means that it will not only remain the case that Edgar's well being is an issue that concerns me, but also that all of my beliefs about Clive, his actions, and the undesirable results of these actions (Edgar's being harmed) remain.

Given that all this is still in play, we can ask what my behavioral dispositions might be in the absence of anger. First, take the general case. As removing the anger involves removing the mood-like awareness component, nothing is globally affecting my behavior and we should expect my behavioral dispositions towards the majority of objects in the world to be as normal—I will chat normally to my wife, stroke my cat, and so on. What about the Clive-specific cases—what if I were to come across Clive at a social event? While it may be true that, in the absence of anger, I may no longer feel inclined to abuse or physically attack him, his failures still matter to me. Because of this, I may well take the opportunity to civilly express to him my displeasure at what he has done, my disagreement with the actions he has taken, and so on. But these expressions of displeasure would still be directed at Clive, and not to anyone else present.

So while removing the anger from the situation might well change the nature of my Clive-directed behavior, it would not remove it altogether. I still believe Clive to be the agent of an undesirable state of affairs, and these beliefs ensure that I still have explicitly Clive-directed behavioral dispositions.

What is especially telling is that if we add back the mood-like awareness of the world, we find that all the angry targeted behavior we are trying to account for comes with it. What happens is that the globally affective nature of the mood-like awareness ensures that my actions in general take on a more irritated, aggressive quality. In the general case, this explains why I no longer chat to my wife, but shout at her; why I no longer stroke my cat, but kick it, and so on. And as this mood-like awareness is globally affective, it will not only transform my general behavioral dispositions, but also my underlying Clive-specific behavioral dispositions. Whereas in the absence of the mood-like awareness I might merely be inclined to take the opportunity to verbally express my displeasure to Clive, when this component is present these dispositions will take on a more aggressive and confrontational character.

So I suggest that the onset of anger does not create Clive-directed behavioral dispositions *ex nihilo*—on the contrary, my beliefs about Clive and his actions would have ensured that some Clive-directed dispositions obtained even if those beliefs had not made me become angry. Once we recognize this, we can see that an explanation of the Clive-directed angry behavior does not oblige us to endorse an additional intentional mode of anger, but can be fully explained by the transformational nature of the relevant mood-like awareness acting on the underlying behavioral dispositions. Moods do not yield such directed behavioral dispositions because the absence of a perceived ground ensures that, in the underlying behavioral dispositions, there exist no directed dispositions to transform.

These considerations suggest that in order to explain the evidence that leads us to claim that emotions are targeted, we do not need to appeal to an independent kind of intentionality enjoyed by emotions but not moods. When it comes to explaining subject testimony, we find that we need only appeal to the agent's beliefs about their reasons for being in an emotional state. In the case of targeted behavior, we need to appeal both to the agent's beliefs about the genesis of their emotion, and to the particular directed behavioral dispositions that these beliefs result in. Then, to explain the angry behavioral dispositions that obtain, we need to appeal to the way the globally affective transformational nature of the relevant mood-like awareness acts upon these targeted behavioral dispositions.

In conclusion, I suggest that the first step towards getting an adequate picture of the intentionality of moods and emotions is to follow Crane in treating intentionality as the way in which the mind apprehends the world. This enables us to thereby bring both emotions and moods under the umbrella of intentionality. But I suggest that we treat them, not as additional intentional modes of awareness, but as characteristic modifications of our other (perceptual/conceptual) modes of awareness. Once we have made this move, I suggest that in order to explain the fact that both emotions and moods are globally affective, we should see that both types of emotional states are of the same kind—they both serve to change the way in which their subject apprehends the world.

The difference between emotions and moods lies not in intrinsic differences between the two states, but in differences in accompanying mental states. Where emotions are concerned, the subject will invariably have beliefs about why he or she is in that emotional state. These beliefs will then enable the subject to testify as to the targets of their emotions, and will provide the subject with target-directed behavioral dispositions. When transformed by the subject's emotional state, these underlying targeted dispositions can then lead to explicitly targeted emotional behavior. In the case of moods, the subject will have no accompanying beliefs, and the state will not be targeted. The absence of these beliefs explains the subject's inability to answer questions about what they are in a mood about, and explains why they have no underlying targeted behavior for the anger to transform.

ACKNOWLEDGMENTS

I would like to thank Laird Addis, Tim Crane, Bill DeVries, Jesse Prinz and the other participants at the Intentionality: Past and Future conference for a stimulating discussion of the issues contained in this paper, and the British Academy whose kind support enabled me to attend this conference. I would also like to thank Greg Currie and Bob Kirk for penetrating comments on an earlier draft.

Four

LOCKEAN IDEAS AS INTENTIONAL CONTENTS

Gábor Forrai

John Locke was not concerned with the problem of intentionality. But to discuss his theory of ideas in terms developed for giving account of intentionality is valuable, for this may help us to a better understanding of his theory. I will suggest that we should regard his ideas as pieces of intentional contents. This sort of interpretation, although not new (Gibson, 1918, pp. 13–28; Yolton, 1984, chap. 5), is not widely accepted (Chappell, 1994, pp. 31–35). My favorable arguments for it are based on charity: this interpretation helps us see why Locke can avoid some fatal and quite blunt errors to which he is often supposed to be subject. First, I distinguish between two different ways of thinking about intentionality, object-theories and content-theories. Then I argue that, contrary to the appearances, Locke's account is not an object-theory. Finally, I explain why Locke's theory is a content-theory.

1. Two Theories of Intentionality

Let me begin with some obvious facts about intentionality. When we think, we think about something. What a thought is about is constitutive of its identity. A thought about a cat is not the same thought as one about a dog. The natural way of capturing this difference, reflected in our grammar, is to treat thoughts as relations. When we think about a dog and when we think about a cat, we enter into the same sort of relation but with different objects.

This relation is quite strange. First, ordinary relations presuppose the existence of their *relata*. For example, you cannot be smaller than a centaur, since centaurs do not exist. But we can think about things that do not exist. Second, ordinary relations do not presuppose a particular way of conceiving their *relata*. Suppose the deflated ball is your son's favorite toy. If the deflated ball is under the tree, so must be your son's favorite toy. But if you want to throw out the deflated ball, a sense remains in which you may not want to throw out your son's favorite toy. In the second case, the way you conceive the object of your thought makes a difference. So thought cannot be a genuine relation to objects.

We can solve this puzzle in two ways. One is to maintain that thought is a genuine relation, but its objects are not ordinary objects. The other is to hold that thought is merely relation-like, but not a genuine relation. Adopting the terms from David Woodruff Smith and Ronald McIntyre (1982, pp. 40–47, 106–108, 141–150), I will call these object- and content-theories. Note that my explanation of the content-theory follows more closely Crane (2001, pp. 13–33).

An object-theory assumes two things. (1) Objects of a strange sort exist, and these objects have two characteristic features. (a) They enjoy a peculiar ontological status in that they do not exist in the ordinary sense; and (b) our way of conceiving them is constitutive of their identity. (2) The objects we think about are these objects. The idea is this. In addition to the deflated ball, a strange object exists, which we can call the-deflated-ball-thought-about. The deflated ball exists, and is identical with your son's favorite toy. The-deflated-ball-thought-about does not exist, and is not identical with your-son's-favorite-toy-thought-about. When you say you want throw out the deflated ball, the object you think about is not the deflated ball, but the-deflated-ball-thought-about. We can explain the apparently strange features of intentional relations in this way. We have no problem with thoughts about non-existing things, since we never think about things that exist. The difference between the thoughts concerning the ball and the ones concerning the centaur is merely this. In the first case, the object of our thought, the-deflated-ball-thought-about, has an existing relative, namely the ball itself. In the second case, the object of our thought, the-centaur-thought-about, is not so privileged. Centaurs do not exist. As for the other difficulty, wanting to throw out the deflated ball is not the same thought as wanting to throw out your son's favorite toy, for they are relations to different objects. The reason why we may still be tempted to regard them the same is that their objects happen to have the same "relative."

In contrast with this, content-theories maintain that (1) no special ontological category of objects-thought-about exists. To describe something as an object of thought is to say that it fulfills a particular role. The things that can fulfill this role form an ontologically heterogeneous group, and include even things that do not exist. (2) We always conceive objects of thoughts in some particular way. No "bare" conceiving of objects exists. We can conceive of the same object of thought in different ways. The way of conceiving is termed "content." In specifying a particular thought, to describe its content is sufficient. We do not have to mention the object, because this is redundant: the specification of how we conceive something automatically contains what is conceived.

On this picture, thinking about non-existing things does not present a problem, because theories of this kind do not assume that all thoughts are relations to objects. Only those thought are relations whose objects exist. Thoughts about balls are relations, but thoughts about centaurs are not. As far as the second problem is concerned, the reason why I can describe you as wanting to throw out the deflated ball and at the same time not wanting to throw out your son's favorite toy, is that I may choose to pay close attention to the content of your thought, to the way you conceive the object of thought in question.

2. The Object-Theoretical Interpretation

We may turn now to Locke. On the usual interpretations, his ideas are regarded as mental objects of some sort. At first sight, his theory appears to be an object-theory. Even though he did not formulate it as a theory of intentionality, the way he describes ideas appears to fit the pattern. (1) Ideas are strange objects, namely, mental objects. (a) They do not exist in the ordinary sense: they are in the mind. For instance, centaurs do not exist; they are merely ideas in the mind; and (b) their identity depends on how we conceive them. The child's rudimentary idea of gold and the chemist's sophisticated idea are two different ideas. (2) What we think about are ideas. In fact, ideas are officially defined as whatever is the object of understanding when we think (Locke, 1975, bk. 1, chap. 1, sec. 8; hereafter in text as 1.1.8).

Tempting as this interpretation may be, I will try to show that it is wrong. The argument will have two parts, one about meaning, and one about knowledge. In both cases, I will point out that Locke's position needs an assumption incompatible with the above interpretation, and Locke makes that assumption. To put it crudely and tentatively, the assumption is this. A sense exists in which the identity of ideas is determined by what is outside the mind and not by what is inside. Sometimes what matters for the identity of ideas is the extramental objects to which they are connected instead of the properties they have by virtue of their being in the mind. On the object-theoretical reading, in contrast, ideas are mental objects, which are conception-dependent, and if ideas have any connections with things outside the mind, these connections are indifferent to their identity.

Let me begin with meaning. Locke believes that words signify ideas, in their "primary and immediate signification," the ideas of the person who uses them. He also explains in detail that, due to the imperfections of language and abuses of its users, words standing for complex ideas may signify different ideas in the minds of different speakers. He thinks that this confusion can be remedied, and describes how in the cases of different kinds of words. But his therapy will not work unless he can guarantee the agreement of our simple ideas, for the complex ideas are all built up of simple ideas.

Here comes the crunch. How do I know that when you say "yellow" you have the same simple idea in mind as I have? If a simple idea is a mental object in the sense of the object-theory, its identity must depend on our way of conceiving it: on its inherent properties, those features that we can discover by introspection. I can know in this way that the idea I associate with the word "yellow" is different from the one I associate with "blue." But I cannot examine your ideas, so I cannot know whether the ideas you and I associate with the word "yellow" are qualitatively identical or not.

This is a standard and serious objection to Locke. If words stand for ideas, and ideas are mental objects in individual minds, we can never know if we understand each other or if it merely appears so. The reason Locke does not address it in connection with meaning is that he addresses it in the chapter "Of True and False Ideas." I will start from afar.

In the beginning of the chapter, he explains that ideas are not propositions, so they cannot be true or false in the literal sense. When we declare an idea true or false, what we speak of is a tacit proposition asserting that the idea agrees with something else. Two things exist with which we can compare ideas: "real existences" and other people's ideas. Let us begin with the first one. Locke argues that, as regards real existence, simple ideas are all true:

> being barely such Perceptions, as God has fitted us to receive, and given Power to external Objects to produce in us by established Laws, and Ways, .. . their Truth consists in nothing else, but in such Appearances, as are produced in us, and must be suitable to those Powers, he has placed in external Objects, or else they could not be produced in us: And thus answering to those Powers they are what they should be, true Ideas. (1975, 2.32.14.)

Expressed plainly, simple ideas are true if they match their regular causes. Since they necessarily do that, they are all true (Ayers, 1991, vol. 1, pp. 60–66). Robert Cummins has suggested that Locke gave what we call today an informational account of mental content (1989, pp. 35–36).

We may worry that a problem about secondary qualities exists, the ideas of which do not resemble their causes. But Locke reassures us: simple ideas are just "Marks of Distinction in Things, whereby we may be able to discern one Thing from another," so what is critical about them is that they fulfill the role of distinguishing the things that are different, and they can do that without resembling their causes. "[T]he name blue notes properly nothing, but that Mark of Distinction, that is in a Violet, discernible only by our Eyes, whatever it consists in" (1975, 2.32.14).

The picture is that simple ideas constitute a network differences, which matches the distinctions in things, and the properties, by virtue of which simple ideas themselves differ—their inherent, qualitative properties—, are relatively unimportant: they have to differ where things differ, but they do not have to resemble them. This suggests the following possibility: if the qualitative properties of ideas were systematically permuted in a way that left the network of distinctions intact, that would not change anything of importance. The marks of the permuted system would be different, but they would mark the same distinctions, so they would not count as false with regard to "real existences."

This brings us to the second sense in which we can raise the issue of truth of simple ideas. If someone's simple ideas are permuted relative to ours, would this mean that his ideas are false with respect to our ideas? This worry about a possible permutation gives rise to the objection we started from: the disagreement between simple ideas may result in an undetectable failure in mutual understanding. Locke examines a case of this kind, namely a systematic and undetectable inversion of blue and yellow, and his conclusion is straightforward:

> Neither would it carry any Imputation of Falshood to our simple Ideas, if by the different Structure of our Organs, it were so ordered, That the same Object should produce in several Men's Minds different Ideas at the same time; *e.g.* if the Idea, that a Violet produced in one Man's Mind by his Eyes, were the same that a Marigold produced in another Man's, and *vice versâ*. For since this could never be known: because one Man's Mind could not pass into another Man's Body, to perceive, what Appearances were produced by those Organs; neither the Ideas hereby, nor the Names would be at all confounded or any Falshood be in either. For all Things, that had the Texture of a Violet, producing constantly the Idea, which he called Blue; and those which had the Texture of a Marigold, producing constantly the Idea, which he as constantly called Yellow, whatever those Appearances were in his Mind; he would be able as regularly to distinguish Things for his Use by those Appearances, and understand, and signify those distinctions, marked by the Names Blue and Yellow, as if the Appearance, or Ideas in his Mind, received from those two Flowers, were exactly the same, with the Ideas in other Men's Minds. (1975, 2.32.15)

This fits quite well with what Locke said about the truth of simple ideas with respect to real existences: what matters about the idea is the distinction it marks, and not its qualitative features that distinguish it from other ideas. So a sense exists in which the identity of simple ideas depends on the qualities and powers they serve to mark. The qualification "in a sense" is necessary. Locke's language and what he says pull apart. He speaks as if it were the qualitative or inherent properties that fixed the identity of ideas: if different people used qualitatively different ideas to mark the same qualities, the identity of ideas would go with the qualities of the mark instead of the quality marked. But what he says points in the opposite direction: what matters for the truth of the idea (either with regard to "real existences" or other people's ideas) is the quality marked. So a sense exists in which the identity of ideas hinges on what they mark.

This sense of identity saves Locke from the objection threatening his semantics and his whole program of rectifying the imperfections of language and its abuses. The undetectable qualitative differences between the simple ideas of different people do not make them different ideas, or they do not make them different ideas in the sense in which mutual understanding demands that we attach the same ideas to the same words. Expressed plainly, the permutation does not change a thing. As a result, we cannot fall victims to undetectable misunderstandings. If the object-theoretical interpretation is right, Locke is not permitted to make this move. If ideas are mental objects, their identity cannot depend on anything outside the mind. In so far as he allows the identity of ideas to depend on things outside the mind, he renders his theory of ideas inconsistent.

This consideration is not sufficient to undermine the object-theoretical interpretation. An advocate of that interpretation might reply that Locke is inconsistent at this point. In order to support his failing semantics—he might say—he deviates from his official line, and falls into inconsistency. I want to block this response by showing that this is not the only place where Locke makes this move. I will argue that the thought that the identity of ideas depends on things outside the mind plays an equally crucial role in his theory of intuitive and demonstrative knowledge. (Sensitive knowledge is irrelevant for my purposes, so I will ignore it.) So let me move over to that territory.

Knowledge of this kind has two characteristics: it is about universal propositions, and it is absolutely certain—except that in long demonstrations the weakness of memory may lead to mistakes. So how can we gain certain knowledge of universal propositions? Locke's answer is the same as René Descartes': by *a priori* inspection of clear and distinct ideas. Once we have obtained the ideas from experience, we do not need further experience for knowledge. Its *a priori* character distinguishes knowledge from mere judgment. We have knowledge, if the examination of ideas alone is sufficient to ascertain their connection. If we need something over and above the ideas—namely, experience or testimony—, what we have is not knowledge but judgment.

Why should the *a priori* inspection of ideas yield certainty about universal truths? As for certainty, Locke takes it for granted that if our ideas are clear and distinct, we cannot go wrong about the connections between the ideas. This is a view he shares with his contemporaries. What is problematic is truth and universality. How the connections among ideas could provide a clue to the connections among their extra-mental counterparts is not obvious.

Why should the arrangements of ideas reflect the ones in the real world? Why should all extra-mental particulars falling under an idea exhibit features that correspond to those of the idea? There must be some linkage between the realm of ideas and the realm of things, one that grounds their isomorphism. There must be something to do the sort of job that God does in Descartes. If Locke's ideas are self-sufficient mental objects, as the object-theoretical interpretation has them, then the problem emerges even more evidently than it otherwise would. If we have two sets of ontologically separate objects, why should the relations between the members of one set mimic the relations between the members of the other? No wonder that representatives of this line often criticize Locke for failing to see the magnitude of this skeptical problem and having a too quick way with it.

But Locke does have a solution, which relies on the concepts of reality and real essence. Reality is the feature of ideas that provides part of the linkage. It also has a central role in the second half of the *Essay*: after its introduction, the earlier, elaborate taxonomy of ideas is replaced with the trichotomy of simple ideas, mixed modes, and substances, and this trichotomy is based on the consideration of reality (1975). To put it plainly, an idea is real if it matches what it should match. Patterns or "archetypes" exist for ideas to follow, and reality is the property of matching the pattern. The key point behind the trichotomy is that different kinds of ideas are directed at different archetypes.

With regard to simple ideas, Locke repeats in nearly the same words what he says in connection with their truth and falsehood. Simple ideas are, "Effects of Powers in Things without us, ordained by our Maker . . . whereby we distinguish the Qualities, that are really in things themselves" (ibid., 2.30.2.). They are "designed to be Marks," "real distinguishing Characters." To fulfill that purpose they do not have to be "exact Resemblances." That they are "constant Effects," if "they answer and agree" with the "Powers of Things" is sufficient. So the requirement is such that it can be met by ideas of secondary qualities as well.

Locke also explains why all simple ideas meet this requirement: we are completely passive during their acquisition. We get them from the lawful operation of things without us, and since we cannot interfere with these causal processes, there cannot be a mismatch between them and their archetypes. So the point is that the inherent qualities of ideas—that may disagree with the inherent qualities of things, as with the inherent properties of other people's ideas—do not matter. What matters is whether the idea marks some quality or power in external things. As simple ideas are received and not created by us, there must be some quality or power to cause them, and this is what they mark. As a result, simple ideas are all guaranteed to be real.

Mixed modes are different from simple ideas in two respects. First, they are voluntary creations. Second, they are arbitrary in the sense that they have no external archetype. They are not designed to capture something given in nature. Let me illustrate this with the two most notable kinds of ideas in this group, geometrical ideas and moral ideas. In the natural world nothing like a Euclidean triangle exists, yet we do not regard the idea of a Euclidean triangle as a monster that should be banished. Alternatively, take a moral virtue, like courage. Courage may have a legitimate claim on governing our conduct even if we all turn out cowards. In neither case would the lack of exemplification in the real world count as a deficiency. We would not feel obliged to revise or banish these ideas.

As mixed modes do not have real world targets, they cannot be faulted for failing to hit their targets. So mixed modes can prove unreal only in one way: if to exemplify them is impossible. And this happens only if they are made up of incompatible simple ideas. So we are free to compose mixed modes any way we want, and as long as they remain within the bounds of logical consistency, they are guaranteed to be real.

The ideas of substances—natural kinds, as we would call them today—, are also voluntary collections of simple ideas, like mixed modes, but they are not arbitrary. They are designed to capture clusters of properties that are regularly coinstantiated. For instance, we find that yellow, malleable, heavy, incombustible, etc. are properties that tend to go together, so we introduce the idea of gold to capture this cluster. We have an obligation to adjust our idea to the real cluster. So here we do have a target, and we may miss it. If we include a simple idea in the collection whose natural counterpart is not a regular attendant of the counterparts of the rest of the collection, our idea is not real. (The opposite kind of failure, when the collection of simple ideas does not exhaust the cluster of properties, does not make the idea unreal. It makes it inadequate.) Even though we do pretty well in this regard, here we do not have the sort of guaranteed reality as with the other two kinds of ideas.

But the idea of reality is not enough to answer the question concerning the isomorphism between ideas and reality. Suppose I have two ideas, both of which are real, and I perceive some connection between them. What guarantees that the real world objects that match the ideas also exemplify the connection? If A and B are real ideas, and I perceive that A is B, why would this indicate that all things that correspond to A also correspond to B?

At this point the concept of real essence enters. The real essence of something is what fixes all its properties (ibid., 2.31.6, 13; 3.3.15, 18; 3.6.3, 6, 9; 4.3.25; 4.6.10, 11, 12). Consequently, if I have an idea of the real essence of something, I have the key to all of its properties. This does not mean that I know all those properties right away. It may require considerable effort to trace the connection between the idea of the real essence and other ideas, to draw out what is implied in the idea of the real essence. But what is imperative for us is that we have a guarantee that the result of the *a priori* inspection of ideas matches the real order. When we see that the idea of a real essence implies an idea of a property, things falling under the first idea must have that property that corresponds to the second idea, because grasping the real essence means grasping what determines the properties.

The next question is whether our real ideas are ideas of real essences. With regard to simple ideas and mixed modes, Locke answers in the affirmative. In this domain, our ideas are reliable guides to truths. As a result, we may have genuine knowledge of mathematics and morality. With regard to substances, he answers in the negative. Our ideas of substances are just collections of simple ideas, and such collections contain no information about the further properties of the things that correspond to the collection. If you have an idea of something yellow, heavy, malleable, etc., you just cannot find out whether the thing you are thinking of is inflammable or not. The only things you can find out is that gold is yellow, heavy, malleable, etc. But then you do not find out anything new. So the only sort of knowledge we may have of substances is trivial. What is not trivial is a matter of judgment and probability and not of knowledge and certainty.

This was a long story to tell, and the point was that herein we find additional reasons to challenge the claim that ideas are mental objects. If ideas are mental objects, their identity should be fixed in terms of their inherent, qualitative properties. But we have learned two things about simple ideas that suggest otherwise. First, their qualitative properties are irrelevant for their reality. Ideas of secondary qualities, which are not resemblances of the powers of things that produce them are just as real as the ideas of primary qualities.

Second, simple ideas are ideas of real essences. They are not haphazard ways of picking out something without picking out what is essential about it. Instead, they pick out the essential being. The power picked out by the idea of red is nothing more than what the idea of red picks out. But the power itself is not red, since power is a secondary quality. So the significance of the qualitative aspect of the idea consists only in being correlated with the power. The ideas that are correlated with the powers should have different qualities so that we can tell them apart ("discern them," as Locke would put it), but it does not matter what qualities are used in telling the powers apart. What is crucial is the distinction marked and not the quality of the mark.

Both of these remarks point in the direction that a sense exists in which the identity of simple ideas is determined not by their inherent properties—by our way of conceiving them—but by their correlation to powers and qualities outside the human mind. If this is granted for simple ideas, it is true also of complex ideas. Complex ideas are composed of simple ideas. Composition is an inherent property, an aspect of our way of conceiving, and it plays an ineliminable part in the identity of complex ideas. But a sense exists in which the identity of simple ideas is fixed from outside, so the identity of complex ideas is not fixed completely by our ways of conceiving them either. Without this sense of identity Locke's claim that the *a priori* inspection of ideas can give us certainty about universal truths would be difficult to sustain. So this sense of identity of ideas is just as essential for his theory of knowledge as for his theory of meaning.

3. Locke's Content-Theory

Now I will explain how we can understand Locke's theory of ideas as a content-theory. This reading makes sense of the features of his account without which his semantics and epistemology would be implausible but which cannot be accommodated within the object-theoretical reading. What we need to show is that his theory of ideas, when construed in content-theoretical terms, provides foundations strong enough to support his semantics and epistemology.

The crucial points of this interpretation are as follows. (1) Whereas the content-theory distinguishes between the object of a thought, and its content, the way the object is conceived, Locke does not make this distinction explicitly, but he tacitly relies on it. He uses the term "idea" to stand for pieces of intentional content. (2) He is an externalist with regard to simple ideas in the following, minimal sense. The existence of simple ideas, in the sense of intentional contents, implies the existence of the objects we conceive when we have simple ideas. He does not claim that simple ideas are individuated in terms of things that are outside the mind. Simple ideas as contents are still distinguished in terms of their inherent properties. But these ideas are world-involving in the sense that we could not have them if some things did not exist.

This construal can cope with those features of Locke's account that fit ill with its object-theoretical understanding. First, consider the case of a systematic but undetectable inversion of yellow and blue. As we have seen, Locke explicitly says that the person who is subject to this inversion (relative to us) does not have false ideas with regard to other people's idea. So the ideas of the subject of inversion are "in conformity with" with the ideas of others. But the language Locke uses suggests that the ideas the subject of inversion has are not identical with our ideas. This may strike one as a contradiction, which is poorly disguised. But it can be easily straightened out with the help of the distinction between content and object. The subject of inversion, and the others, think of the same thing, namely a power in the things themselves. This is to a great extent in line with Locke's argument for the conformity: the ideas of the subject of the inversion are not false, because he would mark with his idea the same distinctions as we do. On the other hand, the way he marks this distinction differs from our way: the appearance he enjoys is not the same as ours. This is why Locke describes him as having ideas that differ from ours. So the object of his thought is the same as ours but the content of his thought is not.

Second, consider the related cases of the reality of simple ideas and their truth with regard to real existence. At first sight this appears to go against Locke's view on the ideas of secondary qualities. He says that these ideas are not resemblances. But he also says that they are real, that is they match their archetype, and that they are true; that is they are in conformity with what exists. How can simple ideas match their archetype and at the same time fail to resemble them?

We can also answer this question with the help of the distinction between object and content. Locke's claim about the failure of resemblance pertains to simple ideas as contents. The way we conceive the powers inherent in things does not match the way things are. Take away our way of conceiving, and no color is left: color is reduced to its causes (ibid., 2.8.17). But take away our way of conceiving size, and size still remains. In contrast, reality and truth have to do with the object of thought and not with its content. Locke is an externalist about simple ideas. We cannot create a single simple idea. So something must exist that causes us to have this simple idea. So the existence of the simple idea implies the existence of its object. Hence, all simple ideas are true. Their reality can be explained in a similar way. Simple ideas are not required to fit anything else than what causes them. As a result, they necessarily match what they should match, that is their archetypes. Hence, reality.

Looking at what changes if we move over from simple ideas to complex ones is instructive. The object of complex ideas is what we think of when we have them in mind. The content—if you wish, the idea—is a structure composed of simple ideas. Consider the issue of truth and falsity with regard to other people's ideas. Suppose your idea of gold differs from mine. Your idea is composed of the simple ideas of yellow and shiny; mine includes malleability and incombustibility also. Your idea picks out a different set of objects from mine. The objects of our thoughts disagree. This is why we face a genuine possibility of falsehood. Falsity is possible even if the objects of our thoughts do not exist. If you think of a centaur and I think of a unicorn, we are still thinking of different things. These were examples of ideas of substance, but the same goes for mixed modes.

Consider reality and truth with regard to real existence. In this respect substances and mixed modes are different. The first have extra-mental archetypes, sets of properties that are regularly coinstantiated. Suppose I join simple ideas of properties that are not coinstantiated, like when I form the idea of a centaur. Then the object of my thought does not exist. Whatever I wished to capture with my idea, I did not capture it. So my idea is chimerical and false.

Mixed modes do not have extra-mental archetypes. When we think about mathematics and morality, we make no assumption about the existence of our objects of thought. So only one way exists in which our idea may fail to match what it should: when we fail to think about anything, when our thought does not a proper object at all, for example when an idea is put together of incompatible parts. Apart from that, mixed modes are bound to be real and true. What is crucial about these considerations about complex ideas is that they show that the objects of thought do not form a special ontological category. Some of the things we think about exist, others do not.

The last issue we have to take up is real essence. Having an idea of the real essence of something is to conceive that thing in such a way that encapsulates all its properties. Simple ideas are ideas of real essences, because their object is a single quality or power. A single quality does not imply other properties. So if we conceive them, no property can be missing from our idea.

Mixed modes are ideas of real essences for a different reason. They are our arbitrary creations. Once we created them, it turns out that they imply properties, which are unintended side effects. But these properties are implied by the idea we created, so they are automatically encapsulated. The objects we conceive by the ideas of mixed modes are the objects that correspond to these ideas. These objects may have individual characteristics that are not encapsulated by the idea, but these are not characteristics of the kind, they are not "essential," so they do not have to and should not be represented in the idea. Like in the case of simple ideas, nothing is missing.

The situation is different with the ideas of substances. Here the object we conceive with the idea is given beforehand and independently of the idea. Observable properties exist that form stable clusters. Wherever we find a cluster, we naturally assume the existence of an underlying structure responsible for the cluster, something that holds the observable properties together (Locke, 1823, vol. 4, p. 91; 1975, 3.6.6., 3.6.36). As a result, in principle, we could conceive the same object in two ways, by way of the observable properties and by way of the underlying structure. The first is the nominal essence. But the properties that we include in our ideas of substances do not exhaust the cluster. The things that are similar in the ways we record in the idea are also similar in ways that are unknown to us. In addition, these similarities are not captured by our ideas of substances. As a result, they are not ideas of real essences. This is why an *a priori* inspection of these ideas does not lead to new insights.

Finally, let me respond to three possible objections against the line advocated here. The first is this: ideas are images, and images are mental objects, so Locke is an object-theorist of some sort. It true that several Lockean ideas have properties characteristic of sense perception and sensory imagination, namely visual, tactile etc. properties. In this sense, they may be images. (I doubt that all ideas are images in this sense, but I will not argue this here.) This much can be granted by the content-theoretical interpretation, since content does not have to be propositional or conceptual. We can regard images as mental objects in the formal sense of having properties and being referred to by noun phrases. Even the contents of the content-theory are objects in this minimal sense. But the fact that ideas are objects in this minimal sense is far from implying a commitment to the object-theory. The reference to the image-like character of ideas can also be easily accommodated within the content-theory: our ways of conceiving objects are visual, tactile, etc. All this does not show that in Locke's view the objects we think of are images.

However, Locke wrote passages that suggest that ideas are the objects of thought. For example, ideas are first introduced as, "whatsoever is the Object of the Understanding when a Man thinks, . . . whatever is meant by Phantasm, Notion, Species, or whatever it is, which the Mind can be employ'd about in thinking" (1975, 1.1.8.), and towards the end of the *Essay* we read, "since the things, the Mind contemplates, are none of them, besides it self, present to the Understanding, 'tis necessary that something else, as a Sign or Representation of the thing it considers, should be present to it: And these are Ideas" (ibid., 4.21.4). But these passages are not conclusive. First, contents are also objects in a minimal sense.

Second, Locke is not careful when he talks about ideas. John W. Yolton (1984, p. 90) cites many of Locke's passages (1975, 1.4.21, 2.1.5, 2.1.9, 2.1.23, 2.10.2, 2.32.1, 3) in which ideas are identified with sensations or perceptions, which should be regarded as mental acts and not mental objects. In addition, Yolton refers to Locke's (1823, vol. 9, pp. 211–254; vol. 10, pp. 247–259) criticism of Nicholas Malebranche, and his remarks on Malebranche's British follower, John Norris. This sort of carelessness is fairly easy to understand in light of his project, which is semiotical, not physical. What Locke wants to find out is not the nature of ideas, but the way signs—ideas and words—are used in the understanding of things. In the first draft of a reply to John Norris, who has criticized Locke for not making apparent the ontological status of ideas, whether they are substances or modes, Locke puts in exasperated terms that he should not like to be exercised about questions that are none of his concerns (Acworth, 1971, pp. 7–11).

The final objection is the one Michael R. Ayers raises against Yolton. In Yolton's view, as recapitulated by Ayers, Locke uses the term "idea" with a harmless ambiguity to stand for both the thought of an object ("intentional act") and the object thought of as the object is thought of ("intentional object"), but he does not use it stand for an object that stands between the real object and the mind. Ayers's objection is that ideas do not fit the role of intentional objects. Intentional objects are intrinsically intentional, by which he means that they possess representational power in themselves, they do not owe it to anything outside them. To this he objects by saying that ideas do not have their representational powers intrinsically. Instead, they represent the powers and qualities of things in virtue of the fact that they are caused by those powers and qualities. So their representative power is not intrinsic; not due to the way they are in themselves but to the way they are caused (1991, vol. 1, pp. 62–64). The reason is that simple ideas—the whole discussion is focused on simple ideas—are nothing else than the "blank effects" of qualities and powers outside the mind.

I think this controversy can be clarified with the resources of content-theory. What Ayers calls intentional objects are what we called contents: ways of conceiving objects. Contents are "intrinsically intentional" in the way Ayers suggests: a content represents an object, since ways of conceiving are always ways of conceiving something. But this sort of "intrinsic intentionality" does not clash with the fact that simple ideas are "blank effects." Ayers's point is that we can only have simple ideas due to the actions external things. This is exactly why I called Locke an externalist in a minimal sense: he holds that we could not have simple ideas if there were not qualities and powers to cause them. Minimal externalism is the idea that the existence of some contents implies the existence of the object they specify. No contradiction exists between the claims that contents intrinsically represent objects, and that some contents would not exist without the causal work of the objects they represent. The first claim describes the character of contents. The second has to do with their origins or, if you wish, the necessary condition of their existence.

Five

NORMATIVITY AND MENTAL CONTENT

Jussi Haukioja

1. Introduction: Normativity as Possession of Correctness Conditions

The imaginary philosopher widely known as Kripke's Wittgenstein—that is, Ludwig Wittgenstein as interpreted by Saul Kripke (hereinafter, Wittgenstien as interpreted by Kripke will be indicated by KW)—is usually read as arguing that a naturalistic account of word meaning and mental content is impossible (Kripke, 1982). I am not convinced that KW's argumentation was aimed at naturalistic theories in general, but he was arguing against the viability of the widespread naturalistic strategy of accounting for content in terms of a speaker or thinker's dispositions.

Everyone working on the subject agrees that normativity had a central place in KW's rejection of semantic dispositionalism. There is no general agreement on what he believed constituted normativity. The literature has different accounts. Many theorists follow Paul A. Boghossian's account of normativity as possession of conditions of correct use, or, in short, correctness conditions:

> Suppose the expression "green" means green. It follows immediately that the expression applies correctly only to these things (the green ones) and not to those (the non-greens). The fact that the expression means something implies, that is, a whole set of normative truths about my behavior with that expression: namely, that my use of it is correct in application to certain objects and not in application to others . . . . The normativity of meaning turns out to be, in other words, simply a new name for the familiar fact that, regardless of whether one thinks of meaning in truth-theoretic or assertion-theoretic terms, meaningful expressions possess conditions of correct use. (1989, p. 513)

Here Boghossian is writing about the normativity of meaning, but he obviously intends his remarks to carry over to mental content as well (Boghossian, 1989, pp. 516–517; Miller, 1998a, pp. 178–181). In this respect, Boghossian is following Kripke, who also took it as given that the same argumentation would apply equally to dispositionalism about meaning and dispositionalism about content. The problem is supposed to arise from the notion of correctness conditions, and such conditions exist for mental contents and linguistic entities. For example, correct and incorrect instances of applying the concept RED to objects in one's environment exist. Similarly, the thought that, say, George Walker Bush is wearing pink boxer shorts has correct and incorrect instances (when one takes into account thoughts with that content that appear in other possible worlds.) In this paper, I will also speak mostly of predicates and the normativity of meaning, but I could give a parallel argument for concepts and content.

This understanding of the normativity constraint is, compared to other accounts, minimalist. Nearly everyone would agree that content is normative in this sense, and our everyday folk conception of meaning and content clearly includes the thought that meaningful predicates and concepts do possess conditions of correct use in this sense. As such, this conceptualization is not controversial.

Recently some theorists have claimed that KW must have had something more substantial in mind. For example, José L. Zalabardo reconstructs the "Standard Normativity Argument," based on this account of normativity (1997). He claims that no textual evidence exists in Kripke for a key premise which is needed for the argument to work, and suggests another reading of the normativity requirement.

Scott Soames gives a related analysis (1998). I respond to both Zalabardo's and Soames's arguments in detail elsewhere (Haukioja, 2002). Other theorists such as John McDowell (1984) and Robert B. Brandom (1994) take the normativity of meaning to be the claim that meanings confer obligations on us, that to use a term with a specified meaning is to be committed to a particular way of using it. Since these obligations and commitments are supposed to be semantic in nature, these views go beyond the minimal notion of normativity, as possession of correctness conditions.

My intention in this paper is not to come to any conclusions about what KW (or Wittgenstein, for that matter) meant to say about content and normativity. Instead, I suggest that we may have dismissed too lightly the arguments we can construct taking normativity to consist of possession of correctness conditions. There is an argument to be found in, or suggested by KW, that, if successful, does present a real problem for many influential theories of meaning and content. In the end, I do not think that this argument damages the prospects for a naturalistic theory of content, but it does force us to reconsider some of our conceptions about semantic theories in general. For the rest of this paper, I will take the claim that meaning is normative to mean the following:

(*N*) If *S* means something by predicate *P*, then there exists an unbounded range of actual and non-actual cases to which *P* correctly applies, and an unbounded range of actual and non-actual cases to which *P* does not correctly apply.

This definition bears a strong similarity to the definition of normativity given by George M. Wilson (1994, p. 381). The correctness conditions for the application of meaningful predicates are, at least in some cases, determined in advance. When agents mean something by a predicate and form judgments about whether the predicate applies to previously unencountered entities, the correctness or incorrectness of their judgments is, at least in some cases, already determined before the agent make the judgment.

I take (*N*), thus stated, to be a platitude about meaning. There are theorists who would deny (*N*). Meaning finitists such as David Bloor (1997) and Barry Barnes (1982) deny that meanings "reach ahead of actual application" in the manner suggested. Crispin Wright (1980) takes Wittgenstein's rule-following considerations to refute (*N*) (called the objectivity of meaning by Wright).

The terminological differences can be more than a bit confusing: both Bloor and Wright insist on "the normativity of meaning," but they do not take this to include advance determination of correctness in new instances. It appears to me that when Boghossian takes normativity to be, "a new name for [a] familiar fact" about meaning, advance determination is an inseparable part of this "familiar fact." Wright does think that correctness conditions exist for the application of predicates, for an individual in a community. The finitists would agree. But Wright explicitly denies that correctness conditions exist for the community as a whole, "we shall reject the idea that . . . the community goes right or wrong in accepting a particular verdict on a decidable question; rather, it just goes" (1980, p. 220).

I believe that Wright, like the finitists, feels compelled to reject (*N*), because they wrongly equate (*N*) with Meaning Platonism, the view that correct application is determined by an abstract intermediary such as a set or a property (Miller, 1998b). I do not think that meaning finitism, the view that correct application is never fully determined in advance, or Wright's (early) closely related view, are tenable positions, but to argue against them here is beyond the scope of this paper.

This reading of the normativity constraint may seem to overlook the many passages in KW that stress the justificatory or action-guiding role of meanings. I am prepared to accept that KW may have had another conception of normativity in mind as well, and that this other strand might be developed to present a powerful argument against naturalistic semantics. I will not be concerned with this possibility here. I tend to think that we can plausibly read the passages where he writes about semantic justification or guidance in a sense that supports my reading of the normativity requirement. I will briefly return to this issue at the end of this paper.

On this reading, semantic norms are constitutive instead of prescriptive or regulative. A sign counts as meaningful if and only if it has conditions of correct use. Similarly, a concept or a thought counts as having content if and only if it has correctness conditions. I do not think that more substantial, semantic "oughts" exist. Because a predicate has a specified meaning, it follows that it applies correctly to some things, and not to others—agents do not count as competent users of the term unless they are aware of this—but it does not follow from this that we "ought" to, in general, apply it to the entities to which it correctly applies. In different situations, and for different reasons, agents may have obligations to apply predicates to entities to which they do not correctly apply.

2. Correctness and Extension

On the reading of the normativity constraint that I have adopted here, KW's normativity argument against dispositionalism is that dispositionalism cannot account for the correctness conditions of predicates (Kripke, pp. 29–37). There is a quite natural response to this, given by Jerry Fodor and echoed by many others:

> [Requiring] normativity to be grounded suggests that there is more to demand of a naturalized semantics than that it provide a reduction of such notions as, say, extension. But what could that "more" amount to? To apply a term to a thing in its extension is to apply the term correctly; once you've said what it is that makes the tables the extension of "table"s, there is surely no further question about why it's correct to apply a "table" to a table. (1990, p. 135)

This response relies on what we could call an "indirect" explanation of predicate or general term reference. We account for the correct applicability of a general term by postulating an intermediary abstract object—in this case, the extension of the term. Other indirect explanations make use of other intermediaries such as properties or universals.

I do not deny that we find it natural to say that, for example, "predicates refer to properties," or that "the meanings of terms determine their extensions," and similarly for concepts. It does not appear to be a big step from these commonplace expressions to saying that the task of a semantic theory is to explain how these referential relations between predicates and properties, or predicates and sets (extensions) arise. If we take predicates primarily to denote abstract objects, and only derivatively particular entities that bear relations to these abstract objects, we are committed to what I would call Meaning Platonism:

> Meaning Platonism: If S means something by predicate P, something about S determines an abstract object A as the referent of P. When S correctly applies P to individual x, this correctness consists in the appropriate relation obtaining between A and x.

A could be, for example, a universal, and the appropriate relation that of instantiation. Alternatively, as in the assumptions behind the quotation from Fodor, *A* could be a set (the extension of *P*) and the relation that of set membership. The key idea is that to be a competent user of predicate *P* is to instantiate a set of facts, which determines an abstract object to be the referent of *P*. Correct use of *P*, on the other hand, consists in successfully tracking the requirements placed by this abstract object.

In Meaning Platonism, the intermediary abstract objects are seen as truly constitutive of predicate reference, and not merely as a convenient way of speaking about the predicate being applicable to new, unencountered instances. Giving intermediaries an explanatory role leads to difficulties for Meaning Platonism. As Anthony Quinton put it nearly half a century ago:

> What . . . is the explanation of re-applicability? The usual procedure is to assert the existence of some species of abstract objects, either universals in the world or concepts in the mind . . . . Either the assertion that there are intermediaries says something more than that there are re-applicable words or it does not. If it does then the theory is viciously regressive; if it does not then no real explanation has been given. (1957, p. 39)

The vicious regress, which, according to Quinton, plagues theories that posit intermediaries, is a variant of the Third Man:

> To find out that some individual, *a*, is *F*, I must first discover that *a* stands in some relation *R* to an intermediary *x*. To find this out I must first discover that the pair of individuals (*a*, *x*) stands in some other relation *S* to the intermediary pair (*y*, *z*) and so on. (1957, p. 39)

I am not convinced that this regress argument works when the explanatory intermediary is an extension—in this case, the relation *R* is just the relation of set membership, and we do not obviously face a vicious regress. But KW can be interpreted as finding another kind of flaw in the theory which posits intermediaries: To find out that predicate *P*, as used by *S*, correctly applies to *a*, I must first discover that *P*, as used by *S*, stands in some relation *R* (reference) to an intermediary *x* (the property of *P*-ness or the extension of *P*). I suggest KW directs his criticism at this relation.

On this reading, KW's arguments against dispositionalism aim at showing that the total dispositional state of an agent cannot determine an intermediary (such as an extension of "table" or the addition function) such that it truly explains re-applicability. KW points out two problems for dispositionalism. (Many commentators find, in KW, three objections to dispositionalism: the finitude objection, the normativity objection, and the objection from error. On my reading of the normativity constraint, the last two coincide.)

First, the dispositional state, which constitutes grasp of a meaning, must be finite, while extensions are infinite (Kripke, 1982, pp. 26–28). Most commentators appear to think that this so-called finitude objection is not especially damaging. There is no limit to the range of situations in which dispositions (mental or non-mental) could be displayed (Blackburn, 1984, p. 289). The finitude of my total dispositional state does not seem to be in conflict with the claim that predicates can be applied in a potentially infinite range of situations.

On a non-Platonist theory such as the one I will sketch in the next section, this reply seems appropriate. But the finitude objection seems more promising as an argument against the dispositionalist theory which is also committed to Meaning Platonism—a theory which claims that the (total) dispositional states of speakers pick out determinate intermediaries for their predicates. The claim is that, here and now, my dispositional state grounds a relation between, for example, my use of "green" and the property of greenness, or the set of all actual and possible green things, or what have you. Unless we are willing to accept a Lewisian inegalitarianism with respect to properties (however they are understood), too many properties or sets exist, KW claims, for such a determinate meaning relation to be grounded.

We can use KW's own "skeptical paradox" about the signs "+" and "plus" to illustrate this reading. A dispositionalist theory which also accepts Meaning Platonism would claim that my dispositional state picks out one determinate function as the intermediary which determines correctness conditions for my use of "+" and "plus." The dispositionalist owes an explanation of why my dispositional state picks out the addition function, and not one of the countless plus-like functions, which are also compatible with my finite past usage of the "+"-sign. KW claims that this cannot be done without circularity.

The second problem is the normativity objection. To say that Platonistic dispositionalism fails to account for (N) is to say that it does not deliver the right intermediaries. Crude dispositionalism will wrongly equate actual use with correct use. We are all disposed to make errors occasionally. To account for (N), we need a way of filtering out incorrect applications. But sophisticated dispositionalism can, according to KW, only be made to seem to work by making it viciously circular, bringing in the intended properties or functions in the specification of ideal conditions. KW's dismissal of sophisticated dispositionalism is notoriously quick: "A little experimentation will reveal the futility of such an effort" (Kripke, p. 31). But KW's argument has, I believe, been convincingly amended by Boghossian (1989, pp. 539–540; cf. Miller, 1998a, pp. 181–189; Miller 2003).

I claim, then, that KW should (or plausibly can) be read as arguing against Meaning Platonism. Alexander Miller (1998b) and George Wilson (1994; 1998) have proposed similar interpretations of KW. The normativity argument is a central part of KW's argument against dispositionalism, which in turn is meant to show that currently influential theories of meaning cannot explain reference to the intermediaries postulated by Meaning Platonism.

Read this way, KW does not claim that a successful dispositionalist reduction of extensions would be inadequate as a theory of meaning, because it would still leave out normativity. Instead, KW is claiming that a dispositionalist reduction of extensions, if we give extensions the role of intermediaries, is not possible, because the resources available to a dispositional theory are not sufficient (without circularity) for picking out the right extensions. With Meaning Platonism out of the picture, we should no longer think of extensions as having explanatory value. Instead, we should see the specification of correctness conditions as a precondition for the specification of extensions. One might say that, according to KW, extensions are (covertly) normative, in a minimalist sense, because they are just the sets of entities to which a predicate correctly applies. I believe KW would agree with Fodor that nothing would be left out if we had a reduction of extension—if we reject Meaning Platonism, such a reduction would already have to include a "grounding" of (*N*).

It may be helpful to elucidate these issues by seeing how similar claims would apply to our grasp of the rules of chess. The rules of chess are constitutive rules that distinguish between correct chess moves and incorrect chess moves (non-moves). The voluntary movement of a piece on a chessboard counts as a chess move because we perform it in a context where the distinction is made between correct moves and non-moves. The correctness of the correct moves available in any given position on the chessboard is also determined in advance of any judgments about correctness. As such, they play a role analogous to semantic norms, as I have explained them above.

Of whatever grasping the rules of chess consists, this grasp has to enable an agent to play chess (though not to play chess well). Agents grasp the rules of chess if and only if they are able reliably to distinguish between moves and non-moves. Suppose we wanted an explanation of the competence of a chess player and asked, How is it that some possible moves on the chessboard are correct and others are not? An analogue of Meaning Platonism would be that something about a chess player determines an abstract object—perhaps the Platonic object LEGAL CHESS MOVE, or the set of all legal chess moves—as the standard by which the correctness of particular moves is determined. In analogy with the quotation from Fodor, we could then argue, "To perform a move which belongs to the set of all legal chess moves is to make a correct chess move; once you've said what it is that determines the set of correct moves, there is surely no further question about why it is correct to make one."

I doubt that anyone would take seriously the claim that this argument shows that chess is not a rule-governed activity. We do not find the Platonistic pattern of explanation intuitively compelling in the context of the rules of chess—we are used to thinking of competence in chess as a practical ability.

Giving an account of the competence of chess players is, primarily, to give an account of how they make the distinction between correct moves and non-moves. We could say that a player's ability, in a way, picks out the set of all legal chess moves, but only derivatively. The Platonic explanation seems to get things the wrong way around. But, in philosophy, the analogous explanation of semantic competence is quite wide-spread.

This account of KW's argumentation gives a plausible reading of his "skeptical" solution, as well. With Alex Byrne (1996), I find the standard reading of the skeptical solution as a projectivist theory of meaning attributions difficult to square with the apparent minimalism about facts and truth-aptness found in KW. On my account, the claim that meaning attributions do not have classical truth conditions would turn out to say the following. We cannot establish the truth of "Jones means addition by 'plus'" by showing that "Jones" refers to Jones, "addition" to the addition function, "'plus'" to the word "plus" and "means" to the meaning relation which obtains between Jones, "plus" and the addition function. Read this way, KW's point is that meaning is not a relation between a person, a sign, and an intermediary such as a function. No facts about an agent could ground such a relation in a determinate way. Instead, meaning attributions make claims about how it would be correct for the agent to apply the sign in question, in particular actual and counterfactual situations. The challenge for a theory of content would then be to show how the distinction between correct and incorrect use could arise on such a theory. In the next section, I will present the outlines of what I take to be the most promising theory.

3. Dispositions and Corrective Practices:
The Response-Dependent Account

If what I have presented above is on the right track, the task of a semantic theory is then to show how correctness conditions can come to exist for the application of concepts and meaningful predicates in an unbounded range of particular cases. To account for (N), we would have to show how the correctness of some applications could be determined in advance of anyone's judgment about the applicability of a concept. In this section, I outline a theory of this sort, the response-dependent account of the possession conditions of basic concepts and the mastery of semantically basic terms.

To restrict our attention to basic concepts, ones acquired from examples, will be helpful. The possession of basic concepts does not consist in knowledge of a definition, but is recognitional in nature. In the case of adults who understand a natural language, the majority of new terms are undoubtedly acquired via definitions or descriptions that make use of antecedently possessed concepts. Obviously, not all concepts can have been acquired in this way since the process has to start somewhere. We do not need to assume that what is semantically basic for one speaker or thinker is basic for all of us—what matters is that for each individual some concepts must be basic. To explain how non-basic concepts have content we already have to have an account of how basic concepts have content.

On a response-dependent account (Pettit, 1991; Jackson and Pettit, 2002), the following holds for any basic concept, *F*:

(RD) It is *a priori* that: *x* is *F* (concept *F* correctly applies to *x*) if and only if *x* is such as to seem *F* in favorable conditions.

(RD) follows quite straightforwardly from a natural story of how we acquire basic concepts. Being basic, *F* can only be acquired by ostension—by exposure to exemplars, things to which *F* correctly applies. Any such set of examples is finite. To apply *F* to new cases, we have to develop the appropriate extrapolative disposition—we have to come to see the exemplars as saliently similar to each other in some respect, such that we can recognize of new cases whether they are similar to the exemplars in this same respect. But this is just to say that one has to develop the disposition to react in a uniform way in response to things which seem *F*; the disposition to apply *F* to all and only the things which seem *F*, should the question arise. Our patterns of response, then, pick out one continuation of the series among the countless possibilities.

Sometimes, the way things appear can be misleading. Because a not *F* thing can sometimes appear *F*, or a thing *F* can appear non-*F* for some reason, the qualification "in favorable conditions" is included in (RD). What, then, are favorable conditions? One idea would be to give a list of factors that must be present or absent—if *F* is a color concept, for example, one might require that observations be made in daylight, that the observer shouldn't be under the influence of a drug that affects color vision, and so on. This way of defining favorable conditions fails, I think, due to the holistic nature of our belief systems. (Boghossian, 1989, pp. 539–540)

A more plausible suggestion, I think, is Philip Pettit's idea that favorable conditions are those that survive our practices of correction and approval (1990; 1999). For a criticism of Pettit's view, see Frank A. Hindriks's work, "A Modest Solution to the Problem of Rule-Following" (2004). When we find that intertemporal or intersubjective discrepancy exists in our classifications, we take this to be a sign that someone has made an error because of some perturbing factors. To resolve the discrepancy, we assume that the conditions were not favorable for making the relevant class of judgment, and the deviant judgments are discounted. We try to identify the perturbing factors that caused the discrepancy—we do not discount deviant judgments for the sake of maintaining consistency. Instead, we assume that, when discrepancies arise, some judgments were made in conditions where judgments of the relevant kind tend to be unreliable.

According to this theory, we would need to develop, in addition to the extrapolative dispositions, also meta-dispositions to revise one's extrapolative dispositions when such discrepancies arise. Having these meta-dispositions enables one, then, to take part in the discounting practices.

It might appear as if the appeal to meta-dispositions would make the account circular, but it does not. The question of the correctness of the meta-dispositions need not be raised when we are explaining how the first order dispositions can lead to either correct or incorrect judgments. That we have the meta-dispositions, and that we share them widely, is enough. We can raise the question of the correctness of our meta-dispositions by forming meta-meta-dispositions, but this is not required for the discounting practices that give rise to the distinction between correct and incorrect first order judgments.

On this view, our concept F correctly applies to x when and only when x is such that, in circumstances which do not give rise to the kind of discrepancy explained above, x would fit our dispositions to generalize from the exemplars. Therefore, (RD) holds. In addition, (RD) is *a priori* because our responses fix the extension of F: F correctly applies to whichever entities do fit our extrapolative inclinations. The property in question may be a different one in different possible worlds in which F is used to refer to things which seem F under favorable conditions, but whichever world happens to be actual, F will correctly apply to the property which fits the speakers' dispositions in that world.

The talk of extension-fixing and properties may seem Platonistic in the sense discussed earlier, but Meaning Platonism is not implied. The correctness conditions of a basic concept are not explained here by a connection with an intermediary abstract object—instead, whether a term applies to an entity is settled, one might say, on a case-by-case basis. To speak of a concept's extension, or of a predicate referring to a property, is perfectly appropriate, as long as this is not taken as explanatory of correct application.

The response-dependent story also accounts for the advance determination of correct applicability. To take an example, suppose I am making a judgment about whether a particular object, x, is red. We might think that, on the response-dependent account, the correctness or incorrectness of my judgment is not determined in advance. According to (RD), RED applies to x if and only if it appears red—but whether it appears red is just a matter of how x happens to strike me, of how I classify it. But this claim would overlook that appearances are grounded. Object x has the relational property of being such as to seem red to us in favorable conditions in virtue of the non-relational properties of both x and us.

If RED is response-dependent, then the question of which non-relational property of objects grounds the relational property of being such as to appear red will depend on our nature. But once our nature, our extrapolative dispositions, and the nature of object x are fixed, the correct answer to the question "Is x red?" will, vagueness aside, exist in advance of anyone's judgment. If our extrapolative dispositions were completely random, and there were no constraints on how and why we revise them, correctness would not be determined in advance. But considerable convergence in our tendencies to generalize exists, both across times and across persons. Without such convergence, the response-dependent account could not get off the ground, because we would instinctively generalize in wildly inconsistent ways across times and persons. The question of whether RED correctly applies to an unencountered object x can be determined in advance of our judgments.

In some cases, the correct usage may be indeterminate, for one of two reasons. First, many concepts are vague in the familiar sense of having borderline cases, such as our color concepts. Second, when concepts are used outside their normal range of application, there may be alternative ways of extending the usage, such that none of these is determinately correct. These two sources of indeterminacy correspond to what Mark Wilson calls expected and unexpected vagueness, respectively (1982, pp. 551–552). Cases of the second kind are sometimes used in arguing for finitism (Barnes, 1982), but these cases do not threaten the advance determination of cases within the normal application range of a concept—and this range will contain as yet unencountered cases (and be unbounded).

To accommodate for the second kind of indeterminacy, we do need to acknowledge that our concepts may not have determinate correctness conditions outside their normal range of application. Nonetheless, we can think of them as having partial denotations or partial extensions in the manner described by Wilson (1982), following Hartry Field (1973).

What about the community as a whole? Can the response-dependent framework allow for community-wide error? Wright argued that, since we can only become aware of going astray from the pattern of correct use by communal assessment, the community as a whole cannot go right or wrong, it "just goes" (1980). Within the response-dependent account, we can accept Wright's starting point if we hold that favorable conditions are those which survive our discounting practices, as described above. Only disagreement in judgments can give us reason to think we have gone astray, although I believe that the assessment need not be communal: intrapersonal assessment of one's judgments concerning the same object over time is sufficient.

But on the response-dependent account, for the community as a whole to go astray for a time is also possible. We can easily imagine events in which, say, the color perception of all members of a given community are temporarily affected in such a way as to cause disagreement over time. For example, suppose all red things were to appear green, and *vice versa*, to everyone for some time. (That we do not find this supposition self-refuting shows that we do assume that the community as a whole can go wrong for a time.) In such a situation we would find ourselves, as a community, in inter-temporal discrepancy—our usage of color concepts rests on the tacit assumption that the colors of objects are, by and large, stable. We would then seek to find an explanation for this discrepancy, and discount the deviant judgments as erroneous. Thus, we might discount all judgments made during the period, which is just to say that the community went wrong as a whole.

What if we could not find any explanation? If a community-wide discrepancy of the kind imagined here was a single occurrence, we would be justified in discounting the deviant judgments even without an adequate explanation. Were such occurrences to recur often, our whole color discourse would be undermined. Yet, one could say that the community "just goes," in another sense, though not the one Wright had in mind. It would seem unfair to ask for a justification for why we pick out this property as the referent of, say, RED, and not some other property. At this level, correctness and incorrectness do not apply—we pick out this property just because we happen to have these extrapolative dispositions and not some others. That is just the kind of creatures we are. But, given that we are creatures of this kind, and not some other, correctness conditions will exist for (many) new applications of a concept, for individuals in a community and for the community as a whole.

Finally, a word on the more "substantial" accounts of semantic normativity mentioned at the beginning of this article. While I do not believe strictly semantic "oughts" or prescriptive semantic norms exist, if semantic competence is seen as a practical ability, I think we can account for some of the intuitions about the justificatory or action-guiding force of meaning. Agents do not count as competent users of a predicate unless they show (and would show, in counterfactual circumstances) responsiveness to correction, and are prepared to correct themselves. It is constitutive of being a competent speaker or of possessing concepts that one be (implicitly or explicitly) aware of there being correct and incorrect uses of one's terms and concepts. In a fundamental sense, their grasp of meanings guides competent speakers—we count as competent speakers only if we leave open the possibility that we or others may later overthrow our judgments about the applicability of a term to new instances.

Six

THE ONTOLOGICAL AND INTENTIONAL STATUS OF FREGEAN SENSES:
AN EARLY ACCOUNT OF EXTERNAL CONTENT

Greg Jesson

Knowledge and sensation ... must be either the things themselves or their forms. The former alternative is of course impossible: it is not the stone which is present in the soul but its form. It follows that the soul is analogous to the hand; for as the hand is a tool of tools (that is a tool for using tools), so the mind is the form of forms and sense the form of sensible things. (Aristotle, 1941, 431b24–432a3)

The referent of a proper name is the object itself which we designate by using it; the idea which we have in that case is wholly subjective; in between lies the sense, which is indeed no longer subjective like the idea, but is yet not the object itself. (Frege, 1980, p. 58)

1. Introduction

No field of human thought exists in which thinkers are more motivated by realism than in mathematics. Unlike philosophers of mathematics, mathematicians are almost universally convinced that they are describing mind-independent realities that are not in any way human inventions or constructs. So it was with Isaac Newton, Gottfried Wilhelm Leibniz, Georg Cantor, Ernst Zermelo, Karl Weierstrass, Pierre de Fermat, Augustin Cauchy, Richard Dedekind, and Kurt Gödel. Consequently, it is significant that Gottlob Frege and Edmund Husserl, widely considered to be the founders of the two dominant schools of contemporary western philosophy—the analytic and phenomenological movements—received their doctorates in mathematics. Both began their academic careers as mathematicians attempting to understand how math and logic could be mind-independent, yet presented within the subjective mental life of the individual. Frege spent his entire academic career in the mathematics department at the Friedrich Schiller University in Jena, Germany. Husserl studied under Karl Weierstrass at the University of Berlin and later wrote that Weierstrass gave a series of lectures on the theory of functions that kindled in him an interest concerning "a radical grounding of mathematics" (Willard, 1984, p. 21).

It was Frege's and Husserl's early conviction of the reality of mathematical and logical entities, and the objectivity of mathematical and logical judgments, that grounded their Platonism, epistemological realism, ontological dualism, anti-empiricism, anti-psychologism, and fervent rejection of skepticism.

Throughout this study, I will quote extensively from all periods of Frege's writings to show that Frege struggled with the same problems and reworked his solutions over decades, and to provide a context in which to illuminate Frege's influential paper of 1892, "On Sense and Reference" (1980). Although "On Sense and Reference" is widely considered a paradigm of analytic methodology, paradoxically great disagreement exists about what constitutes the article's subject. I argue that Frege's paper is best understood as an account of intentionality that bridges the continental and analytic movements by introducing an innovative methodology to address several perennial philosophical problems. I maintain that the most perspicuous interpretation of what Frege is attempting in "On Sense and Reference" is to illuminate what Brentano called the "reference to a content" in every mental phenomena. Frege does this by providing an explication of the cognitive difference between informative and non-informative identity statements. Although he does not use the word "intentionality," this pointing phenomenon of consciousness, as revealed in thinking and language, is what drives Frege to offer his account of referring by means of *Sinn* ("sense") to *Bedeutung* ("meaning").

To avoid confusion between thoughts as abstract objects and thoughts as individual mental events, in this work I will refer to the propositional subset of abstract objects with upper-case, "Thoughts." Abstract modes of presentation will be indicated by the upper-case "Sense," or "Senses," or the German *Sinn* or *Sinne*.

Sounding like Aristotle, near the beginning of his career Frege claimed in his 1893 book *The Basic Laws of Arithmetic*:

If we want to emerge from the subjective at all, we must conceive of knowledge as an activity that does not create what is known but grasps what is already there. The picture of grasping is very well suited to elucidate the matter . . . that which we grasp with the mind also exists independently of this activity, independently of the ideas and their alterations that are a part of this grasping or accompany it; and it is neither identical with the totality of these events nor created by it as a part of our own mental life. (Frege, 1967, pp. 22–24)

And near the end of his career, in his 1918 article, "The Thought," Frege wrote:

The grasp of a thought presupposes someone who grasps it, who thinks. He is the owner of the thinking, not of the thought. Although the thought does not belong with the contents of the thinker's consciousness, there must be something in his consciousness that is aimed at the thought. But this should not be confused with the Thought itself. (1984, p. 369)

Much current Frege scholarship often appears adrift and cut off from textual moorings. Any attempt to interpret specific doctrines such as *Sinn* and *Bedeutung* apart from Frege's motivations and overall philosophical framework will necessarily misconstrue his work.

2. Language as the Alleged "Clothing of Thought"

Many contemporary commentators claim that Frege was concerned not with mental acts and their properties and relations but with the properties and relations of language. Some consider one possible exception to be Frege's essay "The Thought," but this is explained away by claiming it was written near the end of his career. Contradicting the popular philosophical myth that Frege was not concerned with mental acts, Frege went to great lengths to maintain a fairly plain and consistent distinction between mind-independent realities and psychological realities throughout his writings. "The Thought" merely distills and summarizes what had been present in his early and middle writings. More often than not, interpretations of Frege are uprooted from all textual evidence because, as Joan Weiner puts it, "He turns out to be positively hostile to some of the most prominent views attributed to him, and widely held by our philosophic peers" (1990, p. 11). Take for example Frege's thoughts on the conceptual, explanatory limitations of a naturalistic account of human life, the theory of natural selection, to explain the objectivity of logical judgments:

In these times when the theory of evolution is marching triumphantly through the sciences and the method of interpreting everything historically threatens to exceed its proper bounds, we must be prepared to face some strange and disconcerting questions. If man, like all other living creatures, has undergone a continuous process of evolution, have the laws of his thinking always been valid and will they always retain their validity? Will an inference that is valid now still be valid after thousands of years and was it already valid thousands of years ago? (1979, p. 4)

The all-too-common trend to interpret Frege as primarily interested in language while ignoring the mental act and the mind-independent realm of abstract entities, such as numbers, functions, concepts and Thoughts, is simply without foundation. Michael Dummett, for example, claimed, "Frege was the founder both of modern logic and of modern philosophy of language" (1978b, p. 116). Fair enough, but Dummett meant far more than that Frege was merely concerned with the well-recognized limitations of natural language. Dummett claims:

> [A]ccording to Frege, natural languages are incoherent in the sense that no complete systematic account of the use of sentences of such a language could be framed . . . . [W]here Frege diverged from his predecessors was in the methodological remedy he adopted. Others have thought that the philosopher's task is to divest thought of its linguistic clothing, to penetrate all forms of mere expression to the pure thought which lies beneath: Frege was the first to attach weight to the fact that we cannot have a thought which we do not express, to ourselves if not to others. Any attempt to scrutinize our thoughts, taken apart from their expression, will therefore end in confusing the inner experience of thinking, or the merely contingent mental accompaniments of thinking, with the thoughts themselves. (ibid.)

But exactly how can this be reconciled with what Frege actually said? Frege wrote, "To think is to grasp a thought. Once we have grasped a thought, we can recognize it as true (make a judgment) and give expression to our recognition of its truth (make an assertion)" (1979, p. 185).

And:

> Therefore two things must be distinguished in an assertoric sentence: the content, which it has in common with the corresponding propositional question; and the assertion. The former is the thought or at least contains the thought. So it is possible to express a thought without laying it down as true . . . Consequently we distinguish:
>
> (1) the grasp of a thought—thinking,
> (2) the acknowledgement of the truth of a thought—the act of judgment,
> (3) the manifestation of this judgment—assertion. (Frege, 1984, p. 355; see also Frege 1979, pp. 139, 142, 269–270)

Further, if Frege gave the argument that we can have access to our thoughts only by means of language, this appears to generate insurmountable problems. Either we can have direct apprehension only of language, or we can only have indirect access to language through some other language to which we have direct access. The first option needs to provide an explanation of what it is about language that dictates that we can only have direct apprehension of language, because, after all, language is just another object (either printed or spoken) in the world. The second option tilts dangerously close to generating a vicious infinite regress in which we will need language to represent language, which represents language, and so on. In order to prevent a regress, an explanation needs to be given why only language can be directly apprehended. More importantly, to think that language *per se*, however specified, can do cognitive work apart from the mental lives of individuals is just a confusion. Language must be intended or somehow incorporated into the mental life of the individual. Therefore, mere language cannot be the explanation of how the mental act intends or interacts with other objects.

Gregory Currie, in his article, "Frege on Thoughts," makes a claim similar to Dummett's:

> Frege's puzzlement about how we grasp Thoughts is really a puzzlement about how a use of language—an event which takes place in the physical and mental worlds—enables us to grasp an abstract Thought. (1980, p. 239)

Barry Smith also followed Dummett in his article, "Husserl's Theory of Meaning and Reference," when he remarked:

> And how does logic come to be applicable to our actual thinkings and inferrings? Frege seeks to solve these problems, in effect, by assigning to language the job of mediating between cognitive events on the one hand and thoughts and their constituent meanings on the other. Unfortunately however he does not specify how this mediation is effected. (1994, p. 164)

and:

> Frege sees no contradiction in the assumption of a being who could grasp thoughts directly, without linguistic clothing, even if for us humans it is necessary that a thought of which we are conscious enters into our consciousness always with some sentence or other. (ibid., p. 165)

But perhaps Frege provided no explanation of how language connects our internal experiences to objective thoughts, "an event [according to Currie (above)] which takes place in the physical and mental worlds," because he never made such a claim. Frege went to great lengths to distinguish the mere private experience of thinking, the grasping of a Thought, from the activities that presuppose such thinking, judging a Thought to be true or false, and expressing a Thought by means of spoken or written language or by means of hand or facial gestures.

Psychologism and formalism commit similar errors. Psychologism confuses the activity of thinking with the Thought that the thinking is grasping. Formalism confuses the sign, written, verbal or otherwise, with what is signified. Frege was not especially interested in the linguistic or mathematical sign *per se* but what such signs signify. Confusing the particular signs with which we often express Thoughts, and the Thoughts, generates, according to Frege, utter confusion. Consequently, Frege despised formalism because it identified the sign with the signified:

> Now the objects of arithmetic, i.e., numbers, cannot be perceived by the senses. How do we come to terms with them? Simplicity itself! We pronounce the numerical signs to be the numbers. Then in the signs we have something visible, and that is naturally the chief thing. Of course the signs have totally different properties from the numbers themselves, but what does that matter? . . . Of course it is a puzzle how there can be a definition where no question is raised about the connection between sign and thing signified. So far as possible we knead sign and thing signified indistinguishably together . . . . Sometimes, it seems, the numerical signs are regarded as chess pieces and the so-called definitions as rules of the game. The sign then does not designate anything: it is the subject matter itself. To be sure, in all this one trifling detail is overlooked: namely, that with "$3^2 + 4^2 = 5^2$" we express a thought, whereas a configuration of chess pieces asserts nothing. Where people are satisfied with such superficialities, of course there is no basis for any deeper understanding. (1967, pp. 10–11)

To be sure, Frege stated, "the world of thoughts has a model in the world of sentences, expressions, words, and signs" (1984, p. 378), but if A is a model of B, then A and B are not identical. Frege saw Thoughts and their mental expressions, ideas, as things distinct and separable from language. Therefore, we can have ideas that are not expressed in written or spoken language, or in any other way. According to Frege, because language can model logic, language can, when it correctly models logic, reveal logical structure. But language should never be confused with logic. He wrote, "If our language were logically more perfect, we would perhaps have no further need of logic, or we might read it off from the language. But we are far from being in such a position" (1979, p. 252, see also 269–270). Succinctly stated, if, "the business of the logician is to conduct an unceasing struggle against psychology and those parts of language and grammar which fail to give untrammeled expression to what is logical" (ibid., 1979, pp. 6–7), then logic cannot be identical to psychology, language, or grammar.

Many similar examples abound. Perhaps no contemporary philosopher has done as much to rediscover the historical Frege as opposed to his mythological, contemporary counterpart as Tyler Burge. Considering the industry of re-reading Frege as an idealist, Burge said:

> It is dubious historical methodology to attribute to a philosopher with writings that stretch over decades, a large, controversial doctrine, if he nowhere plainly states it in his writings. If Frege had believed in any such idealism about physical objects (or any doctrine qualifying their ontological status), he would have surely said he did. Doing so would have been necessary for a philosopher to balance the flat-out statements about mind-independence that Frege makes. (1996, pp. 355–356)

3. Frege's Project

It is simply a mistake to read Frege as not providing an ontological structure to explicate how the mental gets hold of the non-mental. According to him, every investigation into what mental and linguistic acts signify is an investigation into the Sense/referent nexus or the Thought/referent nexus. Of course, the terms "*Sinn*" and "*Bedeutung*" have become part of the familiar jargon of contemporary philosophy, but Frege's purpose in writing about these entities is only revealed in the context of describing the act of knowing, of coming to be in a state of knowledge where one's subjective experiences apprehend what is objective. The point of Frege's discussion concerning the cognitive differences between informative and non-informative identity statements is that some of our most important pieces of scientific knowledge are informative identities. Near the middle of "On Sense and Reference," Frege claimed that we are not concerned with the referent alone, but the Thought united with the referent in the act of knowledge (1980, p. 65). Similarly, in the final paragraph, Frege (ibid., p. 78) returns to the issue of the differing cognitive values of uninformative and informative identities to provide an account of knowledge wherein the meaning of a sentence is integrated with the referent of the sentence, its truth-value.

Further, central to Frege's project was his desire to defend the claim that it was only within the context of his three-fold distinction that mental life was even possible. He rejected accounts of mental life that were inadequate to describe what we all experience. For our mental lives to be merely the unconnected flow of subjective ideas in the way that David Hume claimed is not possible. Nor is it possible that we only have access to what is private. Such accounts are mere philosophic yarns that are driven by philosophic commitments made prior to, and independent of, the evidence that is present to each of us. As Frege put it, "I do not create a tree by looking at it," and I do not, "generate a thought by thinking . . . still less does the brain secrete thoughts, as the liver does gall" (1979, p. 137). Similarly, we cannot combine visual, auditory, and tactile ideas with the auditory ideas associated with the use of words to adequately describe our commerce with Thoughts. "The result," wrote Frege, "would no more be a thought than an automaton, however cunningly contrived, is a living being" (1979, pp. 144–145).

From a prephilosophical and pretheoretical point, as Frege scornfully proclaimed in "The Thought," "A man who is still unaffected by philosophy" knows that our experiences have a particular character (1984, p. 360); that ultimately our experiences are about a specific subject matter; and that we utilize a perspective, out of many possible perspectives, to get hold of the subject matter. He took it as indisputable that in order to indirectly perceive, we must first directly perceive something, and we must always think or conceive of things in a specific way, or from a particular perspective. Second, the same object can be apprehended in a multitude of ways. Third, the same object could be apprehended by the same person at different times and by different people at the same time, and at different times. From this, Frege sought to account for our experiences of meaning, referring, and knowing, by means of the well-known threefold distinction of ideas, Senses and referents.

Attempting to avoid psychologism, Frege insisted that Senses exist independently of the psychological lives of individuals and yet are involved in the explanation of how ideas and expressions, in mental and linguistic acts, have the referential character that they do. We cannot account for the difference between informative and non-informative identity statements by means of expressions and referents alone. Frege argued that the only way to explain the epistemic difference between these is by finding some way to bring the same object before the mind by means of different modes of presentation. The burden of his project was to give sufficient weight to both the objective and subjective linked together by the Senses that are on the objective side of the Thought/referent nexus.

Frege's three realms are then:

(1) Ideas: Thinking is a private, subjective internal process that consists of having ideas which grasp Senses and the propositional combinations of Senses, and Thoughts (1979, pp. 2, 142; 1984, p. 368). Grasping a thought takes place in our inner world of experience (1979, p. 137; 1984, p. 137).

(2) Senses: Senses and Thoughts are mind-independent (1984, pp. 133–135, 137, 148–149). Senses are non-spatial and non-temporal (1984, pp. 135, 148). Thoughts are not properties of an individual (1984, p. 133).

(3) Referents: Physical objects are mind-independent and are not properties of humans (1984, p. 137).

Although the Sense and the referent are always distinct, Frege had to claim that there must be a close connection between them, for by means of the Sense the appropriate and singular referent is selected. Different mental acts and different expressions having different Senses can refer to the same object via different "aspects" that the referent has. Different Senses will contain different "modes of presentation" and thus allow for different ways of determining the referent. Senses are meant to be like a lens through which we view the world, but Frege was ultimately concerned to demonstrate the mind independence, and therefore the objectivity, of Senses and Thoughts as the only way to avoid complete mental sequestration. He maintained:

> The thought we have expressed in the Pythagorean theorem is timelessly true, true independently of whether anyone takes it to be true. It needs no owner. It is not true for the first time when it is discovered; just as a planet, even before anyone saw it, was in interaction with other planets. (1984, p. 363)

Senses (*Sinne*) are, "timeless, eternal, and unvarying," and are between the individual's particular, private ideas (*Vorstellungen*) and the referents (*Bedeutung*). Psychologism implies that we are always confined to our individual repository of subjective ideas. For Frege, such unqualified isolation within the "inner world" would be a, "blurring of the boundary between psychology and logic," and the breakdown of all science (1984, pp. 352, 368).

Often the emphasis in interpretation is put only on the three types or levels of realms and not upon the relationship they have to each other. Frege realized that it was not sufficient to list the three different kinds of entities involved in the mental act and leave it at that. Instead, he sought to explain how they are connected in the formation of the epistemic act. As Dallas Willard remarked:

> We do not in reality have complexes of sense/reference/*Vorstellungen* floating about doing interesting semantic or epistemic things. We have persons representing, inquiring and making judgments about objects, and occasionally coming to knowledge of them. (1994, p. 237)

The crucial questions for Frege's account of the mental act center on two issues: first, what is the connection between the private, subjective ideas and the public, objective Senses, and in particular the propositional subset of Senses, Thoughts? Second, what is the connection between the Thought and the referent?

4. The Ontological and Intentional Status of Fregean Senses

I suspect that Frege's notion of Senses, as functioning between the psychological representations in individuals and the objects of reference, turns out to be deeply problematic. I argue that Frege faces a dilemma: Either Senses are not as objective as he wishes, from which it follows that he lacks an account of why we are not marooned in the psychological realm; or Senses are as fully objective as he maintains, from which it follows that they are not suitable to be the means by which ideas and expressions obtain their capability to refer to the kinds of things we ordinarily take our mental and linguistic acts to be about. If Senses are incorporated into the psychological realm to explain the intentionality of acts, they will be incapable of accounting for objectivity; if Senses account for objectivity, then there exists no explanation of how our mental and linguistic acts refer to the kinds of commonplace objects we take them to be referring to. Frege revealed the weight of this dilemma in that he held that our subjective ideas are required to accomplish many of the tasks of Senses. But if our apprehensions of Senses are the means by which we subsequently apprehend referents, we seem cognitively removed from those objects in a way that is incompatible with our experience.

Concerning the first horn of the dilemma, Frege required ideas to perform functions that are supposedly unique to, and are reasons for positing, Senses. Ideas, images, and impressions have an explanatory advantage by being embedded in the individual's mental life. But as Frege emphasized, such entities could never account for the objectivity of knowledge because they are necessarily private. However, the grasping of a referent is not possible without the mental or linguistic act grasping a Sense. In "The Thought," Frege claimed, "Although the thought does not belong with the contents of the thinker's consciousness, there must be something in his consciousness that is aimed at the thought" (1984, p. 369). At this level, intentional inexistence is impossible—every idea grasps a Sense. The objectivity of Thoughts precludes their isolation within consciousness, yet to avoid the skepticism Frege so rigorously attacks, consciousness must grasp something besides itself and its contents: ideas, images, and impressions.

There must be some way for the individual's private stream of ideas and images to select Thoughts. Out of the infinite number of Thoughts how do we get hold of the appropriate Thought? What is it about our mental life that makes it possible to grasp the right Thought? It can't be that just any Thought we get hold of is the appropriate one. This view would utterly undercut all thinking and therefore be self-defeating. Frege claimed, "to the grasping of thoughts there must then correspond a special mental capability, the power of thinking." This should not be identified with Thoughts because "in thinking we do not produce thoughts we grasp them" (1984, pp. 368–369). Similarly, he wrote:

> The metaphors that underlie the expressions we use when we speak of grasping a thought, of conceiving, laying hold of, seizing, understanding, of *capere, percipere, comprehendere, illigere*, put the matter in the right perspective. What is grasped, taken hold of, is already there and all we do is take possession of it. (1979, p. 137)

This immediately complicates matters because this appears to require two levels of intentionality. Subjective ideas grasp Senses, and Senses lay hold of the referent. But if this is the case then Senses cannot be the explanation of how referents are grasped since they themselves must be grasped. It would appear *ad hoc* to maintain that every mental act requires a Sense in order to grasp, except when what is being grasped is a Sense. What is it about Senses that absolve them from requiring another Sense to grasp them? If Senses require another Sense to be apprehended then why stop there? A vicious infinite regress lurks. Perhaps Frege could fend off the vicious regress by arguing that Senses do not admit of differing modes of presentation, that they are one-dimensional. But we are still left with the question: How do our subjective ideas intend these one-dimensional objects?

Frege was aware of such problems, yet he felt he had been driven to this point and there was no turning back. In a most remarkable passage he admitted:

> [T]he grasping of this law [a thought] is a mental process! Yes, indeed, but it is a process which takes place on the very confines of the mental and which for that reason cannot be completely understood from a purely psychological standpoint. For in grasping the law something comes into view whose nature is no longer mental in the proper sense, namely the thought; and this process is perhaps the most mysterious of all. (1979, p. 145)

What could it mean to be, "a process which takes place on the very confines of the mental," and yet not part of the mental? Does getting the object very close to the mental make intentionality any easier to explain how the mind grasps objects? Are the problems of perception alleviated in the slightest if I can touch the object in question to my eye?

George Berkeley's strategy for eliminating every possible epistemological and ontological gap wherein skepticism might root was to demonstrate that it was logically impossible for anything to exist without being either perceived or a perceiver. Berkeley found a way to secure a necessary connection between sensations and objects, and between concepts and perceptions. However, in doing so, Berkeley also eliminated the intentionality of the mental.

Ideas do not intend objects; they are the objects. Bringing the objects into the mental does not solve Frege's problem, because this is just a restatement of the first horn of the dilemma: If Fregean Senses are incorporated into the psychological realm to explain the intentionality of acts, then they will be incapable of accounting for objectivity. For Frege being a part of the realm of the mental just is what it means for something to be private. Obviously, he cannot get Senses and Thoughts that close to the mental without losing sight of the question that started his intellectual quest: How is objectivity possible?

Concerning the second horn, I argue that insofar as Frege holds that apprehension of the referent necessitates, the grasping of Sense, this results in puzzling philosophical consequences because it excludes direct access to the world that he wanted to secure reference to in the first place. If designation to the referent is always mediated via Sense, then it appears that we have only *de dicto* apprehension of the common objects of consciousness and *de re* access only to Senses. But why should this be? We do not directly or definitely get hold of the referent, because, according to Frege, our access is always mediated by means of a Sense, a mode of presentation. We never grasp the bare referent itself, but only secure it indirectly, by means of one, out of an infinite number of possible descriptions.

The concepts of *Sinn* and *Bedeutung* were introduced to account for the differences between informative and uninformative identity statements. According to Frege, singular terms such as "the fountain of youth" are meaningful just insofar as they have a Sense, but from this, it does not follow that they have a referent. The theory was expanded to include predicates and sentences. The referent of a predicate is a concept and the referent of a sentence is a truth-value. Frege insists that the *Sinn* of an expression is neither a common physical object in the world nor the stuff of our mental lives. The Sense of "the morning star" is not an astronomical body nor is it an idea. What grounds the intersubjectivity of Senses is that they are abstract objects. This is especially crucial in Frege's account of the Sense of a sentence that is embedded in a context expressing a propositional attitude. Such a sentence refers not to the customary referent, namely a truth-value, but to the *Sinn*, which the sentence expresses when not so embedded. So from the fact that the morning star is identical with the evening star, it does not follow that if Smith believes that the morning star is bright then Smith also believes that the evening star is bright. Co-referring terms cannot be substituted within such intentional contexts because the sentences in such contexts do not refer to the ordinary objects, such as stars or planets, but to abstract objects, Senses and Thoughts. Under such circumstances, the Thought that in non-intentional contexts mediates reference, becomes the object which is being referred to. Frege put it this way:

In order to speak of the sense of an expression "*A*" one may use the phrase "the sense of the expression '*A*.'" In reported speech one talks about the sense, e.g., of another person's remarks. It is quite clear that in this way of speaking words do not have their customary reference but designate what is usually their sense. In order to have a short expression, we will say: In reported speech, words are used *indirectly* or have their *indirect* reference. We distinguish accordingly the *customary* from the *indirect* reference of a word; and its *customary* sense from its *indirect* sense. The indirect reference of a word is accordingly its customary sense. Such exceptions must always be borne in mind if the mode of connexion between sign, sense, and reference in particular cases is to be correctly understood. (1980, p. 59)

Frege's point applies not only to describing another person's cognitive events but also to one's own cognitive events. Speaking of indirect reference, Frege said, "If one says 'It seems to me . . . ,' one means 'it seems to me that . . . ,' or 'I think that . . . ,' we therefore have the same case again" (1980, p. 67). In such intentional contexts, terms that are co-referential in extensional contexts cannot be freely substituted without the possibility of changed truth-value. Sentences which express such cognitive events are not about the common objects of the world but about abstract objects—Senses—and replacement of any expression with a different expression having a different Sense will result in a sentence expressing a different Thought.

In their book, *Husserl and Intentionality*, David Woodruff Smith and Ronald McIntyre argue that in such propositional contexts, we will only be left with indefinite or *de dicto* ascriptions because we are not picking out any particular object. G. E. M. Anscombe argued in her essay, "The Intentionality of Sensation: A Grammatical Feature," that several differences in the logic of intentional and non-intentional sentences exist. To substitute co-referential terms while preserving truth-value and the possible indeterminacy of the object being thought about is not possible. Anscombe pointed to another significant feature:

[I] can think of a man without thinking of a man of any particular height; I cannot hit a man without hitting a man of some particular height, because there is no such thing as a man of no particular height. (1965, p. 161)

According to Anscombe, we should, "not be hypnotized by the possible non-existence of the object." (ibid.)

Although Frege never discussed the problem of quantifying into intentional contexts, his doctrine of indirect reference explains why a failure of existential generalization exists in such act contexts. Smith and McIntyre presented this case: from the sentence, "Sherlock Holmes believes that the murderer used belladonna," we cannot infer that "There is an X such that Sherlock Holmes believes that X used belladonna" (1982, p. 72). Sherlock Holmes can mistakenly believe that the murderer used belladonna, or even mistakenly believe that there was a murderer without affecting the truth-value of, "Sherlock Holmes believes that the murderer used belladonna." What his mental state of belief is about is not about any particular object in the world, but an abstract object, a Sense. Smith and McIntyre (1982, pp. 69–82) concluded that there is no genuine *de re* reading of act-sentences that are about objects in the world, since such sentences are strictly speaking about abstract Senses. Given Frege's account, in intentional contexts, the objects that are always accessed are the abstract Senses and Thoughts, never the ordinary objects that we think we have within our cognitive grasp.

If, in order to grasp a Sense it must be mediated by another Sense, and that, by another, and so on, then we would never have any *de re* beliefs; instead all our beliefs would be under a description and be indefinite *de dicto* beliefs. Under such an account, knowledge is not just mediated by Thoughts (or propositions), but is of Thoughts. But perhaps Frege could solve this problem by identifying the Senses with qualities. Frege's ontology divides along one line between unsaturated and saturated entities. Functions (and concepts) are unsaturated while arguments are saturated. An obvious parallel exists here between unsaturated concepts and qualities on the one hand, and saturated arguments and objects on the other. When Frege claimed that concepts are unsaturated, his point was not that they cannot have independent existence; instead it was that concepts and arguments come together to form a unity in the way that qualities and objects come together to form a unity.

So why not just identify concept with quality? The answer is that this creates more problems than it solves. If concepts are construed to be qualities of the object, how can this be an account of intentionality? Exemplification is not intentionality. On the other hand, if qualities are construed to be concepts, are these concepts part of the mental lives of individuals or not? If they are part of the mental lives of individuals, then Frege has decisively moved towards idealism and again lost any possible account of objectivity. If they are not a part of the mental lives of individuals, then we are again faced with the prior problem of explaining how our ideas intend such entities.

These considerations suggest that Fregean Senses are incapable of providing an adequate account of the intentionality of mental acts. Either Senses are incorporated into the psychological realm and so are incapable of accounting for objectivity, or Senses do account for objectivity, but then there exists no explanation how our mental and linguistic acts refer to the commonplace objects amidst which we live. Any theory that entails that we are incapable of directly thinking about the common objects of life must be wrong, for we would not even be able to think about that theory. Frege's *Sinne*, like Hume's ideas, introduced to be the instrumentalities and mediators whereby we gain access to the world, make it impossible to reach that world.

5. Conclusion

The lasting value of Frege's contributions to the issue of intentionality rests in his insistence on drawing the distinction between the psychological and the objective. Where he fell short was in explaining how the objective can be made present within the subjective while maintaining the absolute distinction between the two. Ironically, it was Frege's relentless quest to undermine psychologism that led him to separate the Thought content from the mental act and ultimately this makes his account incapable of linking the act to a mind-independent object. After all, external content is just as external as the objects that Frege sought to reach.

Frege's failure to take subjectivity seriously in that he could not account for the intentional capacities of mental acts ultimately makes his case for objectivity untenable. If cognitive content is in the public world, independent of the mental lives of individuals, then our two problems for Frege will emerge: (1) How can individuals become acquainted with the same public content? (2) How does public content secure the proper referent? My suspicions are that any theory that does not affirm a robust account of mental content will face the same difficulties as Frege's view and lack the resources to resolve them. Husserl attempted to overcome these problems by stressing the explanatory importance of the mental act. He provided grounding for intersubjectivity by treating Senses as universals present in mental acts as properties of those acts.

Having gone this far, I might as well go a little further and end with a general ontological claim. Whatever accomplishes intentionality, whether brain states, mental states, linguistic events, and so on, can do so only by means of its actual properties and relations. Anything else, as Hilary Putnam argued—unknowingly implicating his view—will be magical. Unfortunately, Frege's theory is an example of such magic.

ACKNOWLEDGMENTS

I am greatly indebted to Laird Addis, Dallas Willard, and Ken Williford for many illuminating discussions on the topics of this paper and for their critical comments on earlier drafts.

Seven

SENSE-DATA, INTENTIONALITY, AND COMMON SENSE

Howard Robinson

1. The Problem

It is almost universally believed that the sense-datum theory and common sense realism are incompatible. This is because the only form of realism available to the sense-datum theorist is representative realism that is not commonsensical, because it involves a "veil of perception" standing between the perceiver and the world. In a book I wrote on perception (1994), I accepted that the sense-datum theory—if combined with physical realism—was faced by this problem. I argued that a representative theorist could defend his position against the charge of skepticism by appeal to an "argument to the best explanation," but I did not deny that the sense-datum theory, combined with a realist approach to the physical world, led to a counter-commonsensical "veil." I am no longer so sure that this is true. What I say in this paper is tentative, because, for reasons that will emerge, I am not entirely convinced that the physical realist does not face a "veil," but neither am I convinced that he does.

The expression "veil of perception" is both metaphorical and recent. What it means is plain enough. We can best understand the phrase by considering the way that G. E. Moore (1918–1919) and Henry Habberly Price (1932) introduced the term "sense-datum." If something appears to me to be red, I can ask myself whether that red patch is the surface of a physical object, or something else. This approach, which involves reifying the contents of "seemings," is a mark of the sense-datum theory. The idea that it is correct to reify contents in this way, I have called "the Phenomenal Principle," (PP) to which all sense-datum theorists subscribe:

Phenomenal Principle: If someone, S, appears to perceive something F (where F is a sensible quality and not a substance term) then there is something F of which S is aware. (Robinson, 1994)

For the case in question, if something appears to me to be red, then there is something actually red of which I am aware. For the kind of reasons gathered under the label "argument from illusion," it will be plain that the red patch the subject appears to see is not actually the surface of a physical object. The red patch is what one is aware of, so one is aware of something other than the physical world. The best that can be the case is that this thing stands between me and the physical world, as its representative.

This conflicts with common sense because the core of the commonsensical theory of perception can be stated simply:

Common Sense Realism: In perception, we are aware of physical objects themselves, and not merely of some surrogate or representative.

Our suspicions might be aroused at this point. Something strange is going on, because Common sense realism is being pitted against things appearing different under different circumstances—which is mainly what the "argument from illusion" says. Common sense recognizes that objects appear in different ways without themselves changing. Can it be the case that these facts—that we are aware of objects themselves and that things appear differently under different circumstances—are incompatible with each other? To cope with this apparent conflict, and reconcile common sense realism with "perceptual relativity," or "illusion," the simple statement of common sense realism is augmented by The Intentionality Thesis: (1) the subjective content of experience ("how the world appears") is not to be reified, so that (2) even when an object appears other than the way it actually is, that object is still the direct object of awareness and the only thing of which we are aware.

The Intentionality Thesis can be taken as standing proxy for all those idioms which were appealed to by "ordinary language" philosophers in their attempt to show that all phenomena can be characterized without resort to sense-datum talk. The intentional idioms such as "seems," "looks," and "appears" lie at the center of this whole family.

The theory that results from combining Common Sense Realism and the Intentionality Thesis—augmented common sense realism—appears, at first sight, to be wholly at odds with the sense-datum theory, for the sense-datum theory reifies how the world appears and makes these reified objects into objects of awareness, which prevent us from being aware of physical objects directly. The sense-datum theory also appears to directly contradict Intentionality Thesis (1). How could two theories be more in opposition, for Intentionality Thesis (1) says that we should not reify the subjective contents of experience and the sense-datum theory does precisely that? But perhaps this conflict is more illusory than real. Perhaps the Intentionality Thesis and the Phenomenal Principle can be reconciled.

2. Reasons for Being Suspicious

First, I want to draw attention to an interesting historical fact. The attack on the common sense theory—under the label "naïve realism"—at the beginning of the twentieth century, was largely based on the argument from illusion. That argument, in effect, said that the common sense was incoherent, because it both affirmed the directness of perception and acknowledged that things look different when they have not changed intrinsically. This is held to be inconsistent because you cannot both see something directly and not see it as it is in itself.

The historical interest in this argument is that the philosophers who used it—Moore (1918–1919), and C. D. Broad (1923), for example, were at the forefront of the analytic attack on idealism, but the argumentative strategy of trying to show that our ordinary concepts—in this case, perception, common-sensically understood—have contradictions in them, is a strategy typical of the Hegelian idealists. For example, Francis Herbert Bradley tried to show that there cannot be relations (1930, chap. 3), and J. M. E. McTaggart attempted to show that there cannot be time (1921/1927, chap. 23).

The early analytic philosophers were doing the same thing for our ordinary notion of perception. This does not undermine the argument—stated baldly, this is just guilt by association—but it does suggest that the argument may be too quick, and that perhaps there ought to be another way of explicating our common sense concept. The apparent antinomy that the argument from illusion exposes is, after all, far more obvious than those supposedly uncovered by Bradley or McTaggart.

The usual way around the problem in the last fifty years has been to accept the Intentionality Thesis and deny the sense-datum theory. The exercise I am engaged in is seeing whether we can accept them both. After all, I do not believe that the protagonist of common sense would wish to deny that there is a perfectly good sense in which, if an individual hallucinates a pink rat, or sees a white object that appears pink, the individual is genuinely aware of pink. The challenge is not to set up the two theses of common sense as alternatives to the sense-datum theory, but to reconcile them with it, as far as is possible.

3. First Moves in Reconciliation

Even the sense-datum theorist accepts that taking our experience in the common sense realist way is both natural and inevitable. Price's (1932) account of taking or acceptance is a good example of this. We can express this acceptance in the following propositions:

(1) Our sense-data are naturally and inevitably conceptualized and interpreted as appearances of a physical world and this is the only way they

can be made sense of and how they are "meant" (by evolution, God, or both) to be interpreted.

This commits us to speaking the language of perceptual realism, and, in so far as I am speaking of the physical world, when I report an hallucination, nothing pink exists, only the appearance of pink exists. The same applies when the white wall looks pink: within the physical interpretation, there is nothing pink. This gives us:

(2) Within the scope of our common sense realist interpretation of the sense-data, the Intentionality Thesis holds. This thesis is at the core of the "logic" of the perceptual realist interpretation of experience, which we cannot—and should not wish to—avoid.

But this does not constitute a reconciliation of common sense and sense-data, for it is still ambiguous how we can be aware of objects in the physical world, not surrogates, and yet be aware of logically private sense-data. Indeed, (1) and (2) above look more like an idealist attempt to explain how we construct a physical world out of our sense-data, than like a reconciliation with common sense. It is a common sense of a distinctly Berkelian kind. (1) and (2) are, after all, an account of how our sense-data are interpreted and conceptualized as perception of an external world: the sense-data are there and the external world is just a way of interpreting them.

Although I would be quite sympathetic to this conclusion, I do not think that we can easily come to that conclusion. It is, indeed, an account of how our conception of the physical world is constructed, but it does not follow from that, that it is a construction of the physical world itself, as it would be if the position were idealist.

Let us call the interpretation of our sense-data enshrined in (1) and (2), the Canonical Interpretation, because it expresses how the data are meant to be interpreted. If we are to understand how something like direct realism is to be infused into the canonical interpretation of sense-data, we must look at what is involved when other cognitive states, such as thought and judgment, are taken to be directly and really of real objects in the world.

If I think about Heroes' Square, in Budapest, I think using words with meaning, but no one thinks that these vehicles of thought—the words—constitute some sort of veil between me and Heroes' Square itself. The thought is about Heroes' Square, *simpliciter*. We might attempt the following parallel. If we can take perception as being a form of judgment, represented not in language but in a sensorial way, can it not be thought to be just as much of its object as is a verbal thought?

It is crucial to see how integrated the sense-data and the judgment are in perception. Consider the perceptual judgment involved in perceiving and recognizing that there is a bottle of red wine in front of me. What is the relation of the judgment to the phenomenal episode with which it is connected? It is tempting to think of them as accompanying each other—side by side, so to speak, or with the sense-datum first, swiftly followed by the judgment. But it is also possible to think of them as synthesized into one event, with the phenomenal content contained within the judgment.

Just as some judgments have words as their vehicle, perceptual ones have phenomenal contents. The judgment is about the bottle of wine, which is an object in the external world. This is no more a "projection," in a sense that carries the derogatory overtones of illusion or unnoticed mistake, than it is in the case of the way the words, with their meanings, refer to the Heroes' Square: the phenomenal features, when structured into a judgment, refer to the bottle, in a way analogous to that in which the meaningful words refer to the Square.

4. First Objection: This is Not the Sense-Datum Theory

The natural suspicion is that these suggestions constitute a relapse into a wholly intentional theory. I want to deny this, because we can refer to the sense-data, just as we can refer to the physical objects of perception. I can identify a reddish, bottle-shaped datum, and I can judge perceptually that there is a physical bottle present. But, someone skeptical about my supposed reconciliation might argue, does not this give us two competing objects of awareness, one a sense-datum in private space, and the other a physical object in public space? I am not convinced that it does.

The pure intentionalist is obliged to claim that, when an experience is hallucinatory, or a feature of experience non-veridical, there is no phenomenal object to be an object of reference. The comparison with thought is instructive here. When a thought fails of reference, there is, we might accept, for purposes of argument, no real proposition, but there is a meaningful sentence or thought with a definite character. If I try to refer to "that star over there" when it is only a speck on the telescope lens, even if one concedes—for purposes of argument—that there is no reference and no proposition, that there is a perfectly meaningful sentence, and we know, in the context, what the speaker is "trying to say" uncontroversial. I can pick out and refer to the individual words and their meanings irrespective of whether the sentence succeeds in making a reference in the world, and say what would have to have been the case for there to have been a genuine proposition. What is more, without the meaningful words there would be no propositional thought in the case of successful reference (assuming the thoughts of this kind to be verbal or dependent on words). The words and their meanings are identifiable independent of their contribution to that particular proposition, if there is one; and, in an obvious sense, the word meanings are prior to what is said by means of them in that individual case. Similarly, if I see a white wall looking yellow, or hallucinate the bottle altogether, the experience has a character and a content that I can individuate perfectly easily, and it involves the sense-data, without which the judgment delivered by the canonical interpretation would not be possible. I use the word "character" in this context deliberately. David Kaplan attributes "character" to demonstratives even when they are failing to refer (1978). This is the same for sense-data, regardless of whether they are representing reality as it actually is. The analogy with the relation between word meanings and their contribution to the content of a proposition shows why the sense-datum in private space and the fully conceptualized experience of a public object are not in competition.

On the other hand, the reservation remains: can sense-data be thought of in this dual way? Can that very thing (I inwardly ostend the sense-datum as picked out by Moore or Price) be both the private datum and the public object? Is it possible that, like the duck-rabbit, I can see it both as a subjective realization of the sensible quality in question, and as an intentional mode of appearance of a physical object? One way of trying to explain how this can be is by mobilizing the contrast between the extensional and intensional senses of "aware." According to traditional sense-datum theorists, the competition is between naïve realism, which involves extensional awareness relations to the surfaces of objects, and extensional awareness of logically private objects. You cannot have both, at least in the same area of the visual field. But why cannot you have extensional awareness of a sense-datum and intensional awareness of how an object seems to be or appears, the second occurring by means of the first? The question "is that very thing private or public?" is ambiguous, depending on whether the demonstrative "that" in the question is situated within a thought structured by the Canonical Interpretation or is understood extensionally. What is, in core respects, experientially the same, can be conceptualized in either way, but the intensional interpretation would not be available if the extensional one were not. The sense-datum, considered as an extensional object of awareness is like the word as sound or mark: the intentional interpretation is parallel to the word as meaningful and making a definite contribution to the propositional thought. The reference "that word" can mean either.

5. Second Objection: Sense-Contents are Not Vehicles According to Common Sense

The following reservation might remain. I have no inclination to take the vehicle in the case of thoughts—that is, the words, considered as either sounds, marks or meanings—to be the objects of those thoughts themselves. But in perception this is what I naturally do with the sense-contents. The sense-datum theory tells me that this identification is false, and this subverts common sense.

To reply to this, we must make a distinction that common sense does not make, but which is consistent with it. As we will see in a slightly different context below, the failure of an issue to be raised in common belief does not mean that common belief opposes the issue. The distinction is between identifying sense-contents with external objects *simpliciter*—which is naïve realism, with all its problems—and identifying the contents with how the object appears. The sense-datum theory does say that sense-contents are not identical with objects, *simpliciter*, but it does not say that they are not identical with how objects appear: indeed, it says just the opposite.

6. Sense-Data Have a "Blocking Function" Which Supports the "Veil of Perception" Metaphor

This objection can be thought of as a version of the objection presented in section 5 presented, because it is a way of expressing the worry that sense-data masquerade as, but are not, external objects. It is also an argument against intentionalism that I have used elsewhere:

> [I]f S is aware of a square patch of red in the center of his field of vision, then he cannot also be aware of a blue patch of similar shape and same or smaller size on the same line of vision. Most especially, if he is aware of a red patch which is not in fact the colored surface of an object but, e.g., an hallucination, then he cannot be aware of the color of a blue physical object on this line of vision . . . . [This] shows that such objects possess what might be called a blocking function, i.e., the capacity to constitute a "veil of perception" after the traditional manner of sense-data. (1974, pp. 308–309)

One premise of this argument is that a hallucination—assuming it to be opaque—blocks out from our visual field the objects that are actually present in the world. The other premise—though not so explicit—is that, accepting a causal argument for sense-data, the ontological status of normal sense-contents is the same as that of some hallucinations. The conclusion is that normal sense-contents also block out from our visual fields the objects that are actually present in the world. The premises are not controversial. To resist the conclusion we must maintain that the blocking function of hallucinations does not follow directly from their being subjective, for they share this, if the sense-datum theory is correct, with all sense-contents. This is indeed the case. The role of hallucinations as blocking out the world is a cognitive function: that is, they block out the world because they are not the modes of appearance, enshrined in a perceptual judgment, appropriate to the objects that are actually present, not because they are subjective entities. Normal sense-data are the modes of appearing, located in perceptual judgments, appropriate to the objects present and so do not constitute a cognitive block. The argument as I originally presented it is effective against a traditional naïve realism, which requires that sense-contents be ontologically identical with facets of external objects. The whole argument of this paper is that that is not the right way to characterize the directness of our perceptual contact with the world.

7. So Where Is the Traditional Problem?

Does this mean that the traditional "problem of perception," according to which acceptance of the arguments for sense-data leads to a "veil of perception," is misconceived? I think that it probably does and that the traditional problem rests on the failure of the empiricists to have any understanding of thought and intentionality. When John Locke stated in the introduction to the *Essay* that he meant by idea "whatever is meant by phantasm, notion, species, or whatever it is that the mind is employed about in thinking," he was not declaring idea to be a generic notion, but instead claiming that there was no serious theoretical difference between the different concepts that it was used to replace (1689).

In particular, that sense-contents and intellectual contents are, *in re*, the same kind of thing. The assimilation is from the intellectual to the sensory, for both are mental images. Locke may have been ambiguous in what he was doing, but Berkeley and Hume understood. For empiricism in general from that point on, thought was either the association of ideas (images), or later, in the pragmatists as exemplified by Alfred Jules Ayer, the situating of those ideas in an appropriate behavioral or functional role. For discussion of Charles Sanders Peirce's account of signs, see Ayer's discussion (1968, chap. 4).

The reconciliation I am proposing between the sense-datum theory and common sense rests on taking the intentionality of thought to be as real and intrinsic a feature of perceptual judgment as is its phenomenal nature. Any theory that treats intentionality reductively, as a function of external relations of the data, cannot see it as an intrinsic part of the phenomenology, which is essential to saving common sense.

In a sentence, my claim is that the apparent clash between representative realism and common sense derives mainly not from the role of sense-data in the first, but from the crudity of empiricist accounts of judgment: repair this shortcoming and the conflict is much diminished, or even entirely avoided. Notice that the mediaeval philosophers, though believing in phantasms, which are sense-data, never seem to have worried about a veil, as opposed to a vehicle, of perception. This, I would suggest, is because they were not tempted by a reductive approach to form and thought, and, hence, intentionality.

On the other hand, those traditions that later revived intentionality and took it non-reductively, seem to have believed that this involved avoiding reifying sense-contents, not merely in the context of the "canonical interpretation," but altogether. Franz Brentano, for example, maintains that if one treats phenomenal color as existing one would be obliged to do the same with other contents of possible thought, such as the round square. This is a quite bizarre *non sequitur*, which fails to allow for the wholly different nature of the presence of qualities in perceptual experience from their involvement in thought. The prejudice carried over into Edmund Husserl and the phenomenological tradition, emerging back into analytical philosophy in the form of percept theory and Roderick Chisholm's adverbialism (1957). I am not convinced that we cannot avoid both the reductive crudities of the empiricists, and Brentano's howler, thereby reconciling the sense-datum theory and an adequately direct and commonsensical realism, as did the mediaeval philosophers.

8. Veridicality and Common Sense

I may have under-described common sense. Its two components so far— Common Sense Realism and the Intentionality Thesis—ignore the question of how, according to common sense, the way things appear is related to how they actually are. Without question, common sense suggests that in standard conditions—"normally"—things appear roughly as they are. Let us call this the veridicality condition. The veridicality condition can be interpreted in a weakly or strongly realist way. The weaker claim is that, normally, objects look the way they should look, given the conditions. The stronger interpretation is that normally objects look the way they actually are, where this interpretation is to be understood without reference to perception or appearance. At its strongest, this realist version of veridicality is equivalent to naïve realism, and collapses in the face of the argument from illusion.

But the strong claim can be presented in a weaker version which might be characterized as holding to the veridicality of the manifest image of the world in a general way, not in the way required by naïve realism. According to this theory, objects look different colors in different lights, and, to some degree, different shapes from different angles. For example, railway lines appear to converge in the distance. But things in themselves, independent of perception, are quite like the way they appear under the best conditions of observation. In sense-datum terms, this is a representative theory, with a realist account of secondary qualities. So the weaker, more plausible, version of the strong veridicality condition holds to the general accuracy of the manifest image of the world as a representation of the world as it is independently of how we perceive it.

The properly weaker veridicality condition says nothing about the objects in themselves, beyond the implicit claim that perception does individuate them—they are there as separate things—and that they tend to appear as they should. What they are like intrinsically, independently of appearance, and according to the best scientific or metaphysical account, is not something on which it has a view.

I believe that untutored common sense gives us no guidance on how we might understand the veridicality condition. The various forms that the veridicality condition might take only emerges as a result of philosophical reflection.

Someone might raise the following problem about my contrast between things looking the way they should and looking the way they intrinsically are, apart from appearance. Such an objector might say that he can attach no other sense to things looking the way they should that does not appeal paradigmatically to looking the way things intrinsically are. But the notion of a thing looking the normal, standard or proper way can be explained and indicated by reference to how that thing appears usually, or in some conditions, these conditions being explained experientially.

The situation is as follows. Three propositions are uncontroversially part of our commonsensical conception of perception.

(1) Common-sense realism.
(2) The intentionality thesis.
(3) The weak veridicality constraint.

These can be strengthened either by:

(3a) Strong realism about veridicality, which is classic naïve realism as portrayed by its opponents.

(3b) Weakened strong realism about veridicality: the world as it is in itself, wholly in abstraction from how it appears, is broadly as it appears. The manifest image is, in general terms, strictly veridical.

(3a) is obviously false, but the others are compatible with the sense-datum theory. Perhaps more interestingly, (1), (2), and (3) are all compatible with idealism, though not with Kantianism, nihilism, or radical skepticism. All three propositions require that there are objects individuated as perception would lead us to believe. This rules out the object in itself being an undifferentiated Kantian *noumenon*. It also rules out that no objects exist. But so long as what underlies the appearances ascribed to a particular object explains and sustains those appearances, then common sense is satisfied. The explanation that the nature of an individual object is a permanent possibility of sensation (appearances), or a Divine intention to sustain appearances in some way, or simply lacking all sensible qualities as we know them, as in the "scientific image," may come as a surprise to common sense, but common sense is not averse to surprises, so long as they do not subvert the essential framework.

9. Conclusion

My position can be summed up in the following five propositions.

(1) Perceptual judgments—the kinds of things that might be expressed verbally in such sentences as "I see a wine bottle" or "that is a wine bottle," though these judgments are not themselves verbal—refer to the object perceived in the external world, if the experience is not hallucinatory.

(2) The relation between the sense-datum or sensation, on the one hand, and the judgment on the other is not external or causal, but the judgment is embodied in the sense-contents, in a way analogous to that in which other judgments are embodied in verbal forms.

(3) The sense-contents can be regarded—in abstraction from the judgment—and, as such, instantiate sensible qualities.

(4) The belief that (3) is not consistent with (1) and (2) rests on errors made by philosophers from the seventeenth to the nineteenth centuries concerning intentionality, and its relation to sense-contents.

(5) The reference made to objects in these judgments carries commitments to how they sensibly are, but not to how they are intrinsically, as this might be conceived in science or metaphysics. The conclusions from these disciplines can be surprising and go beyond common sense without actually contradicting it.

ACKNOWLEDGMENT

The problem discussed in Section 5 was pointed out to me by Bill Fish.

Eight

THE CONTENT OF
PERCEPTUAL EXPERIENCE

János Tőzsér

1. Introduction

There is something odd in philosophical discussions about perception. For example, during the first two thirds of the twentieth century, discussion centered on whether any such things as sense-data exist at all. Commenting on the nature of this discussion, George A. Paul said, "some people have claimed that they are unable to find such an object, and others have claimed that they do not understand how the existence of such an object can be doubted." (1936, p. 67)

Contemporary discussion on the nature of perceptual experience is similar to the arguments on the existence or non-existence of sense-data. One camp considers as self-evident that perceptual experience is primarily of a subjective nature. According to this view, in perceptual experience we have direct awareness of some subjective entities, which is independent of the mode of representing the mind-independent world. The second camp believes that perceptual experience is of a representational nature, that perceptual states are intentional states. According to this view, the content of perceptual experience is the mind-independent world *per se.*

We could naïvely think that there is nothing equivocal about how objects appear to us, and what the content of our perceptual experience is. To the contrary, these widely divergent views illustrate that perception remains a peculiar philosophical problem for which no consensus exists.

I am not in possession of any knock-down arguments against these theories. Nor will I say if one is better than the other. I do believe that perception is better framed in terms of the disjunctive theory of perception. In the present paper I will sketch a philosophical theory of perception that I take to be a special version of the disjunctive theory. I will demonstrate that the disjunctive theory involves less intellectual discomfort than the others, and that it provides a salutary way beyond widely accepted conventional standpoints about perceptual experience that leave us with such opposing views for the same phenomena. First I will describe some other widely-held views and my objections to them, and then I will provide my version of the disjunctive theory and the most important motives for it. I will not defend my view against possible objections. My sole aim in this paper is to demonstrate its plausibility.

2. The Camps

The members of the camp emphasizing the subjective character of perceptual experience can be divided into two groups according to their conception about the nature of non-physical, mind-dependent entities. There are those who hold that in the process of perception we are immediately aware of sense-data, as mental objects, and those who hold that we are aware of certain sensational qualities (qualia), as mental properties. According to the first view, when I perceive, for instance, a red tomato, then this should be interpreted as the following:

> [T]here *exists* a red patch of a round and somewhat bulgy shape, standing out from a background of other color-patches, and having a certain visual depth, and that this whole field of color is directly present to my consciousness, [and] that something is red and round then and there I cannot doubt . . . , and that it now *exists*, and that I am conscious of it—by me at least who am conscious of it this cannot possibly be doubted. (Price, 1936, p. 3)

In the course of perception I stand with this object in a relation of "seeing," or "having."

According to the second view:

> [T]he adjective "red" in "I am aware of a red appearance" and "I am experiencing a red sensation," is used adverbially to qualify this undergoing, [and] we could say that such a sentence as "I am aware of a red appearance" tells us *how* the subject is sensing, or in what *way* he is sensing. (Chisholm, 1994, p. 103)

While for the adherents of the sense-datum theory the proper expression of the relation is "I see (or I have) a red sense-datum," the adverbialists hold that we should say, "I sense redly," or, while according to the sense-datum theorists we should formulate a sentence about a mental state of *P*—for example about his being in pain—in the following way: "*P* feels a sharp pain in his leg," according to the adverbialists we should express this as, "*P*'s leg pains him sharply." In a word, according to the sense-datum theory, perception has a relational nature, consisting of a relation between a subject and a sense-datum, and according to the adverbial theory, perceptual experiences are nothing other than, "*modifications* of the person who is said to sense those appearances" (Chisholm, 1994, p. 104). These two views agree on the most important point, that the content of perceptual experience, that of which we are immediately aware in the process of perception, should not be identified with the mind-independent objects and properties of the external world.

The members of the other camp, who emphasize the intentional content of perceptual experience, can also be divided into two groups according to how radical their views are about the representational nature of perceptual experience. There are those to whom perceptual experience has a fundamentally representational character. In the course of perceptual experience, we are aware of the objects and properties of the mind-independent world, but beyond this the experience also has its subjective qualities. For example:

> [W]e can draw a distinction between sensational and representational properties of experience. Representational properties will be properties an experience has in virtue of features of its representational content; while sensational properties will be properties an experience has in virtue of some aspect—other than its representational content—of what it is like to have that experience. (Peacocke, 1994, p. 341)

Or, "When I look at my blue wall, I think that in addition to being aware of the color I can also make myself aware of what it is like for me to be aware of the color" (Block, 1994, p. 689).

But there are also philosophers in this camp who think that the perceptual experience has exclusively representational character. The perceptual experience as conscious mental state has no subjective characteristics. Perceptual experience involves nothing apart from the way of representing the mind-independent world. For example, "Phenomenal character (or what it is like) is one and the same as a certain sort of intentional content" (Tye, 1995, p. 137). Or, "[The] mind has no special properties that are not exhausted by its representational properties, along with or in combination with the functional organization of its components" (Lycan, 1996, p. 11).

The first group may be termed a weak, and the second, a strong intentional theory. The difference between the two positions is that the strong intentionalists maintain that the phenomenal character of experience is fully determined by the representational content of experience; that is, if two (metaphysically possible) experiences differ in phenomenal character, then they differ in content as well. The weak intentionalists hold that the representational content does not fully determine the phenomenal properties, because it is possible that (1) two experiences differ in phenomenal character but have the same content (Shoemaker 1994), or that (2) two experiences do not differ in phenomenal character but have different contents (Block 1994).

3. An Argument for Subjectivism

The strongest argument for the subjectivist views (more exactly for the sense-datum theory) is the "argument from hallucination." The argument in its plainest form is as follows:

(P1) There could be hallucinations. (Empirical fact.)

(P2) When somebody has a hallucination, then it appears to him that he perceives something, while he does not really perceive anything. (Analytical statement.)

(P3) When somebody has a hallucination, then that which he is aware of is not part of the mind-independent world. (Analytical statement.)

(P4) When somebody has a hallucination, then it appears to him that there exists an object with particular sensible qualities. (Phenomenological fact.)

(P5) When somebody has a hallucination, then the object which he is aware of is a sense-datum. (The definition of the word "sense-datum.")

(P6) There is no difference between a particular veridical perception and an appropriate hallucination with respect to their phenomenal character. (Phenomenological fact.)

(P7) If a particular veridical perception is indistinguishable from an appropriate hallucination with respect to their phenomenal character, then the subject has the same mental state in both cases.

(C) The thing which somebody is aware of in the course of veridical perception, is also a sense-datum.

According to Howard Robinson, we get much stronger argument from the original "argument from hallucination" when it is connected with the "argument from causation" (1994, pp. 151–163). Consider the following: Suppose that a person P sits at the table on which there is a red tomato. P's sense-organs function properly, light conditions are normal, and the visual experience is the result of reliable cognitive processes. In a word, P sees the tomato. Further, suppose that we fix this state of P's brain, we hold P's brain artificially in the same state in which he originally was, seeing the tomato, and at the same time we remove the tomato from his visual field. In that case, P will be precisely in the same mental state with regard to its phenomenal character as in the case in which he had perceived veridically the tomato, he will just have a hallucination. However, if P's veridical perception and his hallucination, above the subjective indistinguishability, have the same immediate cause (and we saw, that they in fact have the same cause, for we stipulated this at the beginning of our thought-experiment: we fixed the brain-state of P), then we should give the same description of the two cases, and it is not plausible to say that in the case of hallucination P is related to sense-data, while in the case of veridical perception he is not. What follows from all this, Robinson says, is, "[P]erceptual processes in the brain produce some object of awareness which cannot be identified with any feature of the external world" (ibid., p. 151).

Intentionalists deny this conclusion:

> In order to see that such arguments are fallacious, consider the corresponding argument to searches: "Ponce de Leon was searching for the Fountain of Youth. But there is no such thing. So he must have been searching for something mental." This is just a mistake. From the fact that there is no Fountain of Youth, it *does not follow* that Ponce de Leon was searching for something mental. (Harman, 1994, p. 665)

Or, "Consider the following parallel. Paul wants a blue emerald to give to his wife. There are no blue emeralds. It *does not follow* that Paul wants the idea of a blue emerald to give to his wife" (Tye, 1992, p. 162).

The core of these arguments is that if we take perceptual experiences to be intentional states like beliefs, judgments, willings, searchings, thoughts, etc., then the "argument from hallucination" collapses. Since just as it does not follow in any way from my belief that "Santa Claus was born in Finland" that there exists something (a mental object) of which I believe that it was born in Finland, in the same fashion, from my hallucinating that there is a red tomato in front of me, it does not follow that there exists something which is red. Instead, every intentional state (including perceptual experience) represents a given state of the mind-independent world, which means that the world is in such and such a state to the subject having the intentional state. The content of perceptual experience is none other then the way the world is represented to the subject.

If, for instance, I have the perceptual experience that on the table in front of me there is a red tomato, then this perceptual experience represents the world in a such way as if there were a red tomato on the table in front of me, and from that on, it depends on the world, conceptually independent from my perceptual experience, whether I hallucinate or perceive veridically. In this sense, perceptual experience is directed at the mind-independent world both in the case of veridical perception and in that of hallucination. The difference between the two cases is that while in the case of hallucination the subject's experience represents the mind-independent world falsely, in the case of veridical perception, the subject's experience represents the world correctly. Therefore, we have no reason to commit ourselves to the existence of sense-data that mediate between the mind and the world.

To make it explicit: the controversy between sense-datum theorists and intentionalists consists in whether one should accept the following statement:

> Phenomenal Principle (PP): If there sensibly appears to a subject to be something which possess a particular sensible quality then there is something of which the subject is aware which does possess that sensible quality (Robinson, 1994, p. 32).

The sense-datum theorists accept, while the intentionalists reject PP. How do the intentionalists reject it? Consider the following two sentences:

> (1) If P believes that a is F, then there is something a, which P believes is F.

> (2) If P knows that a is F, then there is something a, which P knows to be F.

According to the intentionalists, PP resembles proposition (1) instead of proposition (2), and it is wrong for precisely the same reasons for which (1) is wrong. This is so because just as it does not follow from my belief that there is a red tomato in front of me that there exists something which is red and round, in the same manner, the existence of something red and round does not follow from the fact that it appears to me that there is a red tomato in front of me.

So, the argument of intentionalism against the "argument from hallucination" works like this:

> (P1) Perceptual states are intentional states.

> (P2) An intentional state is either narrow or broad. If it is broad (or long-arm) then it entails the existence of its object. (For example: knowing.) If it is narrow (or short-arm) then it does not entail the existence of its object. (For example: believing.)

> (P3) Perceptual states (like beliefs) are narrow (or short arm) intentional states.

> (C) A perceptual state does not entail the existence of its object.

In this way:

When Paul hallucinates in the above case he has an experience *of* a pink square object. This experience has content—it represents a pink square object. *There is*, then a defined content to Paul's hallucinatory experience. But there is no object, mental or otherwise, that Paul hallucinates. Furthermore the fact that Paul's experience has a certain content no more requires that there really be a pink square object as a picture's representing a three-headed monster, say, requires that there really be any monster. (Tye, 1992, p. 162)

But we are faced with a problem. Namely, it is far from obvious that the intentional theorists' answer to the "argument from hallucination" does not beg the question. The sense-datum theorists could say that the intentionalists do nothing else but treat perceptual states (like our beliefs) as narrow intentional states, without supporting the analogy between our beliefs and perceptual experiences with independent arguments. Provided that this analogy is justified, and our perceptual experiences relevantly resemble our beliefs, then our perceptual experiences can be regarded as narrow intentional states, since our beliefs are beyond doubt such states, and the "argument from hallucination" indeed collapses.

The question is precisely whether there is such a close analogy between our beliefs and our perceptual experiences as the intentionalists claim, since the intentionalists admit, too, that several differences or disanalogies exist between perceptual experiences and beliefs. To see a horse galloping across a meadow on the one hand, and on the other hand to have the propositional attitude, "I believe that a horse is galloping across the meadow," is a quite different matter. The contents of perceptual experience are much richer in detail, and contain a gamut of additional information, than our beliefs; for example, "the galloping horse is gray," "there is a rider on the horse," and so on. Furthermore, our perceptional experience may come into conflict with our beliefs. Let it be enough here to mention the Müller-Lyer or Ponzo illusion. One of the equal length segments will be perceived as being longer than the other, even if we know them to be equal. Therefore, while it is exceptionally peculiar to say, "I believe that *p*, but not-*p*," to say, "I perceive that *p*, but not-*p*," can be quite natural. In addition to the two disanalogies, most intentionalists accept the thesis that while our beliefs are of a conceptual nature, our perceptual experiences are non-conceptual (Evans 1982; Peacocke 1992; Crane 1992; Bermudez 1998). In contrast to having beliefs, having a perceptual experience does not require concepts, "to be in a non-conceptual state with content *p*, one does not have to possess the concepts which one *would* have to possess if one *were* in a conceptual state with content *p*" (Crane, 2001, p. 152).

The question then is whether these three differences, if taken together, do not destroy the close analogy between beliefs and perceptual experiences the intentionalists hold to obtain, and the existence of which they need so as they can avoid the conclusion of the "argument from hallucination." The problem is that while the intentionalists refute (or believe to refute) the "argument from hallucination" by invoking the significant similarities between beliefs and perceptual experiences, they point to some relevant differences between beliefs and perceptual experience as though they have forgotten their argument against the "argument from hallucination."

The intentionalists could reply that this contradiction or tension in their argument does not threaten the crux of their theory. For the crux of the theory is that "*P* has a particular perceptual experience" must be understood as "it is for *P* as if the world be in such and such a state." If it appears to *P* as though there was a red tomato before him, this amounts to: *P*'s perceptual experience represents the world as if there was a red tomato before *P* at that moment in time and in that place.

In a word, as Colin McGinn puts it, "the content of an experience determines what it is *as of*—how the world *would* actually be presented *if* the experience were veridical" (1989, p. 58). The emphasis is on the as-if structure of experience, that, according to the intentionalists, the experience is not object-involving. The main analogy between beliefs and perceptual experiences, too, resides in this as-if structure, and in this respect the three disanalogies mentioned above are irrelevant.

I am ready to concede this much to the intentionalists. But I claim that there is one such distinctive feature of perceptual experience that distinguishes it from propositional attitudes and which clearly shows why perceptual experience may not be understood after the manner of beliefs.

I fully agree with Robinson, who argues:

It can hardly be disputed that experience reveals the nature of objects—at least as they are conceived to be in our naïve conception of the world—in a way that other mental states or attitudes do not. They are characterized by the fact that they do not require the presence of the object in question; whether an object is there when you think of or desire it is immaterial to the phenomenology of thought and desire as such. They are essentially acts tailored to the absence of their objects. This is shown in the fact that the experiential differences between other intentional states—between fearing, loving or desiring, for example—do not consist in any difference in the manner of the presence of the object, but in the manner of the subject's response to the object. The object is present purely intellectually, that is, as an object of thought, in all these cases. But in sensory experience the role of the object is quite different. In contrast to its absence in the other cases, experience is something by which the object is (apparently) made present, and which without the (apparent) presence of the object could not take place. Furthermore, we take this presentational aspect of perception to be intimately related to the distinctive phenomenology of perception: perception is experientially as it is because of the apparent presence of the empirical features of things in the experience itself. So whereas the intentionalist claims that in perceptual experience things are conceived of, albeit in a uniquely sensible way, our ordinary assumption is that they are present in experience in a way indistinguishable from that in which we naïvely think them to be present in the external world. (1994, pp. 165–166)

Let me first clarify what I understand by the object's being presented in perceptual experience. Assume that I see now a red tomato and then, after a few moments, I close my eyes and imagine it. Assume, furthermore, that I have an excellent imagination, and the image imagined by me is exactly like the one I had while seeing the tomato. The imagined image resembles the seen one as a photograph resembles that of which it is a photo; they possess the exact same shades, light conditions, shadows, figures, etc. Nevertheless, I can discern, through introspection, a difference between the two mental states. I claim that the only difference that I can discern is that while in the first case the object was presented to my mind, in the second case it was not so presented. Let me rephrase this in David Hume's terminology. The first mental state, the one called "impression" by Hume, differs from the second one, called "idea" by Hume, in that the second, "may mimic or copy the perceptions of the senses; but they never can entirely reach the force and vivacity of the original sensation" (1975, p. 17). The second is a mere dull copy of the former. What Hume means under the expression "dull" is not that the colors of the imagined object are less lively, for instance, that red is almost pink or that black almost fades to gray, but that in the second case, the object is not given so robustly than in the first one. I call this robust givenness of the object in perceptual experience the object's being presented to the mind.

I hold two arguments against the intentionalists' explanation of perceptual experience. First, return to the case wherein I see a red tomato, and then after a few seconds I close my eyes and imagine it. Assume again that the imagined image is exactly like the one I had while seeing the tomato, even though introspectively I can distinguish beyond doubt between the mental states of seeing and imagining. I ask whether the intentionalists can account for the introspectively discernible difference between the two mental states without invoking the object's being present to my mind in the first case, and its absence in the second case. Can they account for the difference in their terms?

I take it for granted that the strong intentionalists cannot account for this difference. According to them, the phenomenal character of perceptual experience is fully determined by the representational content of experience, which is the same in the two cases, for the seen and imagined images, being exactly alike, give exactly the same representation of the mind-independent world. Therefore, the strong intentionalists must contend that the phenomenal characters of the two mental states are indistinguishable, which is clearly false according to the testimony of my introspection. All this is meant to show that perceptual experience—as opposed to imagining—possesses such a characteristic—the object's being presented to the mind—which cannot be explained in terms of the representational properties of experience.

In the view of the weak intentional theory, over and above their representational properties, perceptual experiences also possess sensational properties (or qualia); that is, the phenomenal character of experience is not fully determined by its representational content. The weak intentionalists may claim that the representational content of the mental state I have while seeing the tomato, and the representational content of the mental state I have while imagining it, are the same, but we are able to introspectively distinguish them precisely because their sensational properties are different.

I do not think this description is tenable. If the imagined image is exactly like the seen one, then the sensational properties of the two mental states must be the same also—provided that there are such properties at all. Why? Because the two images have the same sensible qualities: they have the same redness, roundness, visual depth, etc. Therefore, if I am only concerned with the sensible qualities the tomato appears to me to have, then the two mental states are indeed indistinguishable. I can discern a difference between them through introspection only at a different level. It is not that I manage to discover some hidden sensible quality in which the two images differ after all, that is, that I discern such a difference, which implies a difference in the sensible qualities the tomato appears to me to have. Instead, it is the mode of givenness of the object, which is different in the two cases. Once again: the sensible qualities the object appears to me to have are exactly the same in the two cases, but the way it is given to me is different. All this shows that perceptual experience might not be fully accounted for by representational plus sensational properties, for in that case we would not be able to distinguish between the two mental states. This appears to prove that perceptual experience during veridical perception is essentially of a relational nature, and that perceptual experience during veridical perception may not be accounted for without reference to the object that is being presented during the experience. With this, I come to my second objection.

As we have seen, the object to which the subject's mental state is directed is given in perceptual experience during veridical perception in a way that is different from all other mental states—presented to the subject's mind directly. I claim that the presentative character of object-givenness peculiar to perceptual experience and only to perceptual experience cannot be explained by the intentionalists' formula of "it is for the subject as if . . . ," for the "as if" expression occurring in this sort of statement is all too vague to do the job. I concede to the intentionalists that the formula, "it is for the subject as if . . . ," is adequate for explaining cases like "*P* believes that *p*," or "*P* thinks that *p*," but only because these mental states (or events) obtain (occur) only when the object to which the subject's mental states is directed is not presented to the subject.

Since perceptual experience during veridical perception, in contrast with beliefs, is impossible without the object's being presented to the mind, it cannot be accounted for without reference to its objects as the necessary *relata* of perceptual experience. But the intentionalists try to do exactly this when they consider perceptual experience generally in the fashion of beliefs as as-if structures, and view perceptual experience, like the adverbialists, as mere modifications of the mind.

The feature that distinguishes perceptual experience from all other mental states—the object's being presented to the mind—is missing from the intentionalist account. This means that the intentionalists are unable to explain the distinctive phenomenal character of perceptual experience. If there exists such a characteristic of perceptual experience that characterizes only it and nothing else (and we have seen that there is such a characteristic), then we must commit ourselves to such a theory that explains this feature. Some intentionalists agree and make a distinction between representation and presentation. John Searle says:

> If, for example, I see a yellow station wagon in front of me, the experience I have is directly of the object. It doesn't just "represent" the object, it provides direct access to it. The experience has a kind of directedness, immediacy and involuntariness which is not shared by a belief I might have about the object in its absence. It seems therefore unnatural to describe visual experiences as representations . . . . Rather, because of the special features of perceptual experiences I propose to call them 'presentations'. The visual experience I will say does not just represent the state of affairs perceived; rather, when satisfied, it gives us direct access to it, and in that sense it is a presentation of that state of affairs. (1983, pp. 45–46)

I fully accept what Searle says. But the intentionalists' arguing in this manner gives rise to problems. If intentionalists accept that in perceptual experience an object is presented to the subject, and maintain that in perceptual experience we have direct access to the perceived object itself, and state that perceptual experience is object-involving, then I cannot see how they evade the conclusion of "argument from hallucination." Since, if they accept that (1) in the case of veridical perception, perceptual experience is object-involving, (2) veridical perception is subjectively indistinguishable from an appropriate hallucination, (3) when two mental states are indistinguishable, then they are the same, and (4) in hallucination we are aware of something which is not part of the mind-independent world, then it would follow that (5) in the case of veridical perception no less than in the case of hallucination, what we are aware of is not the mind-independent world but some subjective entity. Therefore, intentionalists cannot maintain that perceptual experiences are about the mind-independent world and at the same time adhere to the view that perceptual experiences are related to their objects in a way that is different from that of beliefs.

Holding on to both views and having both be true would be convenient, but—and that is my main objection—intentionalists are unable to do that. For if they evade the conclusion of the "argument from hallucination," then they cannot explain the distinctive character of perceptual experience that distinguishes it from any other mental states, that is, presentation of its object. If they accept the presentation of an object in perceptual experience, then they cannot escape the conclusion of the "argument from hallucination." The disjunctive theory I will propose is capable to do both, and as such is intellectually more comforting then the intentional theory of perception.

4. An Argument for Strong Intentionalism

The strongest and most evident argument against the subjectivist views is that they are in contrast with the introspectible evidence of what it is like for us to perceive. In short, the sense-data (or equally qualia) are absent from any introspection of our mind and this fact conflicts with the hypothesis that such entities need to be posited as objects of our awareness in explaining the phenomenal character of the perceptual experience. Instead, those objects, qualities, facts, and relations, which are revealed by introspection in perceptual experience, appear as the objects, relations, etc. of the mind-independent world. As shown by P. F. Strawson, we are doomed to failure if we should wish to describe our perceptual experience without referring to the objects of the external world (1979). When I would like to describe what it is like for me to be looking at a red tomato in front of me, while introspecting my current visual experience I have to employ the very same vocabulary as I would use to describe the scene perceived. It is usual to formulate this observation by the phrase that perceptual experience is transparent to its content. By definition:

Transparency Thesis (TT): Introspections say that when somebody has a perceptual experience of something then he is not aware of his perceptual experience having sense-data (or equally certain intrinsic qualities), rather this experience is transparent to its content where the content is the object, qualities etc. of the mind-independent world.

Strong intentionalists argue in harmony with TT, for example, Michael Tye says:

Standing on the beach in Santa Barbara a couple of summers ago on a bright sunny day, I found myself transfixed by the intense blue of the Pacific Ocean. Was I not here delighting in the phenomenal aspects of my visual experience? . . . I am not convinced. It seems to me that what I found so pleasing in the above instance, what I was focusing on, as it were, were a certain shade and intensity of the color blue. I experienced blue as a property of the ocean not as a property of my experience. My experience itself certainly wasn't blue. Rather it was an experience that represented the ocean as blue. What I was really delighting in, then, were specific aspects of the content of my experience. It was the content, not anything else, that was immediately accessible to my consciousness and that had aspects I found so pleasing. (1982, p. 160)

What is the goal of Tye's argument? According to Tye, introspection reveals only represented facts about the ocean, that the content of perceptual experience (*viz.* the ocean *per se*) is blue. To generalize, all introspection reveals facts about how things are represented to be or what is represented in our perceptual experience.

According to the subjectivist camp, this "argument from introspection" is mistaken. We must differentiate between the sensory core of perceptual experience as a brute fact from its interpretation built on it. Berkeley says:

For instance, when I hear a coach drive along the streets, immediately I perceive only the sound; but, from the experience I have had that such a sound is connected with a coach, I am said to hear the coach. It is nevertheless evident that, in truth and strictness, nothing can be *heard* but *sound*; and the coach is not then properly perceived by sense, but suggested from experience. (1965, pp. 167–168)

When we introspect, we report interpreted data, and not brute facts that are directly given to the mind in perceptual experience. In this sense, the initial (or natural) introspective reports are misleading.

We could, without a doubt, create quite a discussion on this point, similar to the discussion on "top-down" and "bottom-up" theory of perception in psychology. I will not enter into the complexities of this discussion, because there is a straightforward consideration that evinces that the differentiation between the concepts of "directly given to the mind" and "naturally given to introspection" is fatal to the subjectivist party, especially to the sense-datum theory. To wit, if we state that in perceptual experience the mind is in direct contact with some sort of data more elementary than those accessible by introspection, then we shall not be able to explain the phenomenal character of experience with the concept "directly given to the mind" (this being the original definition of "sense datum"), as this by definition is reserved for the concept "naturally given to introspection."

Denying that what is accessible to introspection is what it is like to be for us to perceive is difficult. If an adherent of the sense-datum theory were to accept the above differentiation, but at the same time were to maintain the idea that the phenomenal character of experience may be determined by sense-data, then he or she would have to abandon the original definition, according to which sense-data denotes, "objects directly given to the mind," as these—*ex hypothesis*—are not accessible to introspection, and are, therefore, not suitable for the explanation of the phenomenal character of experience.

While the strong intentional theory is in absolute harmony with our initial introspective reports of experience, the sense-datum theory (equally the abverbialist and weak intentional theory) can only be correct if our initial impressions were incorrect or misleading. Our goal is to find a theory that best fits our introspective beliefs, or TT, as "introspective fitness" is the most important criteria by which we may chose between the different theories concerning what it is like to be for us to perceive.

5. The Disjunctive Theory: The Redistribution of Perceptual Concepts

In the previous three sections, I have described various theories concerning perceptual experience. I have tried to show that none of them is able to provide us with a satisfactory solution. The sense-datum theory is in harmony with our introspective evidence that in perceptual experience, in the case of veridical perception (in contrast with other mental states) some object is presented to our mind, but it is in conflict with our introspective beliefs or reports that the contents of perceptual experience are objects and qualities of the mind-independent world. The adverbial and weak intentional theories are similarly in conflict with the latter. The strong intentional theory, on the other hand, is in harmony with our introspective beliefs or reports that the contents of perceptual experience are objects and qualities of the mind-independent world, but it is in conflict with our introspective evidence that in perceptual experience, in the case of veridical perception (in contrast with other mental states) there is an object that is presented to the mind. The adverbial and weak intentional theories are in conflict with the latter.

There is nothing unexpected in this fact, as the sense-datum theory accepts PP and denies TT, and strong intentional theory accepts TT and denies PP, and *prima facie* TT and PP are incompatible with each other. PP may seem to lead to the conclusion that what we are aware of (in veridical perception as well) are subjective entities, and TT may seem to lead to the conclusion that we are aware of (in hallucinations as well) are mind-independent entities.

I claim that the disjunctive theory (DT) I advocate is in complete harmony with our introspection of perceptual experience. In contrast with sense-datum theory and strong intentional theory, DT is able to explain both the fact that the content of perceptual experience during veridical perception is an object or quality of the mind-independent world, and the fact that in perceptual experience during veridical perception there is an object that is presented to the mind. Consequently, if we accept DT, then we may distribute the perceptual concepts in an intellectually more comforting manner than in other theories.

Their differences notwithstanding, the above theories of perceptual experience agree on one point. All of them consider as evident the seventh premise of the "argument from hallucination," according to which, if a particular veridical perception is indistinguishable from an appropriate hallucination with respect to their phenomenal character, then the subject has the same mental state in both cases. All these theories accept the following general thesis:

Sameness of mental states = indistinguishability of mental states.

If they accept this thesis and claim that a veridical perception is the same mental state as an appropriate hallucination with respect to their phenomenal character, then—since the individuation of hallucinations is naturally independent of the subject's immediate physical environment—they are committed to the claim that the individuation of veridical perceptions too, is independent of the subject's immediate physical environment. Therefore, all of them claim that the subject, and the subject alone (to be more exact, his brain) constitutes perceptual experience. In a word, all these theories are internalist. By definition:

Internalist Thesis (IT): Sameness of mental states = indistinguishability of mental states. *A fortiori*, the individuation of mental states is independent of the immediate physical environment of the subject.

My position differs from the standard definition of internalism, which is that—in opposition to externalism—we have to individuate our mental states independently of the immediate physical environment of the subject. In my version, I reverse the logical order, and take this standard definition as consequence of the "indistinguishability of mental states" = "sameness of mental states" thesis, and not vice versa, as it is usually done. My position was greatly influenced by Katalin Farkas's paper, "What Is Externalism?" (2003).

Alternatively, as Michael Martin puts it:

If you could have had the same state of mind as you now do while looking at the [red tomato] even though you were suffering an hallucination, then it cannot be essential to your being in such a state of mind that any object independent of you should have certain qualities or be perceived by you (1995, p. 465).

Now we call those theories disjunctive which deny IT in respect to perceptual experience. By definition:

DT: It is not true that perceptual experience forms a common factor kind of mental state among veridical perceptions and of hallucinations. Consequently, (1) it is not true in the case of perceptual experience that "sameness = indistinguishability," and *a fortiori*, (2) it is not true in the case of perceptual experience that its individuation is independent of the subject's immediate physical environment.

As the DT denies the "common factor view," it must offer different explanations to veridical perception and hallucination. In contrast with the "big camps," which all have accepted IT, according to DT the properties of the perceived mind-independent object are also constituent elements of perceptual experience during veridical perception. When one is perceiving veridically, then what is manifest to him is the mind-independent object, and this object is constitutive of his mental state.

But what is the case with hallucinations? This question may be answered by the adherents of DT in two different ways, depending on whether they are nearer to sense-datum theory or to intentional theory. One of the answers, represented by John McDowell, is that in the case of hallucination the object of experience is "mere appearance," (see McDowell, 1982, p. 211), that is a quasi sense-datum. The other, and to my mind more plausible, answer is that experience in this case has no object.

In opposition to McDowell's position, I claim that PP is only true in the case of veridical perception. When I perceive veridically, then—in contrast to what intentionalists say, and in harmony with what sense-datum theorists say—my mental state entails that there exists an object of which I am aware. However, when I have a hallucination, then—in contrast to what sense-datum theorists say, and in harmony with what intentionalists say—it appears to me as if something existed, but it does not. No matter which of these answers we accept with respect to hallucinations, the essence is this: if in the case of veridical perception the properties of the perceived mind-independent objects are constitutive elements of the perceptual experience, then the subject having the perceptual experience cannot be in the same mental state during veridical perception and the appropriate hallucination.

6. The Main Motivation for the Disjunctive Theory

Disjunctive Theory unites the advantages of the theories purported by adherents of the two "big camps" but is free of the disadvantages of those theories. Concerning veridical perception my intermediate combination is described as:

(1) In perceptual experience a mind-independent object is given to the mind (this being what strong intentionalists accept), and

(2) if we have a perceptual experience, then the object of that experience must exist (this being what sense-datum theories accept).

DT is in some respect similar to intentional theories, and in some other respects similar to sense-datum theory. DT is similar to the intentional theories inasmuch as both accept TT, both accept that it is mind-independent objects that are given to the perceiving subject. It differs from intentional theories in that it interprets TT in a different manner. According to the intentionalists, TT = "introspection exclusively reveals facts about how things are represented to be in perceptual experience." DT, in contrast, states that in the case of veridical perception, the perceived object must exist, as in the case of veridical perception the mental state of the subject guarantees the existence of the object. Stated differently, in veridical perception the subject has a broad intentional state. The main difference is that while according to DT, in the case of veridical perception the subject's mental state entails the existence of its object, according to the intentionalists, the subject's mental state does not entail the existence of its object. According to the second view, whether the subject has a veridical perception or a hallucination does not affect the sameness of the subject's mental state.

DT is similar to sense-datum theories inasmuch as both accept that perception has a relational structure, both theories claim that the directly perceived object is a constituent element of the subject's perceptual experience. They differ in that while according to the sense-datum theory the existence of these directly perceived objects depends on the subject's being aware of them, the DT claims that what we directly perceive are the objects of the mind-independent world. The main difference is that the DT does not endorse the conclusion of the "argument from hallucination." What it claims is not that the "argument from hallucination" is wrong because perceptual states are narrow intentional states, which do not entail the existence of their objects. Instead, DT denies the seventh premise, according to which it is not true for perceptual experience that "indistinguishable = same."

To sum up, according to DT, in veridical perception the mental state of the subject entails the existence of its object, and it is wrong to understand perceptual experience in the manner of beliefs as narrow intentional states (1), and in veridical perception it is a mind-independent object that is being presented to the mind, and therefore the "argument from hallucination" is wrong (2). My claim is that both (1) and (2) are compatible with our introspective evidence of what it is like to perceive something. It is evident that (2) is compatible with them, since our introspection reveals in perceptual experience neither sense-data nor qualia, but only mind-independent objects, as what we are aware of. On the other hand, (1) is also compatible with the introspective evidence, because the distinctive phenomenology of perceptual experience (as opposed to beliefs, imaginings, etc.) involves the object's being presented to the mind.

The decisive claim is the following: the only way to be in harmony with our introspective evidence in both respects is to give up the "common factor view." For if we maintain that veridical perception is a mental state that is different from the corresponding hallucination, then we are justified in claiming about veridical perception the following:

> If it appears to a subject that an object possesses certain particular sensible qualities, then (1) there in fact exists an object with these sensible qualities, and (2) this object is part of the mind-independent world.

I think that is the most natural description of the common, ordinary perception of what it is like to perceive the world. This is the genuine relation between the mind and the world, and this is the basis of our elementary trust in that we have direct access to the mind-independent world.

The aim of my DT is to show the preconditions of this genuine relation between the mind and the world, and I take it that this precondition is the rejection of the "common factor view." Since, if we hold on to the "common factor view," then due to the similarity between veridical perception and hallucination, we would have to deny certain characteristics from one of them. We cannot say that in veridical perception a mind-independent object is presented to the subject, for in hallucination—which is the same mental state—*per definitionem* it is not a mind-independent object which is presented to the subject. (That is what sense-datum theories are alluding to.) Or, we cannot say that in veridical perception there must exist an object at which the subject's mental state is directed, because during hallucination—which is the same mental state—there is no object at which the subject's mental state is directed. (That is what intentional theories are alluding to.)

The sense-datum theorists—provided that they are not idealists—are forced to admit that during all of our perceptual experience we are aware of mind-dependent objects, and that we never perceive the mind-independent world, only through the "veil of our ideas," and this is implausible. By contrast, intentionalists are forced to admit, in order to escape the conclusion of the "argument from hallucination," that perceptual experiences are to be interpreted after the manner of beliefs; but by this, the intentionalists conflate perceptual experience with beliefs, and are unable to account for the distinctive phenomenology of perceptual experience that distinguishes it from all other mental states.

Let me clarify this point from another angle. According to intentionalists and naturally indirect realists endorsing sense-data, to perceive veridically is to have a perceptual experience which is made true by the mind-independent world, which is conceptually independent from the subject's mental state. This means that both views accept a version of the causal theory of perception. It goes like this:

P perceives veridically an object *o* if and only if:
(1) *o* exists,
(2) *P* has an *e* experience (visual, auditory etc.),
(3) *o* causes *e* to occur, and
(4) the causal chain is not deviant but appropriate.

Against this, I claim that:

P perceives veridically an object *o* = *P* has now a mental state which entails that *o* exists, and *o* exists in such a way as it appears to *P*.

In the causal theory of veridical perception only the (2) condition is in the power of the subject, whereas the other conditions depend—say—on the charity of the world. On this account, to perceive veridically is identical with the circumstance that the subject has an experience, and that the subject is lucky. As opposed to that, in my definition the subject's mental state *per se* guarantees that the world is in such and such a state. If there is no mental state which guarantees in itself that the world is in such and such a state, then there is, in a sense, a gap between the subject and the mind-independent world. Why? Because in this case, the cognitive power of the subject would be exhausted by his coming to have a given mental state. In my definition, no such gap is involved, because I connect conceptually, in the case of veridical perception, the mental state of, "it appears to the subject that there is a red tomato in front of him," with the state of the world in which, "there is a red tomato in front of the subject." I can do that because I claim that the perceived object is a constituent element of perceptual experience in the case of veridical perception, in other words because I reject the "common factor view."

In summary, while the adherents of the "common factor view" take the mind to be at home in the world causally, the adherents of DT take the mind to be at home in the world cognitively.

ACKNOWLEDGMENT

I am grateful to Katalin Farkas, Gábor Bács, Zoltán Miklósi, and Gábor Forrai for their helpful comments on an earlier version of this paper. The research leading to this paper was supported by the Hungarian Academy of Sciences–Office of Supported Research (TKI).

Nine

THE INTENTIONALITY OF REFERENCE IN HUSSERL AND THE ANALYTIC TRADITION

Shannon Vallor

The twentieth century has given rise to many innovative and compelling approaches to philosophy. Viewed separately, the analytic and the phenomenological traditions represent the most fruitful and influential of these new directions in thought. Viewing them side by side, we are confronted with how little, historically, these traditions have had to say to one another. In recent decades, the efforts of a small but growing contingent of committed thinkers to lead these traditions into genuine dialogue have begun to pay real dividends. Yet much still remains to be done.

When initiating a philosophical dialogue that is long overdue, it is helpful to have a sense of the common ground shared by both parties to the conversation, and a grasp of the issues that have kept them apart.

In this work, I will explore one such issue by looking at some features of the philosophical problem of reference. While reference is generally held to be an issue studied exclusively within the domain of analytic thought, no account of reference in the analytic tradition from Gottlob Frege onward has provided a satisfactory explanation of the phenomenon of reference. The classic accounts have either collapsed under formal inconsistencies (Frege, 1967), left entire dimensions of the problem untreated with no program for remedying the omissions (Russell, 1993), or have shortchanged the phenomenon by ejecting or negating those components of it that do not fit their particular philosophical approach (Quine, 1961). More recent efforts have faced similar difficulties (Kripke, 1980; Searle, 1983; Devitt and Sterelny, 1999).

Many of the shortcomings of analytic theories of reference can be ameliorated by examining a different approach, which has roots in a common logical ground—the phenomenological model of Edmund Husserl. To illustrate, I will focus on one aporia found in the literature on reference from Frege onward, namely, the intractable failure of the law of substitutivity in some linguistic contexts. The phenomenological model can be used to explain and resolve the basic cause of such failures, by grounding the phenomenon of reference in its underlying theory of intentionality. I will begin with a broad overview of the history of the problem, and then provide what, in this space, can only be a sketch of the proposed phenomenological solution.

1. Failures of the Analytic Account of Reference

One of the central axioms of Frege's account of reference was a principle borrowed from Gottfried Wilhelm Leibniz. The principle states that if two expressions have the same reference, then either expression may substitute for the other in any statement in which one occurs, without affecting the truth of that statement (*salva veritate*) (Frege, 1892, p. 30). This law of substitutivity is virtually indispensable to any extensional and truth-functional logic. Yet as Frege recognized, several types of statements exist for which this law appears to fail. For example, "Venus is the morning star" is a true identity statement. Suppose that we also have a second true statement, "John is certain that he is looking at Venus through the telescope." What if, using "Venus is the morning star" in accordance with the law of substitutivity, we now replace "Venus" in "John is certain that he is looking at Venus through the telescope" with "the morning star"? Has the truth-value of our second statement been affected? The answer depends on whether John knows "Venus is the morning star" to be true. If he does not, then "John is certain that he is looking at the morning star through the telescope" is false, and the law of substitutivity appears to have failed. The law is subject to failure in all contexts that, as in the example above, introduce propositional attitudes such as knowing, believing, doubting, wishing, etc.

This is not the only context in which the law of substitutivity fails. Consider the following true identity statement:

Burma is Myanmar.

Assume the following also to be a true statement:

Aung San Suu Kyi said last week that she would fight to the end for a free Burma.

If I replace "Burma" with "Myanmar" in this statement, then the statement is no longer true, notwithstanding the identity given in "Burma is Myanmar." In addition to propositional attitudes, contexts containing reported or quoted speech often fail to uphold the law of substitutivity. We run into similar trouble with expressions containing indexical terms or modal operators. But the problem of substitutivity is not restricted to the aforementioned contexts, for it appears even in the most straightforward of linguistic expressions:

Venus is the morning star.
Venus is usually seen at dusk.
The morning star is usually seen at dusk.

We can see by these examples that the problem is manifest in different ways. While some substitutions falsify a true proposition, in other instances, substitution merely introduces an ambiguity where there was none before, or turns a well-expressed statement into an awkward or poorly communicated one. We can attack the problem in different ways. Frege's solution to such counterexamples was to make a distinction between the ordinary reference of an expression and its modified reference. For example, in "John is certain that he is looking at Venus through the telescope" and "Aung San Suu Kyi said last week that she would fight to the end for a free Burma," Frege would argue that the singular terms "Venus" and "Burma" do not have their usual reference (the objects they would ordinarily denote through their meaning). Instead, their reference in these contexts has been modified, and consists of just the meaning itself, or the terms' customary sense. For this reason, we are no longer justified in substituting "the morning star" for "Venus" in "John is certain that he is looking at Venus through the telescope," since the second term no longer has its usual reference (which it shares with "the morning star") but a modified reference (its sense) that it does not share with "the morning star." The power of this solution is that it resolves these difficulties in a way that appears to pre-serve the universal validity of the law of substitutivity. For Frege, these are not true exceptions to the law, but situations where one of the law's requirements (identity of reference) is not met.

Commentators have pointed out that Frege's solution is less satisfactory than it appears. First, the apparent solution extends only to cases of proposi-tional attitude or reported speech, and does not help us resolve cases such as those illustrated above by "The morning star is usually seen at dusk." Frege's solution also creates scope problems with the reference of pronouns in special contexts and problems with existential generalization. It raises serious difficul-ties in accounting for the indexical components of language, and poses a problem for those who wish to eliminate all talk of special entities called "senses." For this last reason, Bertrand Russell and W. V. O. Quine elected to find other solutions to the problems of substitution.

Russell's solution is rooted in his theory of descriptions, which holds that propositions commonly contain descriptions or denoting phrases masquerad-ing as names. For him, a true name denotes its referent directly, without the mediation of anything like a sense. His view is that terms that appear to be names generally are not (1993, p. 51). Consider the example above with re-spect to Venus and the morning star. According to Russell, "John is certain that he is looking at Venus through the telescope," does not use "Venus" as a true name. Instead, we may take "Venus" to be a disguised description, per-haps in the form "there is exactly one x such that x is the second planet from the sun and x is commonly called Venus." Alternatively, consider "the morn-ing star" not as a name, but as a disguised proposition similar to "there is exactly one x such that x is a star and x is visible at dawn." In this case, neither description directly denotes an object—instead, they are propositions that are either true or false. Since neither has a reference, they cannot have the same reference, and are not subject to the law of substitutivity.

Russell has proposed a workable theory that explains why substitution fails in special contexts. Yet the theory remains unsatisfactory with regard to its broader content and approach and is fundamentally an artificial solution, one that runs counter to the strong intuition that proper names and other singular terms are among the simplest of expressions. Nathan Salmon has made an apt comparison between Russell and Ptolemy, both adding to their theory "ingenious epicycles . . . in order to make it fit the recalcitrant facts" (1986, p. 46). Yet in another way, Russell's theory is an oversimplification. Whereas in ordinary speech the referent of a singular term such as "Venus" can be associated with a vast and perhaps even infinite wealth of properties, Russell's formulation arbitrarily excises all but those specified in the definite description for which "Venus" is said to stand.

Even if we accept Russell's theory for the sake of argument, we are now faced with the question, "Under what circumstances does the law of substitutivity hold?" If ordinary names are disguised descriptions, what exactly counts as a true name, a name that would directly denote something and would behave according to the law? Russell never entirely settled this matter, but demonstratives indicating a direct sensory acquaintance with an object such as "this" and "that" were early candidates for such "logically proper names." As the reference of demonstratives is an even thornier problem than the reference of ordinary names, Russell never arrived at a workable theory of direct reference. This leaves his theory of descriptions without a foundation. His focus led him to reduce everything we call a name to a descriptive phrase, and to subsequently eliminate these descriptions in his notation. So Russell's solution to failures of substitutivity is part of a larger strategy that renders the whole issue largely moot, as we have no ordinary singular terms left to function referentially, and nothing of substance for the law of substitutivity to cover.

Quine's approach, distinct from Russell's, accepts that some constructions do not permit successful reference of the kind that would allow for proper substitution. These constructions (including the problematic types mentioned above) involve positions that are referentially opaque. An expression placed in these positions will not properly refer, though the same expression will refer in referentially transparent or open positions of non-problematic constructions. So a noun or proper name governed by a verb of propositional attitude, for example, will not refer and cannot be reliably substituted for without potentially disturbing the truth-value of the sentence. Quine cannot erase this difficulty of ordinary speech by turning to his and Russell's program for eliminating singular terms, since he discovers that opacity also bleeds into the realm of quantifi-cation after singular terms have been eliminated (1961, p. 148). These problems with opacity and substitution force Quine to choose be-tween the option of abandoning the principle of extensionality and accepting the role of intensions in reference, or ejecting from quantificational logic forms of discourse that are undeniably essential to natural language (such as modal, demonstrative, and indirect speech). Quine chooses the second option without hesitation, partly because he doubts that recourse to intensions will solve the problem without adopting some version of essentialism, and partly because remaining faithful to natural language was never high on his list of priorities (1961, pp. 152–159). The purified language of science Quine was hoping for never fully materialized, so if by his admission ordinary language falls outside the purview of his account, then as a consequence, his explana-tion of reference is drained of much of its relevance and value.

Something about the dimension of sense or "intension" is amiss in all of these accounts. Logic and truth cannot be detached from the intensional prop-erties of things as easily as the champions of extensional logic have assumed. This is illustrated by cases involving significant alterations in the set of prop-erties associated with an object. Truthful predications of an object under one description can become false or ambiguous when the object is identified in a different way. Familiar examples of this include, "The loser of Waterloo was victorious," and "The morning star is seen at dusk." Why is the disturbance of truth by substitution relevant to the problem of reference? Because these distur-bances indicate that something fundamental is missing from extensional logic.

Claire Ortiz-Hill has suggested that Frege and Russell attempted to re-duce intensions to extensions, but ignored that intensions refuse to exit the logical realm, especially with respect to identity (1991, p. 172). As a result, they did not anticipate the well-known group of problems related to Russell's Paradox, in which classes, when treated as ordinary objects, take on contradic-tory properties. As Richard Cobb-Stevens has indicated, the only organic solu-tion to the paradox is to acknowledge that logical analysis is ultimately rooted in the pre-predicative intuitions of speakers, so that to pick out or refer to an ob-ject is something accomplished by persons, not concepts (1990, p. 70). Russell's Paradox arises because while people use intuition to delimit the likely range of application for the concepts they employ in their speech, Frege's self-determining concepts are under no such external restriction.

In all three traditional analytic approaches to reference, Fregean, Russel-lian or Quinean, we find two crucial features in common. The first is a com-mitment to extensional logic, a commitment honored either by reducing inten-sions to extensions or by excluding intensions from truth-functional considera-tions. I argue that this commitment inexorably leads to the second common feature, namely, an inability to provide a logical foundation for meaning and reference that respects and accounts for the structure, variety, and scope of ordinary language use. This is the point on which traditional analytic accounts of reference must ultimately be judged to fail, for the project of constructing a formal, complete and truth-functional language of science to replace ordinary language never succeeded. We are left with ordinary language, from which meaning and reference are not eliminable, and for which these analytic phi- losophers have no adequate account.

Many contemporary analytic thinkers continue to explore different means of getting beyond the impasse. Saul Kripke, Michael Devitt, John Searle, and others have progressed well beyond the narrow constraints of the traditional ana- lytic program, explaining the phenomenon of ordinary language in a better way in the process. But I postulate that the retention of several methodological preju- dices of the analytic tradition continues to block the way to a solution.

2. A Phenomenological Way Out

The first thing we learn from Husserl's analysis of intentionality is that sense never determines reference except as part of an intentional performance, usually a speaker's act. The act provides the context and, more importantly, the cognitive discrimination needed for a valid reference to take place. Russell's Paradox can be avoided as long as we deny what Frege treated as axiomatic—that the search for the appropriate arguments (objects) for a function is, "a context-free search procedure over an absolutely unlimited range of candidates" (Cobb-Stevens, 1990, p. 70). Allowing this search procedure to be subject to prior restriction on the basis of cognitive intuitions would require a radical revision of Frege's ap- proach. If extensional logic's problems with substitution and identity indicate that it is afflicted with an internal flaw, it may be a fatal one. These problems may not be fixable without introducing considerations alien to extensional treatment.

First among such considerations is the understanding of reference as fun- damentally an act. This may not appear so alien to the analytic approach after all, considering the extent to which P. F. Strawson, Searle, and many others stress the significance of speech acts. Contemporary analytic philosophers have recently gone to great lengths to develop the theoretical apparatus neces- sary to relativize the reference of terms to the context of a speaker's utterance. Kripke, Devitt, Gareth Evans, Keith Donnellan, and others have attempted to provide accounts of reference that avoid the pitfalls I described earlier. Some have even acknowledged the essential role intensions play in reference. But none have been willing to focus on the referring act as a subjective phenome- non. Each attempts by one means or another to redescribe the contributions of the first-person intentional act, in order to conform with the analytic methodo- logical preference for reducing "mentalistic" phenomena to observable or standpoint-neutral ones. Even Searle's account, which emphasizes the role of intentional performances in reference, treats the subjective first-person element as largely coincidental to the reference. In his account, a subject refers to an object because the object happens to satisfy conditions of satisfaction contained in an utterance, an utterance that also expresses the content of a speaker's "intentional state." No direct relation between the intentional state and the secured referent is needed or implied (1983, p. 222).

The current literature on problems of reference remains sharply divided among these different approaches, with no sign of a broad consensus on the horizon. But to address this issue in greater detail here is beyond the scope of this paper.

In response, I argue that:

(1) The contributions of the intentional act are an essential and ineliminable part of linguistic reference.

(2) The contributions of the intentional act can be directly accessed only in phenomenological reflection.

(3) Phenomenological reflection upon an intentional act necessarily yields a first-person element that cannot be fully rendered by a third-person objective account of the time, place, or even social context of an utterance.

(4) A complete, reliable and functional explanation of linguistic reference must be able to account for the contributions of the irreducibly subjective, first-person component of the referring act.

If we understand reference as originating in an act so described, then we must begin not with words but with the act of using them, and with the intentions deployed in that act. The phenomenological analysis of acts offered by Husserl is ideally suited to this focus. Two fundamental aspects of intentionality are involved in any referring act—the directionality of intentional acts, and their object-engaging function. The second aspect is present (either actually or potentially) in all intentional acts, so that each act is always engaging something beyond itself, whether the distance crossed is primarily spatial (as in perception of a chair) or strictly temporal (as in self-awareness of its own passing activity). Intentional acts are always relating to an object of some kind. This object-relation is complemented by an equally fundamental directionality. Intentional activity has a virtually unrestricted range of freedom (metaphorically speaking) that allows it to shift, focus, and even bifurcate its attention to an object. Consciousness can direct its attention to one thing or many, to objects immanent or transcendent, simple or composite, present or absent. Its attention can be directed through modes of perception, imagination, memory or judgment. This "attentional ray" as described by Husserl also has what he calls retentional and protentional temporal dimensions. Intentional acts do not take place in a fixed and finite "now." Instead, they unfold in an open temporal horizon that includes both awareness of the receding past (the retentional phase) and anticipation of the approaching future (the protentional phase). As such, a referring act is never a static relation between subject and object, but a mutual and dynamic interaction. By returning to the aporias of reference we indicated previously, we can illustrate the richness this understanding of directionality lends to Husserl's account.

Husserl had a ready solution to problems with substitutivity that Frege thought unacceptable. Husserl argued that relations of equality and identity involve not merely extensions, but also intensions. As a consequence, complex objects bear with them an irreducible and infinite wealth of properties, barring us from concluding that any two such objects are the same in all respects. For we have no way to be certain that we have accounted for all the properties that the objects have. Husserl claimed that statements of equality regarding complex objects must have a limited scope. Such judgments cannot posit equality in all respects, only that the properties forming the focus of interest are equal (Husserl, 1970, pp. 108–109). Problems with substitutivity disappear in Husserl's solution because the scope restriction means that Leibniz's law of substitutivity cannot be applied in the manner that Frege and his followers apply it. "So long as the least difference remains" between two terms in the way in which they present a thing, these terms cannot be reliably substituted for one another *salva veritate* (ibid., p. 104). Though a single entity may be the referent of both, the reference of the terms themselves is not, in the full sense, the "same."

The reason for this restriction becomes even more apparent when we think about reference in terms of the phenomenological model developed by Husserl in his *Ideas* (1982). Though he ultimately concluded that the model of noesis and noema was too static to be entirely satisfactory, it sheds quite a bit of light on the problem of reference. First, we must take into account that the total *noema* as characterized by Husserl is not, as some commentators have held, the equivalent of a Fregean sense, a special entity mediating the relation between my reference to the object and the object itself. For Husserl the total noema is identical with the object of the reference. Husserl is emphatic that the sense, on the other hand, is only a "piece of the noema," its "How" as opposed to its "What" (ibid., p. 315). Taken alone the sense is not an object, and cannot be a mediate object of the reference relation. (ibid., pp. 314–315) Still, the sense is a fundamental piece of the noematic whole and cannot be separated from the object's identity. Husserl's point is that we never have an object before us except as intended, in a determinate way.

Just as all consciousness is consciousness of something, every something is the object of an intending consciousness. If I object by saying that undiscovered planets exist even though we are not yet conscious of their existence, I forget that I am already conscious of their existence, in the determinate mode of possibility, as soon as I raise the objection. Husserl's idealism is not metaphysical. It only acknowledges that even the meaning of a "mind-independent entity" is always already part of an intentional act, and that an entity without meaning is not something we can consider in any coherent way.

Husserl distinguished within the noema an essential structure consisting of layers of sense or meaning, and within those layers a central core. The "outer" layers of sense include those features of the object that are given as perceiver-relative and accordingly subject to change. The "inner" layers, closer to the core, consist of comparatively stable properties or determinations of sense that are given as belonging to the object itself. At the center of the core is something radically different from these layers of sense, something Husserl calls the "determinable X." The determinable X is the unifying support to which the object's concrete determinations and properties adhere—the "What" of the presentation as opposed to the "How." The determinable X is the closest thing to what analytic thinkers mean by a "bare extension," or metaphysicians mean by "the thing in itself," but is identical with neither. For this "object *simpliciter*" can be distinguished from the noematic layers of sense, but never separated from them. (ibid., p. 313)

Husserl recognized that a yet-undetermined X can never be intended or referred to, though we can approach the idea in abstraction by artificially subtracting the given determinations of an actively intended object. The logic of intentionality demands the existence of the determinable X, for a group of properties do not make up an object. They must be unified and anchored as the determinations of some one thing. Yet this thing, this X, is never grasped by an intentional act without bearing with it a complex of given and anticipated determinations. Even the referent of the prior sentence is not a true X but a symbolic stand-in, for it already has determinations—such as "never grasped without determinations." Yet this does not mean that when I refer, my act must pass through an intermediate entity like a sense on its way to the thing. To employ a rough but still illustrative analogy, if I pick up my cat, I am holding the entire cat, even though my hands are only touching her fur. The fur is an integral part of the cat, not something tacked on in addition. Likewise, the X and its given determinations form an objective and indissoluble whole. Once we take this model into account, we see why identity became such a problem for Frege and those who followed his lead. Frege presumed that logic could resolve objects into bare extensions and concepts, and from there he attempted to eliminate concepts altogether and replace them with new objects, namely classes. From this point on, identity is then merely a matter of two objects having the same class membership(s), and differences between their apparent properties or determinations are rendered moot. But Husserl's analysis shows this to be impossible, for the structure of intentionality prevents objects from being stripped down in this way. And this structure is precisely what bites back, so to speak, when extensional logic is applied to the real world of language users.

So why did Frege reject Husserl's solution? First, the solution flatly predicts the failure of extensional logic, since it holds that intensions cannot be excluded from the logician's interest in truth. Just as Frege and his followers later found, intensions infiltrate and muddy up the "crystalline" waters of extensional logic in ways that cannot be prevented except by radical *ad hoc* measures.

Second, Husserl's means of dealing with intensions introduced an element that few self-respecting analytic thinkers could swallow whole, even today. This element is the aforementioned directional focus of intentional activity, which can narrow the act's attention to some properties of a thing while excluding others, allowing two items with differing properties to be equal in the one respect that is currently the focus of attention.

My argument is that the scope and direction of the intentional act ultimately determines the reference expressed through the act. In addition, I see no way that other theoretical apparatus, no matter how descriptively rich or context-sensitive (senses, time-slices, or possible worlds), can do the work of the intentional act. Nor can the scope and direction of the intentional act be "naturalized," if by this we mean imported into a theoretical framework that excludes the first-personal nature of intentional acts.

Statements like, "The loser of Waterloo was victorious" only arise when we blindly substitute a referential term ("The loser of Waterloo") for another ("Napoleon") without realizing that these terms are not always truth-equivalent, even though they have the same extension. For instance, the referential terms in the preceding sentence are equivalent when the intention behind the statement in which they are employed is focused on, say, the subject's stature. "The loser of Waterloo was short" is just as true as "Napoleon was short." Yet these referential terms are not equivalent when the statement is directed toward Napoleon's status as a victor. We know that the terms are not equivalent in this case because the substitution falsifies the statement, and it does so because the reference to the thing is now being simultaneously directed through contradictory properties—"loser" and "victorious."

One important difference between the analytic solutions to failures of substitutivity reviewed in Section 1 and the Husserlian solution described above is that the former generally focus on looking for a way around those failures, without first addressing the question of why the same terms will substitute cleanly for one another in some cases but not in others.

We have no way to explain these failures without acknowledging that the truth of a statement depends on something more than the extension of the referring term falling under a given concept, or even the context of the utterance fulfilling its truth conditions. Its truth depends in part upon whether what is predicated of the referent fits with those features of the referent already captured by the speaker's object-directed interest. To illustrate, we have said that an object is never part of an intentional act without already having a set of determinations, those features of the object "picked up" by the act's focused attention. But these features are not functioning as predicates. The object appears in the act united with them already, and any predicate that appears in a statement the speaker makes about the object is a feature deliberately highlighted and set off from that object. This distinction affects the meaning of the statement. This is why,

"the prize-winning apple is green"

is not semantically equivalent with,

"the green apple is prize-winning"

or even,

"the apple is both green and prize-winning."

Yet in each case both "prize-winning" and "green" are true of the same object. What differ are the direction of the intentional act, the order in which the act picks up the object's features, and the relative degree of its interest in those features.

This difference also explains why, if the apple being spoken of is now also a bruised apple, the substitution into,

"the prize-winning apple is green"
"the bruised apple is green"

will succeed with no disturbance of truth-value while the substitution into,

"the green apple is prize-winning"
"the bruised apple is prize-winning"

suddenly appears problematic. We could make many other substitutions into both "the prize-winning apple is green," and "the green apple is prize-winning," with no difficulty. When a substitution does fail, it fails because the new manner of identifying the object brings into view a property of the object that conflicts with the property or properties already highlighted by the direction and focus of the original intentional act. Yet a habit of unambiguous speech is to identify objects in ways that fit with what we want to say about them. No competent speaker would be likely to utter the sentence, "the morning star is seen

at dusk," given the many other ways of identifying Venus that would not introduce the problem. But extensional logic can offer no formal restriction against
such speech, nor explain coherently why it produces the difficulties that it does.
Analytic approaches that take into account ordinary language practices and
norms can explain how such mistakes are avoided, but not why the norms exclude them. A phenomenological approach, as we will see, explains both.

As a first step, Husserl's approach requires us to conclude that for linguistic purposes, the identity of a thing with itself is conditional—precisely
because our intentional acts, and the language that we use to express them, do
not give us the option of separating the thing from its modes of appearing to
us. The morning star is not identical with the evening star, even though they
share the same extension. But in 1894 Frege rejected the argument that intentional activity has any bearing at all on logical relations, much less the ability
to dissolve or constitute identities just by shifting its focus, "This is possible
only in the wash-tub of the mind . . . [Husserl] took the road of magic rather
than of science" (Frege, 1984, p. 205). Frege's criticism might be more compelling if his logic held together without any magical intervention. But Russell demonstrated that unless propped up by overtly *ad hoc* measures (which
Frege bravely rejected), Frege's system implodes under its weight (Frege,
1967). Husserl knew that a purely extensional logic would be fatally flawed
(1978, pp. 74, 83). As early as 1891, he noted the problem with extensional
logic that eventually led Frege into the paradox, namely, that extensional
logic is "objectless" (1994, p. 64). The logician's extensions are referents
stripped of their intensional richness and their connection with directed intentions, yet these elements are partly constitutive of what it is to be an object. For
Husserl, "so little is it true that the logic of extension is to be treated independently of the logic of intension, and so little is the former 'fixed untroubled by the
latter,' that when doing extensional logic we yet stand within intensional logic,
or subordinate to it" (ibid., p. 68).

Substitutional problems with the opaque constructions of quotation, propositional attitude, and modality can also be solved using the same basic
model of reference that Husserl uses. Consider the question of quotation or
reported speech. Quine's solution, to generally exclude these contexts as non-
referring, ignores the customary purpose of reporting another's speech. Let us
set aside those exceptions where the purpose of quotation is not to communicate
what was said, but to report what words were used. Obviously in such cases the
references made in the original speech are not preserved in the report. But ordinarily, when we report someone's speech (e.g., "Mary says that . . . ."), what we want
to communicate is the meaning—what the person spoke of and what he or she
said about it. The references made are preserved in the report—but fixed with
respect to the original speaker's focus.

This is why in our previous example, "Aung San Suu Kyi said last week that she would fight to the end for a free Burma," it would be false to substitute "Myanmar" for "Burma" in Aung San Suu Kyi's speech. The problem is not with the nature of the construction as a report. The problem is that, although they have the same extension, "Burma" has properties that "Myanmar" lacks (namely, being under legitimate and democratic governance). In political speech, Burma's democratic leader would necessarily be directing her reference to her country through those properties, preventing "Myanmar" from being a valid substitution for it.

Reported speech or quotation only appears to be opaque in ordinary usage because the focus of the intentional act behind the original statement is more explicit. Yet in most cases we can substitute into these contexts, if the focus of the statement allows. For example, if I attend a geography class, and afterward report to a friend a matter of geographical trivia I learned, (e.g., "Professor Jones said that Burma has a very humid climate"), whether I say "Burma" or "Myanmar" is irrelevant to the truth of the report. This is only because the original speaker's reference in this case was directed only through properties both names hold in common.

Likewise, problems with statements involving propositional attitudes and modality can be solved easily with the phenomenological model. Consider first Quine's example of a statement in which a name occurs non-referentially as a result of a propositional attitude,

Philip believes that Tegucigalpa is in Nicaragua.

Quine's point is that since substitution of "Tegucigalpa" with "The capital of Honduras" fails in "Philip believes that Tegucigalpa is in Nicaragua," "Tegucigalpa" must not refer here (1961, p. 141). If we consider this case using Husserl's approach, we see that this conclusion is unwarranted. As in the case of quoted speech, the issue is the particular direction the reference takes. Substitution fails in "Philip believes that Tegucigalpa is in Nicaragua," not because "Tegucigalpa" does not refer, but because the propositional attitude fixes the reference so that it travels the same path as the original believing intention (in this case Philip's), which, as a result of Philip's ignorance, bypasses the property or sense "capital of Honduras" belonging to Tegucigalpa. Any substitution that alters this path runs the risk of disturbing the statement's truth.

Problems of modality are solved in the same fashion. Quine illustrates these by arguing, for example, that although 9 is necessarily greater than 7, and 9 is the number of planets, that the number of planets be greater than 7 is not necessary (since the truth of the latter is not analytic but empirical). But "9 is the number of planets" is not a true identity, just as "Tegucigalpa is the capital of Honduras" is not. These terms are complex unities that share significant properties, and even their extension. But since "the least difference" remains between them, a reference to one is not necessarily interchangeable *salva veritate* with a reference to another. The point in all of these examples is that reference, in relating a speaker's intention to a thing, travels a particular path of sense that cannot be ignored, even if one's concern is restricted to truth considerations.

Reference is not a bare link between a word or a concept and an extension, but an intensionally rich and irreducible relation between a person and an object, *via* an act in which the object is engaged in a definite way. If the law of substitutivity is to be of any logical use, it must be reinterpreted in a way that takes this richer understanding of the reference relation into account.

Because of the analytic tradition's core prejudice against intentional and first-person considerations, the analytic model is unable to explain substitutional problems in a way that respects the contours of natural language. Husserl's model, on the other hand, does not ask us to eject crucial forms of speech from logical discourse, nor to conclude that our references to things are not references at all, but mere "mentalistic excrescences," to use Quine's term. Husserl's model allows us to recognize that each reference to a thing is borne by an intentional act following a directional path, and that along this path definite properties of the referent are highlighted. This path and its associated properties are preserved in the terms we use to make statements about the referent, and as such, the truth of our statements can be disturbed by the blind substitution of other terms for the referent that express a different path to that referent.

If references do bear within themselves a particular direction or path to their referent, then a name might not be a tag for or even a description of an object (the alternatives usually entertained by analytic thinkers), and instead something like a map of a traveler's route. The object is the destination, and the intentional referring act is the traveler, but the name expresses how the traveler is getting there. Just as there can be many possible routes to a destination, a single thing can have many names. Such a model of reference leaves some room for a modified version of Kripke's account of names as rigid designators (Vallor, 2002, p. 183). A name could be taken to designate rigidly as a publicly "posted" marker, not of the object itself but of the direction of a particular path of intention to it (not unlike highway signs or breadcrumbs left on a trail). Use of that name makes public which properties of the thing are most relevant to the reference. The use of names in language helps to communicate to others not just what we are talking about, but the direction from which we view it and what about it interests us. Unrestricted substitution in ordinary speech works about as well as giving a person from Rome and a person from Prague the same directions to Paris. Only someone who did not understand how directions are used would think that because the destination is the same, all sets of directions to it ought to be interchangeable.

Though the analytic tradition has historically contributed the greater part of our understanding with regard to the philosophy of language, it has also been stalled on several fronts by paradoxes and puzzles of the kind I have touched on here. The explanatory power of Husserl's model is not restricted to problems of substitution—it suggests a way out of the puzzle of informative identity statements, Russell's Paradox, and several other lesser known aporias of reference. Perhaps, then, this model is worth a closer look by analytic thinkers, who share a fundamental philosophical temperament with Husserl, if not the same fundamental assumptions.

Ten

HOW TO GET INTENTIONALITY
BY LANGUAGE

Alberto Voltolini

We are often told that sentences expressing or reporting mental states endowed with intentionality—the feature of being "directed upon" an object that some mental states possess—contain contexts that both prevent those sentences to be existentially generalized and are filled by referentially opaque occurrences of singular terms. Failure of existential generalization and referential opacity have been traditionally said to be the basic characterizations of intentionality from a linguistic point of view. I will call those contexts directional contexts.

In what follows, I will argue that this traditional conception is incorrect. First, the above characterizations do not provide both necessary and jointly sufficient conditions for directional contexts. Second, appearances notwithstanding, these characterizations are not the adequate linguistic counterparts of two elements folk-psychologically featuring intentionality, namely existence-independence and the possible apparent aspectual character of the intentional object, the target of a mental state endowed with intentionality. Indeed, they do not retain the *prima facie* ontological commitment to intentional objects the above elements contain.

I will replace failure of existential generalization and referential opacity with other linguistic factors, namely success of mere existentially unloaded particular quantification and pseudo-opacity. I will contend that they provide both necessary and jointly sufficient conditions for directional contexts, and claim that these factors are the adequate counterparts of the above folk-psychological elements, precisely because they retain the *prima facie* onto-logical commitment to *intentionalia* those elements possess.

1. The Inadequate Linguistic Criteria of Intentionality

For the purpose of this paper, I will use "directional contexts" to mean those linguistic contexts contained by sentences expressing or reporting directional attitudes, mental states endowed with intentionality, the feature of being "directed upon" an object that some mental states possess. A directional attitude is either merely objectual—an attitude of, or about, something—or also pro-positional—an attitude about something that such a something is *F*. I see those contexts as a subclass of psychological contexts, namely the linguistic contexts contained by sentences expressing or reporting mental states in general. Consider sentences like, "I think of Nessie" (uttered by me), or "I believe that Superman is charming" (uttered by Lois Lane), and "A. V. thinks of Nessie," or "Lois believes that Superman is charming." In these sentences, the main verb is followed either by a singular term only or by a sentence containing that very term. Let me then speak of an object position and of an embedded position to mean the position that such a term respectively possesses. Put differently, whether such a position is an object or an embedded position depends on whether the expression/report is merely objectual (when the expressed/reported directional attitude is merely objectual as well; that is, a thought of an object O) or also propositional (when the attitude is also propositional: that is, a thought that O is F). These sentences present typical examples of directional contexts because they respectively express and report mental states that are endowed with intentionality insofar as these states are "directed upon" (different) intentional objects—respectively, Nessie, the purported Loch Ness monster, and Superman, the famous superhero.

Starting from the seminal works of Roderick Chisholm (1957; 1967a; 1972), a long tradition in the philosophy of language has taken failure of existential generalization and referential opacity as the main criteria allowing us to single out sentences presenting directional contexts from sentences presenting other linguistic contexts.

In point of fact, this tradition has been self-limited to allegedly circumscribe sentences presenting psychological contexts in general. Yet, as I said before, I am interested in seeing whether linguistic criteria of intentionality manage to single out a smaller class of linguistic contexts, what I have called directional contexts. In what follows, therefore, I will assume that the tradition aimed at the same goal.

The idea is that the context filled by a singular term in either an object position or an embedded position is a directional context insofar as the sentence containing it (1) does not allow inference of an existentially generalized sentence and (2) does not allow substitution *salva veritate* of that term with another ordinarily co-referential singular term.

In the aforementioned papers, Chisholm mentions a third criterion, the non-truthfunctionality criterion. That is, a further test for a directional context is that the sentence containing it be such that its truth-value does not depend on the truth-value of its sentential components. Chisholm formulates this criterion in a different way; that is, another test for a directional context is that the sentence containing the context therein be such that from its truth-value inferring the truth-value of its sentential components is impossible. James W. Cornman's (1972, p. 58) contrary opinion notwithstanding, these two ways of stating the criterion are not equivalent formulations: an ordinarily extensional context may pass the second, but not the first test (take for example disjunctions). Regardless, I will not consider the third criterion in this paper not only because it does not provide necessary linguistic conditions of intentionality (for it cannot apply to reports of objectual attitudes), but also and especially because, unlike the first two criteria, it purportedly matches no folk-psychological feature of intentionality.

Currently no one maintains that failure of existential generalization and referential opacity are linguistic criteria of intentionality, namely are criteria for sentences presenting directional contexts. Indeed, well-known problems exist with taking those criteria as necessary conditions for such sentences. On the one hand, everybody knows that both reports of veridical attitudes of the propositional form, "*S* knows (perceives, remembers . . .) that *Fa*" and reports of the objectual form "*S* knows (perceives, remembers) *a*," where "*a*" is a singular term, respectively allow the generalization, "There exists something which *S* knows (perceives, remembers . . .) that is *F*" and "There exists something which *S* knows (perceives, remembers . . .)." Such sentences appear to present genuine cases of directional contexts (Cornman, 1972). On the other hand, reports of veridical attitudes merely of the objectual form, "*S* knows (perceives, remembers . . .) *a*" appear to allow substitution *salva veritate* of "*a*" with the ordinarily co-referential singular term "*b*" (Kenny, 1963; Crane, 1995, p. 36). If this is the case, then both failure of existential generalization and referential opacity are unnecessary for a sentence to present a directional context.

Assume these problems can be circumvented by endorsing the traditional move according to which, unlike the main verbs in extensional contexts, the main verbs in the above reports—call them cognitive verbs—entail verbs whose corresponding reports pass both criteria. For example, "to perceive" entails "to have a sensory impression," and a report like "*S* has the sensory impression that *Fa*/of *a*" both fails to be existentially generalized and is referentially opaque (Marras, 1972). Yet, as C. B. Martin and Karl Pfeifer (1986) and Chisholm himself (1967a) have stressed, problems remain with taking those criteria as sufficient conditions.

With regard to the first criterion, consider dispositional contexts like the one contained in "This temple is liable to be destroyed by the next approaching barbarian." Definitely, these contexts are not directional. Yet a sentence such as "This temple is liable to be destroyed by the next approaching barbarian" does not elicit an existential generalization such as "there is [exists] an *x*, and only one *x*, which has the property of being a barbarian approaching next and which is such, that this temple is liable to be destroyed by *x*."

Regarding the second criterion, consider modal contexts like the one contained in, "it is necessary that the evening star appears in the sky at dusk." As everybody knows, these contexts are referentially opaque, for we cannot substitute *salva veritate* "the evening star" with the ordinarily co-referential "the morning star" in the above sentence. Yet modal contexts are by no means directional contexts. This was originally pointed out by William Kneale (1968).

As a further result, failure of existential generalization and referential opacity are not even jointly sufficient linguistic conditions of intentionality. Dispositional contexts are a subclass of modal contexts. To say that something is liable to be destroyed is to say that for it, the possibility exists that the something is destroyed. This illustration demonstrates that not only sentences presenting directional contexts, but also those presenting modal contexts are affected both by referential opacity and by failure of existential generalization.

To be sure, what I have just told is a well-known story. Failure of existential generalization and referential opacity are nowadays taken to be sufficient conditions of the different, linguistic, phenomenon of intensionality, not of intentionality (Crane, 1995, pp. 32–36; 2001a, p. 11; Place, 1996).

Independently of whether the Chisholmian idea is incorrect, understanding its *rationale* is crucial. Why has it been supposed that a sentence for which both existential generalization fails and referential opacity obtains *eo ipso* presents a directional context? Failure of existential generalization and referential opacity respectively have appeared to be the linguistic counterparts of what I would like to call the pre-linguistic folk-psychological features of intentionality, the features by means of which we naturally tend to conceive intentionality even independently of the existence of linguistic reports of directional attitudes. On the one hand, the intentional object, the target intentionality "directs" a mental state upon, is existence-independent; that is, any mental state endowed with intentionality has an intentional object that mental state is "directed upon," that may exist or not exist (Crane, 2001a, pp. 13–18; Smith and McIntyre, 1982, pp. 10–12). On the other hand, the intentional object has a possible apparent aspectual character; the intentional object may appear as if it had a perspectival nature, namely as if its role were simply that of disclosing another object beyond it.

The second feature is often described differently, highlighting that the intentional object is presented under an aspect (Smith and McIntyre, 1982, pp. 12–15; Searle, 1992, p. 155; Crane, 2001a, pp. 18–21). Yet this description appears to me incorrect, for it does not match the phenomenology of the situation. First, note that when a non-existent intentional object is what intentionality "directs" a state upon, that object does not present itself as being given under an aspect. If I think of Nessie, the (nonexistent) Loch Ness monster, I merely think of precisely the (nonexistent) Loch Ness monster, but I do not think of it as the Loch Ness monster. If I thought of Nessie as the Loch Ness monster, then it might be thought of by me also under other aspects, for example as the animal "out there" in the fog. Yet this could be the case only if it had turned out that the Loch Ness monster and the animal in the fog are one and the same individual. Since there obviously is no such a discovery, Nessie is not thought of as something, Tim Crane's contrary opinion notwithstanding (2001a, p. 30). Put differently, cases exist in which we can legitimately say that a subject thinks of an object under two or even more different perspectives; for example, regarding the famous Frege case (Geach and Black, 1952), we legitimately say that Venus is thought of both as the morning and as the evening star. Yet properly speaking this is not a phenomenological description, the immediate description of one's experience. The phenomenological description would instead be that one is first "directed upon" a certain intentional object—the thing that he intends to refer by "the morning star," as he would say—and then "directed upon" another intentional object—the thing he intends to refer by "the evening star," he would again say. Indeed again, the original description—a subject thinks of Venus as either the morning or the evening star—is the description we can properly provide only after the discovery that the first intentional object and the second intentional object—the one for which that subject would use "the morning star" and the one for which he would use "the evening star"—are one and the same individual—Venus.

The above considerations also help us to see why the aspectual character of the intentional object is a merely possible apparent one. Only when the epistemological possibility of the discovery that distinct intentional objects are the same individual is realized—as it turns out to be the case in the "morning/evening star" example, but not in the "Nessie" example—are we properly faced with the alleged aspectuality of an intentional object. In the "morning/evening star" example, having discovered that the morning star is the same as the evening star, we may say that one and the same object (Venus) is thought both as the morning star and as the evening star. Yet even in such a case, folk-psychologically speaking we are only entitled to say that the two intentional objects seem to be aspectual, appear to be aspects disclosing another object.

The possible apparent aspectual character of the intentional object matches another feature of such an entity, namely its phenomenological indeterminacy. Indisputably, an intentional object appears as indeterminate with respect to many properties—we think of Nessie neither as having nor as not having a black ring on its tail, of the morning star neither as having nor as not having a particular mass, and so on. The possible apparent aspectual character of the intentional object casts light on its phenomenological indeterminacy. An intentional object appears to be indeterminate insofar as if it may turn out to seem just a facet of another individual it contributed, along with other seeming facets, to disclose. The phenomenological indeterminacy of the intentional object was first noticed by G. E. M. Anscombe, who said, "I can think of a man without thinking of a man of any particular height" (1965, p. 161). Yet Anscombe actually originated the erroneous conflation of this phenomenological indeterminacy with the ontological indeterminacy of the intentional object. On this point, see

Place (1996). Ontological indeterminacy amounts to the so-called incomplete-ness of the intentional object, according to which for some property *F* and its opposite not-*F*, that object has neither. That such an indeterminacy subsists is a controversial metaphysical thesis on which I will remain neutral. Definitely, the phenomenological indeterminacy of the intentional object does not provide enough evidence for it.

So, failure of existential generalization appears to correspond to the exis-tence-independence of the intentional object—we cannot generalize a sentence containing a directional context, for the relevant intentional object may not actually exist—while referential opacity appeared to correspond to the possible apparent aspectual character of such an object—unsubstitutable embedded singu-lar terms match distinct aspectually distinguishable intentional objects.

Once we go back to this *rationale* for the attempt at making those phe-nomena as linguistic criteria of intentionality, we can also see why that attempt ultimately failed. Failure of existential generalization and referential opacity are not the adequate linguistic counterparts of the folk-psychological features of intentionality, the existence-independence and the possible apparent aspec-tual character of the intentional object. The proper linguistic counterparts of these features are indeed different. To look for better linguistic criteria of in-tentionality, we have to look for these linguistic counterparts.

2. The Adequate Linguistic Criteria of Intentionality

I claim that the genuine linguistic counterpart of the existence-independence of the intentional object is that a directional context legitimizes us to infer from a sentence containing it only an existentially unloaded particular quantification, not both an existentially unloaded and an existentially loaded particular quanti-fication. On the contrary, extensional contexts allow us to infer both. I will call this linguistic factor success of mere existentially unloaded particular quantifica-tion. The idea is that, while an extensional context like "*S* beats *a*," where "*a*" is a singular term, authorizes both an existentially loaded particular quantification, "There exists one *x* such that *S* beats it," and an existentially unloaded particular quantification, "There is an *x* such that *S* beats it," a directional context like the one contained in "*S* thinks of *a*" legitimizes us only to infer an existentially un-loaded particular quantification, "There is an *x* such that *S* thinks of it."

In this respect, a directional context differs not only from an extensional, but also from an intensional context. For an intensional context authorizes neither an existentially loaded particular quantification, nor an existentially unloaded particular quantification. At most, that context authorizes a narrow scope existential quantification, whether loaded or unloaded. Take the above example of the dispositional context contained in the sentence, "this temple is liable to be destroyed by the next approaching barbarian." This is an intensional context, insofar as the only quantified sentence that we can infer from that sentence is, "this temple is such, that it is possible that there is/exists an x, and only an x, which has the property of being a barbarian approaching next, and x destroys that temple," where the quantifier has narrow scope.

As a result, unlike failure of existential generalization, success of mere existentially unloaded particular quantification candidates itself to be a sufficient linguistic condition of intentionality. To be sure, it may seem that reports of veridical attitudes would again constitute a counterexample to this criterion being a necessary linguistic condition of intentionality. For "S sees a" elicits not only the inference "There is an x such that S sees it" but also the inference "There exists an x such that S sees it." Yet these apparent counterexamples may again be circumvented in the same way as the one indicated before: cognitive verbs entail verbs whose corresponding reports ("S has the impression of seeing a") also satisfy the new criterion.

In order to appreciate this move, some clarification is needed. First, if the criterion must work as a linguistic criterion of intentionality, there must be some pre-theoretical linguistic evidence that we distinguish between existentially loaded ("there exists") and existentially unloaded ("there is") particular quantification. I claim this to be the case. In ordinary linguistic transactions we use the two second-order predicates "there is" "there exists" almost interchangeably. Yet the interchangeable use does not mean that "there is" means always the same as "there exists." Alternatively put, the interchangeable use does not mean that each of these predicates is not ambiguously used. Let us see these two points in order.

As to the first point, note for instance that in order already to understand the thesis of the existence-independence of the intentional object, we have to presuppose that "there is" does not mean there what "there exists" means. For what the thesis states is that for any mental state endowed with intentionality, there is an intentional object that the state is "directed upon" which may exist or may not exist. If in such a thesis "there is" meant "there exists," the thesis itself would not be understandable at all, as Crane himself acknowledges (2001a, p. 24). For it would entail the incomprehensible claim that there may be a mental state endowed with intentionality such that there exists an object that said mental state is "directed upon" which does not exist.

As to the second point, take Alexius Meinong's famous *dictum* that, "there are things of which it is true that there are no such things." Again, whether such a thesis is true is not in question. I only question whether we can understand the thesis. We can affirmatively address this question only by presupposing that in such a *dictum* the second occurrence of the predicate "there are" does not mean the same as the first occurrence. Otherwise, the statement of thesis would be a contradictory claim. Nathan Salmon claims that Meinong's thesis is a contradictory one (1982, p. 39). I hold that Salmon misunderstands Meinong's point, since Meinong's purpose was definitely to make a (apparently) paradoxical, but not a contradictory claim.

Given the above linguistic data, let me call the use of "there is" which would make the sentence "there is an intentional object which does not exist" perfectly acceptable the paradigmatic use of such a predicate, and correspondingly the use of "there exists" which would make the sentence "there exists an intentional object which does not exist" contradictory the paradigmatic use of this second predicate.

Once we grasp this distinction between these two paradigmatic uses, we are faced with two options. Either we claim that the paradigmatic uses of "there is" and "there exists" respectively refer to two different second-order properties. As a result, logically adequate paraphrases of sentences in which those predicates were so used would respectively contain two distinct existential quantifiers—a "Meinongian" quantifier and an ordinary existential one. Or, we say that just one existential quantifier exists, which occurs contextually unrestricted wherever "there is" is used paradigmatically—it bounds a variable ranging over the overall domain of objects of discourse—and which occurs contextually restricted wherever "there exists" is used paradigmatically—it bounds a variable ranging not over the overall domain of the objects of discourse, but over the subdomain of the objects of discourse which exist. This second option goes along with maintaining that the existence affecting objects of this subdomain is a first-order property that just those individuals, in the overall domain of the objects of discourse, possess.

The possession of such a first-order property meets Crane's requirement of a criterion to tell the subdomain of existents from the overall domain of the objects of discourse (2001b, p. 339). In order for such a criterion to work, we must understand to what this first-order property of existence amounts. Yet we have a lot of candidates here. For instance, we may say that for an object to exist is to be involved in the causal order.

In speaking of existentially unloaded and existentially loaded particular quantification, I already argued for the second option which, I hold, is ontologically thriftier than the first option. Instead of having two distinct second-order properties, two existential quantifiers, we just have one second-order property, just one particular quantifier; but the one and the same particular quantification sometimes works unrestrictedly, sometimes restrictedly. We ordinarily use particular quantification as even more contextually restricted to the subdomain of locally existent individuals—as when I say "Yes, there is butter," meaning not that there exists butter somewhere or other in the actual world, but that there exists butter in my fridge, or in my kitchen. Once things are put this way, we find it easier to understand why the sentence, "A mental state endowed with intentionality may be such, that there exists an object it 'directed upon' which does not exist," would sound incomprehensible, if in it, the predicate, "there exists," occurred in its paradigmatic use. For it would amount to the contradictory claim that, in the sub-domain of the objects of discourse which exist, exists an object of discourse which does not exist.

If a sentence containing a directional context allows us to infer a mere existentially unloaded particular quantification, the relevant occurrence of the singular term figuring in either an object position or an embedded position in that sentence is genuinely referential. What that occurrence refers to is precisely what makes the corresponding quantified sentence true, namely, the intentional object the expressed/reported attitude is "directed upon." Given that the referent of such an occurrence is an intentional object, let me call this occurrence extraordinarily referential. For this terminology allows me to distinguish that occurrence not only from other occurrences of singular terms, the ordinarily referential ones, referring to no object qualified as intentional, but also from further occurrences of singular terms, namely the referentially opaque ones, which do not refer to any individual at all.

These preliminary statements lead me to my second main claim. To my mind, the possible apparent aspectual character of the intentional object is linguistically matched by the existence of extraordinarily non-coreferential occurrences of singular terms in directional contexts. Indeed, unlike the corresponding ordinarily referential occurrences, these occurrences being extraordinarily referential makes them non-coreferential. In this respect, they are similar to referentially opaque occurrences of singular terms, which are again not co-referential. The extraordinarily referential occurrences are however not the same as these latter occurrences. For, unlike the latter occurrences, the former occurrences do refer, though to different individuals. Their extraordinary referentiality makes them pseudo-opaque occurrences.

My second main claim is that pseudo-opacity is another criterion to tell sentences containing directional contexts from other sentences. Take for instance the name "Hesperus" occurring not in extensional contexts like "Hesperus is a planet," but in contexts like the one contained by "*S* thinks of Hesperus." Unlike the first context, "Hesperus" here is not substitutable *salva veritate* by "Phosphorus." To be sure, also "the morning star" is irreplaceable *salva veritate* with "the evening star" in a sentence presenting a modal context like "it is possible that the morning star does not appear in the sky at dusk." Yet in the directional context, "Hesperus" and "Phosphorus" are not referentially opaque, as "the morning star" and "the evening star" in the modal context above; instead, they are extraordinarily non-coreferential, that is, pseudo-opaquely referential.

As a result, unlike referential opacity, pseudo-opacity is a candidate to be a sufficient linguistic condition of intentionality. In order for pseudo-opacity to also be a necessary condition, one has to make a move analogous to the one provided above for success of mere existentially unloaded particular quantification. This prevents cases like "*S* knows *a*," where substitutivity holds, from being possible counterexamples.

Readers familiar with Gottlob Frege's work will recognize his authorship behind the pseudo-opacity claim. He was the first to expressly hold the thesis that occurrences of singular terms in either an object position or an embedded position within sentences containing directional contexts are not opaque, but refer to extraordinary referents—their *Sinne*. Many have claimed that Fregean *Sinne* may be paired with intentional objects. I will remain neutral on this issue, for my purpose here is not to defend a particular theory of intentional objects. I do not want here to claim that *intentionalia* are Fregean *Sinne*; or that they are abstract objects, Meinongian entiti•s, *possibilia*, or else. My purpose is simply to say that, if we want a linguistic criterion that matches the corresponding folk-psychological feature of intentionality, namely the possible apparent aspectual character of the intentional object, we have to take the aforementioned occurrences of singular terms as referring to (distinct) intentional objects—whatever they are.

Moreover, Frege's pseudo-opacity thesis is a general claim regarding not only directional contexts, but also all psychological contexts. He makes no distinction between psychological contexts and directional contexts: with respect to all these contexts, the terms following the psychological verb of the context extraordinarily refer to *Sinne*. On the contrary, I allow for the possibility that a distinction exists between sentences containing directional contexts and sentences containing psychological contexts in general. For example, a sentence like, "A. V. believes that it rains," definitely contains a psychological context, but it elicits no existentially unloaded particular generalization. Its occurrence of the pronoun "it" is not pseudo-opaque, since it has a mere syntactic role. Another case of a sentence presenting a psychological context which is no directional context is provided by the Chisholmian example, "Diogenes looks for a honest man" (1967a). As "a honest man" is an indefinite description, "a honest man" is not a singular term, not even *prima facie*. So, to speak of its occurrence in the above sentence as referentially transparent, pseudo-opaque, or even opaque is inappropriate.

Finally, unlike Frege I allow for different readings of sentences presenting a directional context: not only the pseudo-opaque reading, which is what I have been considering all along, but also a transparent reading, where ordinarily co-referential terms are substitutable *salva veritate* (provided W. V. O. Quine's "quantifying-in" problem is somehow accommodated), and an opaque reading, where ordinarily co-referential terms are not substitutable *salva veritate*, for they do not refer to anything at all, not intentional objects either. For example, I may wait for Godot as much as Hammurabi may wait for the evening star, without waiting for the morning star; yet Smith may also wait for his life's woman without waiting for his life's ruin. Now (*prima facie*), in the overall domain of the objects of discourse there is someone who is identical with Godot and such, that I wait for him. Besides, in the overall domain of discourse there is also something such that Hammurabi takes it to uniquely be a morning star and such that he waits for it, and there is something such that he takes it to uniquely be an evening star but he does not wait for it. As a result, a pseudo-opaque reading of "A. V. waits for Godot," and of "A. V. waits for the evening star," is true, while a pseudo-opaque reading of "Hammurabi waits for the morning star" is false (for although true that there is an intentional object such that Hammurabi takes it to uniquely be a morning star, this object is not waited for by Hammurabi). Yet in the overall domain of discourse there is no one such that Smith takes her to be his life's woman and he waits for her; nor there is someone such that Smith takes her to be his life's ruin and he waits for her. So, we have no true pseudo-opaque reading of the sentences "Smith waits for his life's woman" and "Smith waits for his life's ruin." Yet these sentences are respectively true and false in their opaque reading: Smith waits that there is someone, that is his life's woman, yet he does not wait that there is someone, that is his life's ruin. In these cases, these opaque readings are justified because the attitudes they intend to report are not directional; in the situation at issue, Smith would indeed have no thoughts endowed with intentionality— singular thoughts as it were—but he would respectively have vs. fail to have merely generic thoughts. Put this way, we are tempted to conclude that the specificity of directional contexts is that they allow for a reading that intensional contexts, while also admitting a distinction between transparent and opaque readings, do not allow for; namely, the pseudo-opaque reading.

At this point, we might wonder why there could not be pseudo-opaque readings of sentences presenting modal contexts whose embedded singular terms refer not to their ordinary, but to their extraordinary, referents (which in these cases would amount to *possibilia*). As regards directional contexts, I introduced the idea of a pseudo-opaque reading in order to match a folk-psychological feature of intentionality—the possible apparent aspectual character of an intentional object—which *prima facie* commits us to *intentionalia*. Yet no such analogous feature arises as far as modal contexts are concerned. To be sure, this is not to say that there may be no pseudo-opaque reading of a sentence presenting a modal context. I only say that we have no independent reason to introduce such a reading. Once we have pseudo-opaque readings of sentences presenting directional contexts, we can also have pseudo-opaque readings of sentences presenting modal contexts. An example would be, "*a*, which is thought of by *S* (to be *F*), is necessarily identical with itself."

3. Adequate Criteria of Intentionality Only
Prima Facie Commit One to *Intentionalia*

At this juncture I will issue a caveat about what I have been discussing so far. I said that both success of mere existentially unloaded particular quantification and pseudo-opacity are candidates for providing not only necessary, but also sufficient linguistic conditions of intentionality. It could be the case that neither success of mere existentially unloaded particular quantification nor pseudo-opacity are sufficient linguistic conditions of intentionality. Once we allow for an overall domain of objects of discourse, it might be the case that such a domain is populated by other entities that do not exist (or that do not exist in the same sense as ordinary existents do), for example, fictional objects. Linguistic contexts purportedly about such entities would also allow for mere existentially unloaded particular quantification. Suppose, in addition, that we were able to find further contexts affected by pseudo-opacity. We should then conclude that both success of mere existentially unloaded particular quantification and pseudo-opacity only provide jointly sufficient linguistic conditions of intentionality.

Perhaps even this retreat is not enough. Once we allow for intentional objects, these objects may have modal properties; for example, the property of being necessarily what T is "directed upon," exemplified by an intentional object (for example, the non-existent Hesperus) conceived of in a certain thought T. As a result, there may be a pseudo-opaque reading of modal sentences. While "Hesperus is such that necessarily T is directed upon it," is true, this is not the case for "Phosphorus is such that necessarily T is directed upon it," where "Phosphorus" extraordinarily refers to an intentional object distinct from the extraordinary referent of "Hesperus." Then one such reading would also allow for mere existentially unloaded particular quantification. For instance, if Nessie does not exist, the pseudo-opaque true reading of "Nessie is such that necessarily my thought is 'directed upon' it," merely entails, "There is an x which is identical with Nessie which is such that necessarily my thought is 'directed upon' it." As a result, it would turn out that both success of merely existentially unloaded particular quantification and pseudo-opacity no longer provide even jointly sufficient linguistic conditions of intentionality.

We can resolve this further problem in different ways, for instance, by saying that the above readings of modal sentences entail certain directional contexts, which are directly characterized by the above linguistic phenomena. Yet questions of sufficiency aside, we have a substantial reason as to why what I took as the traditional conception of directional contexts is incorrect. In order for something to be a linguistic counterpart of a feature of any property whatsoever, it must retain all the *prima facie* ontological commitments such a feature involves. Yet the traditional conception fails to do this. For while the two folk-psychological features of intentionality, namely the existence-independence and the possible apparent aspectual character of the intentional object, *prima facie* commit one to *intentionalia*, if sentences presenting directional contexts were characterized by failure of existential generalization and referential opacity, then one would be immediately led to allow for no intentional object. Let us see why.

With respect to a sentence, failure of existential generalization, whether loaded or unloaded, means that there absolutely is no object, not even an intentional one, one is speaking about in such a sentence. Put alternatively, when a sentence fails to legitimize a existential generalization, whether loaded or unloaded, not only there exists, but also there is, in the overall domain of the object of discourse, no object one is speaking about in such a sentence.

Absolutely no such object for the relevant opaque occurrence of a singular term exists because a referentially opaque occurrence of a singular term denotes no object whatsoever, not even an intentional one, insofar as no would-be *denotatum* for it satisfies a proper individuation condition. Take again a genuinely intensional context such as the one contained by the sentence, "it is possible that the morning star does not appear in the sky at dusk." In such a sentence, "the morning star" obviously is unsubstitutable *salva veritate* with "the evening star," although these singular terms are ordinarily co-denotational. As is well known, a modal sentence of the kind "it is possible that *p*" is true iff a possible world exists in which the embedded sentence "*p*" is true. Yet the possible world which makes "the morning star does not appear in the sky at dusk," does not obviously make "the evening star does not appear in the sky at dusk," true, insofar as "the morning star" and "the evening star" do not share their denotation in that world. Although their real denotation is the same, their possible denotations differ.

Yet speaking of possible denotations for the above descriptions is somehow improper, insofar as how many distinct possible denotations one and the same description possesses is indeterminate. But this means that no thing exists, not even in the overall domain of the objects of discourse, which is a certain possible denotation of a description. David Kaplan has raised the problem by saying that we have a problem of insufficient specificity for an actually unsatisfied description to single out a certain possible *denotatum* (1973, pp. 505–506; 1989, p. 609).

Consider, "the morning star." Is the only thing which firstly appears in the sky at dawn in a possible world *W*, namely the denotation in *W* of such a description, the same as the only thing which firstly appears in the sky at dawn in another possible world *W**, namely the denotation in *W** of that description? Stated generally, how many possible denotations does that description possess? Insofar as we have no answer to this question, the possible denotations of such a description are indeterminate. This is tantamount to saying that no thing exists, not even in the overall domain of the objects of discourse, which is a certain possible denotation of that description. Here we are implicitly talking of the intuitive notional reading of sentences containing intensional contexts.

As is well known, Quine (1971a; 1971b) would say that opacity occurs also in the intuitive relational reading of such sentences, unless this reading is not suitably reformulated. Here I would limit myself to saying that the reason opacity allegedly occurs in such a reading is completely different. This may be seen if we shift from modal contexts to directional contexts, whose sentences also admit a plurality of readings. Here the intuitive notional reading is nothing but its opaque reading. In it, opacity occurs because the possible, admittedly indeterminate, denotations of the relevant actually co-denoting descriptions are different. But in the intuitive relational reading of a directional context, the relevant ordinarily co-denoting singular terms occur opaquely because the sentences differing only for the respective occurrence of those singular terms inherit a truth-value difference from their pseudo-opaque reading, where those singular terms have different extraordinary referents. This shows why the intuitive relational reading of directional contexts cannot be the same as their transparent reading, where those terms are peacefully substitutable *salva veritate* insofar as they ordinarily co-refer.

To put in a nutshell, therefore, if failure of existential generalization and referential opacity were the linguistic criteria for intentionality, then there would not be, not even in the overall domain of the objects of discourse, such things as *intentionalia*.

By saying that the adequate linguistic criteria of intentionality must be faithful to the same ontological commitment as the folk-psychological features of intentionality do, I do not mean that there must be such things as *intentionalia*. Both the folk-psychological features and the adequate linguistic criteria express just a *prima facie* commitment to such entities. In the end, it could be that there are no such things. Yet eliminativism as regards intentional objects cannot come out of language analysis, but at most out of genuine metaphysical inquiry. Only an investigation addressed at enucleating the criteria for objecthood can show that intentional objects have the status of mere would-be entities. Suppose for instance that we were to prove that intentional objects did not satisfy suitable criteria of identity (as for instance Fregean *Sinne* manifestly do not). This would be a genuine metaphysical reason not to admit them.

If *intentionalia* were metaphysically unsatisfying, then the commitment to such entities to which language appears to force us would be a merely *prima facie* commitment. In a sense, it would still be the case that directional contexts would both elicit mere existentially unloaded particular quantification and contain pseudo-opaque occurrences of singular terms. Yet this would amount to saying that it would only be fictionally the case that there are contexts whose sentences are qualified by success of mere existentially unloaded particular quantification and pseudo-opacity.

In this sense, these contexts would have to be considered precisely in the same way as fictional contexts are, as far as the conniving uses of sentences presenting these contexts are concerned. As a result, it would turn out that the pseudo-opaque reading of a sentence presenting a directional context would have only fictional truth-conditions, while a genuinely opaque reading would provide the serious truth-conditions. Mark Crimmins (1998) has theorized a similar distinction between fictional and serious truth-conditions of a sentence presenting a directional context. Following Gareth Evans (1982, pp. 365–366), by conniving uses of such sentences, I mean things like the theatrical utterances of fictional sentences, or the very writing of these sentences on a certain author's part. Often, singular terms occurring in such sentences so used are only fictionally referential. We can merely fictionally infer existential generalizations from such sentences so used; or one is merely fictionally prevented from substituting *salva veritate* ordinarily co-referential terms in such sentences so used. Consider a story speaking of Londres and London as two distinct cities, precisely by so connivingly using the ordinarily co-referential "Londres" and "London." Yet only Londres is depicted in the story as a nice city. As a result, a conniving use of "Londres is a nice city" only fictionally elicits the inference to "There is an object it is which is identical to Londres and this object is a nice city," and only fictionally prevents the inference to "London is a nice city."

Yet this possibly unwelcome result stems out of a metaphysical scrutiny showing that we can ultimately dispense with *intentionalia*. In lack of that scrutiny, we may rest content with what makes the analysis of the intentional discourse adequate, namely what folk-psychology suggests. To repeat, a mental state has intentionality iff its intentional object is existence-independent and it possibly appears as having an aspectual character.

ACKNOWLEDGMENTS

Different versions of this paper have been presented at the Universities of Eastern Piedmont, Parma, and Palermo, and at the Fourth European Congress for Analytic Philosophy 2002 Conference in Lund, Sweden. Let me thank all the participants at those meetings for their stimulating remarks. I am deeply grateful to Paolo Casalegno and Marco Santambrogio for their most important comments. Finally, I greatly owe Clotilde Calabi discussing with me the structure of the work in detail.

Eleven

THE INTENTIONALITY OF CONSCIOUSNESS AND CONSCIOUSNESS OF INTENTIONALITY

Kenneth Williford

1. Introduction

Some philosophers think that intentionality is ontologically distinct from phenomenal consciousness, the Thesis of Separation. Terence Horgan and John Tienson call this "separatism" (2002, p. 520). Colin McGinn calls it "the insulation strategy" (1991, pp. 32ff.). On this view, not the intentionality, but the phenomenality of consciousness is essential, its supposedly intrinsic, nonintentional qualitative character. The Thesis of Separation implies that phenomenality bears no essential connection to intentionality. Those who hold the thesis hold that the theory of intentionality and the theory of phenomenal consciousness are independent.

Many more philosophers think that intentionality can be "naturalized," that some adequate theory of intentionality does (or will) locate it squarely in the natural world by identifying it with some physicalistically acceptable relations. This claim is the Thesis of Naturalized Intentionality. These two theses have led some to think that though there has been progress in the theory of intentionality, a satisfactory theory of phenomenal consciousness will demand resources excluded by naturalism. The theses are perhaps behind the near silence about phenomenal consciousness others maintain while continuing to articulate theories of intentionality *sans conscience*.

The theses have many discontents. First Order and Higher Order Representational theorists of consciousness are both in the business of reducing phenomenal consciousness to intentionality. First Order theorists, like Michael Tye and Fred Dretske, seek to construct phenomenal consciousness out of metarepresentations (Tye, 1995; Dretske, 1995; Carruthers, 2000, pp. 114–179). Higher Order Representational theorists, like David M. Rosenthal, William G. Lycan, Rocco J. Gennaro, and Peter Carruthers, seek to identify phenomenal consciousness with metarepresentations meeting some special conditions, conditions that vary from theorist to theorist (Rosenthal, 1990; Lycan, 1996; Gennaro, 1996; and Carruthers, 2000).

These theorists of phenomenal content all deny that the theory of consciousness can be isolated from the theory of intentionality. They also all maintain that the general theory of intentionality as such does not depend on the theory of consciousness proper and that intentionality is susceptible to relatively easy naturalization. All hold that the denial of the Thesis of Separation brings us closer to the naturalization of consciousness by bringing it under the scope of the Thesis of Naturalized Intentionality.

Another way of denying the Thesis of Separation is perhaps of greater significance. McGinn and, more recently, Horgan and Tienson, and others, have defended the view that intentional content and conscious phenomenal content are internally connected to one another (McGinn, 1991, pp. 23–43; Horgan and Tienson, 2002; Addis, 1989, pp. 6–7; Searle, 1992, pp. 130–132, 151–173). According to these philosophers, theories of intentionality that presuppose the Thesis of Separation, while of some consequence, are radically incomplete (McGinn, 1991, p. 41; Horgan and Tienson, 2002, p. 527). On this view, not only is phenomenal content a species of intentional content, all non-derivative intentional content ineliminably involves phenomenal consciousness and its inherent subjectivity. Otherwise put, intentionality and phenomenality are but two sides of the same coin; call this the Thesis of Strong Inseparability. This thesis implies a return to the Brentanian tradition according to which all consciousness is intentional and all intentionality, *sensu stricto*, is conscious intentionality.

The First and Higher Order Representational theorists deny the Thesis of Separation, in their different ways, in order to take another step towards the naturalization of consciousness. But if we deny the Thesis of Separation in the manner of McGinn, Horgan, and Tienson, then the temptation will be to think that non-derivative intentionality is as far removed from naturalization as is phenomenal consciousness. McGinn is notoriously skeptical about the naturalization of consciousness. Horgan and Tienson likewise have doubts (McGinn, 1991, pp. 1–22; Horgan and Tienson, 2002, p. 530).

To summarize this dialectical landscape, if we accept the Thesis of Naturalized Intentionality, but reject the Thesis of Separation because we think that the theory of phenomenal consciousness is but a chapter of the theory of intentionality, then we will think that consciousness is as easily naturalized as unconscious intentionality. If we deny the Thesis of Separation because one thinks that phenomenal content and intentional content are internally connected, then we will think that intentionality is no more amenable to naturalization than is phenomenal consciousness and that the theory of intentionality inherits all of the problems of the theory of phenomenal consciousness. If we are convinced that phenomenal consciousness is a deep mystery, then we will hold that ultimately intentionality is also a deep mystery; and we will deny the Thesis of the Naturalized Intentionality. This is what McGinn, Horgan, and Tienson do.

In this paper, I assume, and do not argue, that McGinn, Horgan, and Tienson are right in their assessment of the relation between phenomenal consciousness and intentionality. But I argue that this thesis is not only compatible with the Thesis of Naturalized Intentionality (though understood in a more limited way), but also that it validates but defangs intuitions that have led some to think that phenomenal consciousness is not in principle amenable to satisfactory naturalization. Far from being a mere return to tradition and to dualism or mystery, the Thesis of Strong Inseparability, properly understood, provides a clue to the naturalization of consciousness—but a version of naturalization that does justice to the "limitative" intuitions encapsulated in Joseph Levine's notion of the Explanatory Gap (1983; 1993; 2001).

2. The Thesis of Strong Inseparability and the Self-Reference of Consciousness

I am assuming, then, that intrinsic intentionality and phenomenal consciousness are inseparable. But what exactly does this inseparability entail? We can approach this question by considering McGinn's argument for pessimism in the theory of intentionality. In "Consciousness and Content," he writes:

> Consider conscious perceptual experiences, such as my now seeing a scarlet sphere against a blue background. We can say . . . that there is something it is like to have such experiences; they have a subjective aspect. That is to say, there is something it is like for the subject of such experiences: subjective aspects of experience involve a reference to the subject undergoing the experience—this is what their subjectivity consists in. But we can also say that perceptual experiences have a world-directed aspect: they present the world in a certain way, say, as containing a scarlet sphere against a blue background. This is their representational content, what states of affairs they are as of. Thus perceptual experiences are Janus-faced: they point outward to the external world but they also present a subjective face to their subject and they are like something for the subject. But these two faces do not wear different expressions: for what the experience is like is a function of what it is of, and what it is of is a function of what it is like . . . . The two faces are, as it were, locked together. The subjective and the semantic are chained to each other. But then it seems that any conditions necessary and sufficient for the one aspect will have to be necessary and sufficient for the other. If we discover what gives an experience the (full) content it has, then we will have discovered what gives it its distinctive phenomenology; and the other way about. But now we are threatened with the following contraposition: since we cannot give a theory of consciousness we cannot give a theory of content, since to give the latter would *be* to give the former (in the case of conscious experiences). Accordingly, theories of content are cognitively closed to us: we cannot say in virtue of what an experience has

the content it has . . . . Intentionality has a first-person aspect, and this
seems impossible to capture in the naturalistic terms favored by the causal
theories and their ilk. If consciousness is a mystery, then so must its content be. So the challenge runs. (1991, pp. 29–30; emphasis McGinn's)

There is always "something-it-is-like" to be conscious of something.
McGinn points out that this always involves a reference to the subject having
the experience. Put otherwise, if one could "shave off" all reference to a subject having the experience, then there would be nothing it is like to have it.
And if there is nothing it is like to have the experience, the experience is not of
anything; it is not intentional, given the Thesis of Strong Inseparability. If
there is no subject undergoing the experience, there is no intentionality. The link
between the subject and intentionality is what we have been calling phenomenality. The experience has the intentional object it has because of what the experience
is like; but if there is "something-it-is-like" to have the experience, there must be
someone for whom the experience is like something. Subjectivity and world-
directedness go hand in hand, or, as McGinn puts it, experience is Janus-faced.

We can make these points in a better vocabulary. Experiences of the
world must involve modifications of our consciousness. Suppose you have
been sitting in silence for some time. Suddenly the silence is broken by a
passing car. Had there been no change in your consciousness, you would not
have consciously heard the car. You consciously perceive a change in the
environment only in so far as there is a correlative change in your consciousness. This should be uncontroversial.

But must you attend to the changes in your consciousness as changes in
your consciousness in order to perceive changes in the environment? I think
this would only be the case if we explicitly inferred changes in the environment from changes in ourselves. It would be erroneous, as far as the phenomenological description is concerned, to say that we perform this kind of inference. Instead, our perceptions of the world are somewhat analogous to our
understanding a language. We rarely, if ever, infer the meanings of words and
sentences on the basis of their sounds or shapes and some established correlation; instead, the words serve as vehicles of thought. We see or hear right
though them to the meanings they communicate. Likewise, I do not exactly
infer the presence of a car from the sounds I hear in the night street; I hear the
car through the sounds.

There is no inference to the intentional content of the experience. Instead,
it is on the basis of this intentional content that I have definite expectations
about the future course of my experience, expectations that can be frustrated.
We can think of these expectations as encapsulating the relevant inferences.
But the point is that intentional content has priority, and any related "inferences" are based upon the grasp of that content.

It takes an act of reflection to attend to the changes in consciousness as such. But does this mean that those changes are not perceived at all when we are only experiencing the world and not reflecting on the experience? Not at all. We are conscious of these modifications of consciousness insofar as we are conscious of the world, but we are only conscious of them as such when we attend to them. Such attention is constitutive of reflection. When I note, upon memorial reflection, that I had such-and-such an experience and thereupon I started to feel a certain way, I am not only noting the different ways the world appeared to me, I am also thereby noting a series of changes in my consciousness itself.

Still, even granting this point about the content of reflections, you might think that while unreflectively undergoing the experiences in question, I was in no way aware of any modifications of myself but only of the world— barring the postulation of genuinely intentional unconscious perceptions of those changes, contrary to our assumption. We might rightly say that when I am not reflecting, I am simply absorbed in the world; in the best instances the absorption is complete, and I myself fade entirely from view. The thesis I am advocating might appear to be stuck in a dilemma: we must postulate genuinely intentional, unconscious perceptions of these changes as such, or we must hold that I am, despite the phenomenological data, always having only myself or changes in myself as the primary intentional object of my experiences. But we reject both of these: *tertium datur.*

What misleads many here is lack of attention to a mode of consciousness that is fundamental and ubiquitous. Aron Gurwitsch called it "marginal consciousness" (Gurwitsch, 1964, pp. 344ff.; 1985), and Jean-Paul Sartre called it "non-positional," or "non-thetic" consciousness (Sartre, 1957, pp. 40–46; 1956, pp. l–lvi). Characteristic of this mode of consciousness is that its objects are present to consciousness but they are not attended to and, in a sense, are not thought about. P. Sven Arvidson has rightly pointed out that much contemporary work on consciousness is marred by the neglect of marginal consciousness (2000). Theorists of consciousness often speak as if consciousness and attention are the same, but they are not.

Marginal consciousness is always present with attentive consciousness. When I am focusing my attention on writing this paper, for example, I do not cease to be aware of the computer screen, of the lighting, of the sounds outside my window. But I do not need to attend to or think about any of these objects as such in order to be aware of them. They are present to consciousness, but they do not occupy my attention. We need posit no unconscious perceptions of them. The perception is fully conscious, but it is not attentive. The phenomenological data are unequivocal. That we do not identify unconscious perceptions with inattentive or marginal ones is key. When we shift attention to objects that were previously objects of marginal consciousness, they are given as having-been-present-but-unattended. When we are suddenly attentively aware of something of which we were formerly unconscious—even allowing unconscious perceptions—the object is given *de novo*. Perhaps this is why our reflections never surprise us but our first-order perceptions often do (Sartre, 1956, pp. lii–liv). I am always marginally conscious of the changes going on in me as I perceive the world. Those changes in me are present to my consciousness, but they are only attended to as such in reflection.

This brings us to a crucial point. It was a thesis of Aristotle (and later of many others) that every state of consciousness involves a kind of consciousness of itself or self-reference (Caston, 2002; Brentano, 1995, p. 127ff.; Husserl, 1991, pp. 122–124; Sartre, 1957, pp. 40–46; 1956, pp. l–lvi; Gurwitsch, 1985, pp. 3–13; Goldman, 1970, p. 96; Smith, 1989; Zahavi, 1999; Kapitan, 1999; Hossack, 2002; Kriegel, 2003; Grinbaum, 2001; Damasio, 1999). This view has met with incomprehension and resistance in many quarters partly because of inadequate reflection on the general phenomenon of marginal consciousness. Put in these terms, then, the thesis is simply that all consciousness is marginal consciousness of itself.

This is but another way of stating that I am conscious of the world insofar as I am (marginally) conscious of the modifications of my consciousness itself. This last claim is another way of stating McGinn's thesis about the Janus-faced nature of experience: experiences point outward to the world, but, as such, they also make ineliminable reference to the consciousness whose experience it is.

I am here construing this "ineliminable reference to the subject" not as an ineliminable reference to an ego, or "homunculus" in or behind consciousness, but as the ineliminable reference occurrent consciousness makes to itself in every instance.

As Cedric Oliver Evans writes:

[T]he idea can be rejected that self-awareness is awareness of the empirical self. This amounts to a rejection of the view that [all] self-awareness is a special act that describes a special reflective experience which does not occur very often . . . . Instead, . . . self-awareness . . . [is] an aspect of all awareness, and as so conceived self-awareness accompanies all our experience. It is this which permits us to view experiences as experiences *to* the self. (Evans, 1970, 169; emphasis Evans's)

I agree with this account construed as a phenomenological description that captures McGinn's point about subjectivity and has as its sole definite ontological consequence that consciousness literally has a self-referential structure. The claim is not that there is an irreducible ego to which intentional objects appear but that the intentionality of consciousness cannot be separated from the self-referential structure of consciousness. The appearance of the world to consciousness necessarily involves the appearance of consciousness to itself.

According to the Thesis of Strong Inseparability, phenomenal consciousness and intrinsic intentionality are internally interconnected. According to the above, consciousness is essentially self-referential. It follows from these claims that self-reference and intentionality are strongly inseparable as well.

3. Naturalizing Phenomenology and the Self-Reference of Consciousness

The self-reference of consciousness has two significant consequences. First, the self-referential structure of consciousness provides us with a clue to what an acceptable model of consciousness must look like. Second, when coupled with the Thesis of Strong Inseparability, the self-referential structure of consciousness allows us to ascertain the proper scope and limits of the theory of content. Once these are ascertained, we can accommodate but defang a common mysterian intuition.

To communicate the first consequence I must outline a research program in cognitive science and the philosophy of mind. The program I summarize is similar to work that goes under the name of "naturalizing phenomenology," work spearheaded by the Centre de Recherche en Epistémologie Appliquée and to which one can find a good introduction in the 1999 volume, *Naturalizing Phenomenology* (Petitot, et. al., 1999). The basic postulates of the research program are these:

(1) Phenomenological Adequacy: There can be no adequate theory of consciousness that leaves out the phenomenology of consciousness, one that leaves out the way the conscious mind appears to itself; accordingly, the phenomenological data must be taken seriously.

(2) Structural Phenomenological Analysis: The most important phenomenological data for constructing such a theory of consciousness are the structural (general and non-trivially formalizable) features of consciousness and not particular qualitative or intentional contents.

(3) Search for Neural Correlates: By phenomenologically ascertaining the general structure of consciousness and describing that structure rigorously, we will be enabled to formulate a projection from consciousness as it appears to itself to consciousness as it should appear when realized in brain processes. The experimental verification of the presence of the relevantly structured brain processes would, in the absence of any compelling arguments to the contrary, ground the informative, theoretical identity claim that those processes, ascertained in a third-person way, literally are the very consciousness ascertained in the first-person, phenomenological way. Once the relevant identity is found, explaining con-

sciousness reduces to explaining how the brain processes in question come about—and that falls to neuroscience.

The distinction between qualitative content and the structure of consciousness is not trivial. If you think of consciousness as a kind of amorphous bag of qualia, then you prevent yourself from getting a handle on features of consciousness subject to genuine modeling. I agree with Joseph Levine that, for example, phenomenal colors, at their cores, exhibit a kind of unstructured determinateness that prevents us from giving a satisfactory structural model of them—taken singly.

This is so even if, as some have argued, phenomenal colors are in part determined by the necessary relations of similarity and difference they bear to other phenomenal colors (Clark, 1993; Van Gulick, 1993; Levine, 2001, pp. 96–104). Sensory spectra or qualitative spaces as such do exhibit a structure that makes them amenable to non-trivial modeling. So these spectra count as phenomenological structures, even if the individual sensory qualities whose interrelations constitute the spectra or spaces do not.

More important than the structure of sensory spectra are those phenomenologically ascertainable features of consciousness that are perfectly general. These features are present in consciousness no matter what its modality or content. They include (at a minimum) the following:

(1) Temporality: Consciousness always exhibits a retentive/protentive structure. That is, as consciousness unfolds, every present state points in a non-memorial way to its immediately preceding states and points in an expectant way to its future ones. This is a dynamic component of consciousness. (Husserl, 1991)

(2) Diachronic and Synchronic Unities: Consciousness itself is always internally unified over time and the manifold properties and objects of consciousness are perspectivaly unified (or coherently bound) at a time. Diachronic unity is connected to temporality. Synchronic unity is necessary for experiencing a coherently arranged world that includes the subject undergoing the experience (Dainton, 2000). My hope is that the diachronic unity of consciousness can be understood on the model of constant, form-preserving auto-replication. The feature of synchronic unity has been used as a guiding principle for neurologically plausible model of consciousness by Gerald Edelman and Guilio Tononi (2001).

(3) Theme-Margin Gestalt Structure: Consciousness is not to be identified exclusively with attentive consciousness. Attentive consciousness of a specific theme (or object) is always accompanied by marginal, inatten-

tive consciousness of a thematic field (those items directly relevant to the theme) and of merely co-present items. Consciousness, that is, is characterized by a figure-ground structure. Some item or other will be the focus of attention; other items will be in the background, though not unconsciously (Gurwitsch, 1964; 1985). My use of the phrase "marginal consciousness" is slightly looser than Gurwitsch's.

(4) Intentionality/Phenomenality As Such: Consciousness is always consciousness of something. Typically it is consciousness of something other than itself. This will mean that these states of consciousness are, in a sense, defined by a relation to what they are not, defined negatively. No structural model of this general feature need have anything to say about how non-structural content elements are constituted. Ideally, a model of the structure of consciousness would find a way to describe intentionality as such at an abstract level. But such a model need not specify anything about particular intentional contents or the external conditions necessary for the possession of content of a designated type. Only the form matters.

(5) Self-Reference: Consciousness is always someone's consciousness of something. This is the subjectivity of consciousness. I have identified it with the marginal self-consciousness of all consciousness. That identification only yields a phenomenological model of the feature. But the feature might be amenable to rigorous description by suitable mathematical means. The mathematics of self-referential and self-membered and otherwise nonwellfounded structures is now significantly developed and should be applied to this problem. I suspect that this feature, via the application of these models, will yield some of the most important insights into the "shape" of consciousness and is therefore the most salient feature of consciousness as far as theory is concerned. For some inspiration, see Hofstadter (1979). Sources for relevant mathematics abound (Smullyan, 1994; Smorynski, 1985; Varela, 1975; 1979, pp. 170ff., 284ff.; Kauffmann, 1987; Barwise and Moss, 1996; Khromov, 2001).

By developing and conjoining rigorous models of these phenomenologically ascertainable structural features we hope to give an abstract characterization of consciousness. From that characterization it might be possible to deduce the structure of consciousness as it would appear via non-phenomenological means of investigation. This would be somewhat analogous to attempting to deduce the general structure of the outside of a building from a description of the general structure of its interior. Suitable experiments for verifying or falsifying the predictions generated by the model should, in principle, allow us to determine whether we have isolated the right brain processes. Given that there is no reason to postulate any further ontology, identifying consciousness with such processes is the most reasonable thing to do.

To summarize: we started with the consideration that the intentionality of consciousness cannot be explained without thereby explaining the phenomenology of consciousness. That is to say, there can be no complete theory of content that does not in some way account for conscious content; and there can be no accounting for conscious content without an account of consciousness itself. McGinn's pessimism about the scope of the theory of content derives directly from his mysterianism with respect to consciousness. I have rejected that mysterianism and offered an alternative proposal. One of the phenomenologically ascertainable structures of consciousness that will be crucial to the project of "naturalizing phenomenology" and for the creation of a physicalistically acceptable theory of consciousness is the one McGinn takes to ground his pessimism, what he calls the "first-person" aspect of conscious intentionality.

I have identified this with the self-referential structure of consciousness that is phenomenologically ascertainable as ubiquitous marginal self-consciousness. My final claim was that the now significantly developed mathematics of self-referential structures (*inter alia*) will be essential to building a precise model of the general structure of consciousness and that that model will enable us to formulate precise hypotheses about the brain processes that literally constitute consciousness. As formulated, there is no theory of content types in this program. If the program were successful we would be accounting for the intentionality of consciousness physicalistically but incompletely.

4. The Self-Reference of Consciousness and the Explanatory Gap

This incompleteness in the theory of conscious content stems from the self-referential nature of consciousness. This is the second significant consequence of its self-reference. This limit constitutes a validation of something quite like Levine's notion of the Explanatory Gap, and it shows why that gap is only epistemological. In his "On Leaving Out What It's Like" Levine writes:

> I have argued that there is an important difference between the identification of water with H_2O, on the one hand, and the identification of qualitative character with a psycho-functional [or physical] property on the other. In the former case the identification affords a deeper understanding of what water is by explaining its behavior. Whereas, in the case of qualia, the subjective character of qualitative experience is left unexplained, and therefore we are left with an incomplete understanding of that experience. (Levine, 1993, p. 130.)

Given the Thesis of Strong Inseparability, this conclusion will extend to all intentional states. Levine appears to endorse the Thesis of Separation (2001, p. 6). The main idea is that even if some set of psycho-physical (or psycho-functional) identity claims contains nothing but truths, an irremediable gap in our understanding of why this is the case will remain. In one sense it is a mistake to seek to explain an identity. In this sense, the fact that water is H_2O no more admits of explanation than does the fact that water is water. But our desire is not misguided in that way.

Instead we are asking for conceptually satisfying reasons for thinking that conscious states of some type are identical with either physical or functional states of some type. (Mere correlations will not do.) Such reasons would allow us to understand why it is that brain states of a given sort have the first-person, phenomenologically available contents they do, even as understanding something about the chemistry and physics of H_2O allows us understand why water has some of its readily observable properties. Levine thinks that psycho-physical (or psycho-functional) theory will never allow us to understand why conscious states have their contents in a way that is analogous to the under-standing of the readily observable properties of water afforded by physics and chemistry coupled with the *a posteriori* necessary truth that water is H_2O.

Physics and chemistry provide a theoretical framework in terms of which this identity claim can be articulated and justified in an epistemically and concep-tually satisfactory way. In the absence of a similar sort of framework, the relevant psycho-physical or psycho-functional identities will look irremediably epistemically brute or "gappy" (Levine, 2001, pp. 84–94). We may find out that conscious states with a given kind of content are identical to brain states with a given profile, but we will never be able to understand, with theoretical satisfaction, why.

I agree with this conclusion (though with a qualification discussed at the end of the paper). But I think it follows from the structure of consciousness and not directly from the conceivability considerations adduced by Levine and others.

Consciousness is self-referential. Self-referential structure is a type of universal, but peculiar in that its general characterization involves reference to the particularity of its instances; and something's particularity is not itself ca-pable of compression or reduction to something general.

As a loose analogy, consider that, strictly speaking, directly self-referential sentences—considered as bearers of content, not as mere strings of sounds or marks—are unrepeatable. In contrast to non-self-referential sen-tences, the content of each token self-referential sentence of the same type is different from the content of every other token self-referential sentence of that type. (Their Kaplanian "character" may be the same.) Each time I say, "This very sentence has eight words in it," I am predicating the specified property of the sentence token. Abstraction away from the token thus entails a loss of some content, to wit, all the information that is bound up with grasping a token as such (when and where it was stated, in what language or medium). If we abstract away from these factors, we cannot recover the full content of a token self-referential sentence. The general theory of directly self-referential sentences entails that the proper grasp of the contents of such sentences can only be attained by grasping matters the theory can ultimately say nothing explanatory about, namely, the "tokenality" or particularity of each token.

If the content of a state of consciousness is inseparable from the self-reference of consciousness, it will follow that abstraction from the particularity of the state precludes the recovery of its full content. If we remove the aspects of a token conscious state that are bound up with its being just that token state, we remove a necessary factor in the determination of "what it is like" to be in that state and thus a factor in the determination of what it is of. But a general theory of consciousness, though it must recognize the self-referential structure of consciousness, must abstract from the particularity of states of consciousness. In this respect the theory is analogous to a general theory of directly self-referential sentences. This means that in specifying the general structure of consciousness, it must systematically abstract from the particularity crucial to the determination of the content of each actual instance of consciousness.

The content of a state of consciousness depends in part upon the particularity of that state. But all general theories (of the relevant kind, in any case) must abstract away from the particularity of the objects in their domains. The theory of consciousness must abstract away from a feature upon which content irreducibly depends. It follows that the theory cannot capture the content of a state of consciousness without a sort of unexplanatory supplementation, the kind of supplementation that only the subject occupying that state of consciousness is in a position to give.

The contents of my states of consciousness cannot be derived from any general theory of consciousness; they must be, so to say, "entered in by hand." We could say that because such supplementation is necessary statements identifying brain states/processes of a designated type with conscious states with content of a designated type are "incompressible" vis-à-vis the general theory of consciousness. The statements do not follow from the theory; they have to be added as axioms. In one sense, they belong to the theory of consciousness; because they are truths about consciousness, many of which we can discover by empirical methods. But because they cannot be derived from the general theory alone, a theory that includes them is an extension. Interestingly, this follows from something that is a part of the general theory of consciousness. In this sense, then, the theory of consciousness entails its own limit and thus explains why there is an Explanatory Gap.

Levine argues that there will remain an Explanatory Gap precisely because we will always be able to conceive of the non-identity of conscious states with a given sort of content with brain (or functional) states of a given type. He thinks that this non-identity will always remain conceivable because no conceivable theory could connect brain states or functional organization to content of specific types in an intelligible way, the way, for example, chemistry and physics establish a conceptually satisfactory connection between some of the micro-properties of water and some of its readily observable macro properties. Levine goes so far as to suggest that this fact stems, in some way, from the subjectivity of consciousness. But he does not say in sufficient detail exactly why this should be the case; he mentions the determinate way in which qualitative contents are present to the subject and that qualitative contents have simultaneously an "act" and "object" status and are, in some sense, their "own modes of presentation" (Levine, 2001, pp. 6ff., 167ff., 176). I think Levine is on the right track. If the story I am offering is correct, then something like the logical basis of Levine's Explanatory Gap has been unearthed.

With the step of abstraction by which we secure the possibility of a general theory of consciousness, we preclude the possibility of giving a theory that would allow us to account for content absent unexplanatory supplementation. This implies that there is a limit to the theory of the content of consciousness that cannot be overcome. But this is not a reason for despair. The feature of consciousness, self-reference, that entails that there is an Explanatory Gap also provides a clue to the general structure of consciousness and thus a clue (perhaps a key) to the construction of a physicalistically acceptable general theory of consciousness.

5. Conclusion

Nothing in the present account implies that objective similarities of content across minds are impossible or that physical duplicates would have different types of mental content just because they are different particulars. It only implies that such similarities cannot be deduced from a general physicalistic theory of consciousness in the absence of unexplanatory supplementation. The general theory is too coarse grained and in an irremediable way.

This brings us to a qualification of Levine's conclusion. We might think the same reasoning will apply to the general, phenomenologically ascertainable features that are to be used in the construction of a general, structural theory of consciousness. If content similarities cannot be deduced from the theory, then does this not hold for these structural similarities as well? It does. But a clarification will render the point innocuous.

We assume that consciousness is like a natural kind. This will mean that, in terms of general structure, consciousness is similar across all instances. Though true that we must begin to develop a structural model of consciousness by using phenomenological means, the more general the properties we use to construct the model, the safer is the assumption that these properties characterize all instances of consciousness. We build in to the model, even at the ground level, in a sense, what the traditional wisdom would dictate that we be able to derive from an independently understood, physicalistically acceptable theory. But given that physicalism is quite plausible on other grounds, there is nothing methodologically suspect about this.

ACKNOWLEDGEMENTS

I would like to thank the organizers, Gábor Forrai and George Kampis, and all the participants of the 2002 Miskolc conference on Intentionality for an excellent and stimulating time both philosophically. I also thank Gregory Landini, Tim Crane, Brian McLaughlin, Willem deVries, David Taylor, Ernani Magalhaes, Ben Hill, Annemarie Peil, Eli Trautwein, Denny Bradshaw, Charles Nussbaum, Harry Reeder, Tim Mahoney, and Evan Fales for helpful comments and Antonio Damasio, Greg Jesson, Laird Addis, Vijay Mascarenhas, Tomis Kapitan, Daniel Dennett, Ruth Millikan, Susan Schneider, Panayot Butchvarov, Oleg Svidersky, and Carla Calargé for helpful discussions. Uriah Kriegel's helpful comments merit special mention. This paper was also presented at the University of Texas at Arlington as part of their 2002–2003 Philosophy Lecture Series. I also thank the UTA audience stimulating discussion.

WORKS CITED

Chapter One: Laird Addis

Addis, Laird. (1986) "Pains and Other Secondary Mental Entities," *Philosophy and Phenomenological Research*, 47:1 (September), pp. 59–74.
———. (1989) *Natural Signs: A Theory of Intentionality*. Philadelphia: Temple University Press.
———. (1999) *Of Mind and Music*. Ithaca, N.Y.: Cornell University Press.
———. (2000) "The Simplicity of Content," *Metaphysica: Zeitschrift für Metaphysik & Ontologie*, 1:2 (October), pp. 23–43.
Bergmann, Gustav. (1960) "Acts," *Indian Journal of Philosophy*, 2:4 (August), pp. 1–30; and 2:5 (December), pp. 96–117. (Reprinted as *Logic and Reality*. Madison, Wis.: University of Wisconsin Press, 1964, pp. 3–44.)
Burge, Tyler. (1979) *Individualism and the Mental*. Midwest Studies in Philosophy: Studies in Metaphysics, vol. 4. South Bend, Ind.: University of Notre Dame Press, pp. 73–121.
Husserl, Edmund. (1971) *Logical Investigations*. Translated by John Niemeyer Findlay from 2nd German ed. of 1921. New York: Humanities Press.
Jacquette, Dale. (1994) *Philosophy of Mind*. Englewood Cliffs, N.J.: Prentice Hall.
Marsh, Robert, ed. (1956) *Logic and Knowledge*. New York: Macmillan.
Meinong, Alexius. (1899) "Über Gegenstände höherer Ordnung und deren Verhältnis zur inneren Wahrnehmung," *Zeitschrift für Psychologie und Physiologie der Sinnesorgane*, 21, pp. 182–272.
Millikan, Ruth Garrett. (1993) *White Queen Psychology and Other Essays for Alice*. Cambridge, Mass.: MIT Press.
Moore, G. E. (1910) "The Subject Matter of Psychology," *Proceedings of the Aristotelian Society*, 10, pp. 36–62.
Putnam, Hilary. (1975) "The Meaning of 'Meaning.'" In *Mind, Language, and Reality*, pp. 215–271. Cambridge, England: Cambridge University Press.
———. (1981) *Reason, Truth, and History*. Cambridge, England: Cambridge University Press.
Russell, Bertrand. (1956) "On the Nature of Acquaintance." In Marsh, *Logic and Knowledge*, pp. 177–282.
Sartre, Jean-Paul. (1957) *The Transcendence of the Ego: An Existentialist Theory of Consciousness*. Translated by Forrest Williams and Robert Kirkpatrick. New York: Noonday.
Searle, John. (1983) *Intentionality: An Essay in the Philosophy of Mind*. Cambridge, England: Cambridge University Press.
Twardowski, Kasimir. (1977) *On the Content and Object of Presentations*. Translated by R. Grossmann. The Hague: Martinus Nijhoff.
William of Occam. (1957) *Philosophical Writings*. Edited and translated by Philoteus Boehner. London: Thomas Nelson and Sons.

Chapter Two: Philip J. Bartok

Albertazzi, Liliana, Massimo Libardi, and Roberto Poli, eds. (1996) *The School of Franz Brentano*. Boston: Kluwer,

Antonelli, Mauro. (2001) *Seiendes, Bewußtsein, Intentionalität im Frühwerk von Franz Brentano*. Freiburg: Alber.

Bell, David. (1990) *Husserl*. London: Routledge.

Brentano, Franz. (1955) *Psychologie vom Empirischen Standpunkt*. Edited by Oskar Kraus. Hamburg: Felix Meiner.

———. (1982) *Deskriptive Psychologie*. Edited by Roderick Chisholm and Wilhelm Baumgartner. Hamburg: Felix Meiner.

———. (1995a) *Psychology from an Empirical Standpoint*. Translated by Antos C. Rancurello, D. B. Terrell, and Linda L. McAlister. London: Routledge.

———. (1995b) *Descriptive Psychology*. Translated and edited by Benito Müller. London: Routledge.

Chisholm, Roderick. (1957) *Perceiving*. Ithaca, N.Y.: Cornell University Press.

———. (1963) "Notes on the Logic of Believing," *Philosophy and Phenomenological Research*, 24:2 (December), pp. 195–201.

———. (1967a) "Intentionality." In Edwards, *Encyclopedia of Philosophy*, vol. 4. Edited by Paul Edwards, pp. 201–204. New York: Macmillan.

———. (1967b) "Brentano on Descriptive Psychology and the Intentional." In Lee and Mandelbaum, *Phenomenology and Existentialism*, pp. 1–23.

Chrudzimski, Arkadiusz. (2001) *Intentionalitätstheorie beim frühen Brentano*. Boston: Kluwer.

Craig, Edward, ed. (1998) *The Routledge Encyclopedia of Philosophy*. London: Routledge.

Crane, Tim. (1998) "Intentionality." In Craig, *The Routledge Encyclopedia of Philosophy*, pp. 816–821.

Dennett, Daniel, and John Haugeland. (1987) "Intentionality." In Gregory, *The Oxford Companion to the Mind*, pp. 383–386.

Edwards, Paul, ed. (1967) *Encyclopedia of Philosophy*, vol. 4. New York: Macmillan.

Gregory, R. (1987) *The Oxford Companion to the Mind*. Oxford: Oxford University Press.

Guttenplan, Samuel D. (1994) *A Companion to the Philosophy of Mind*. London: Blackwell.

Heidegger, Martin. (1985) *History of the Concept of Time*. Translated by T. Kisiel. Bloomington, Indiana: Indiana University Press.

Husserl, Edmund. (1970) *Logical Investigations*. Translated by John Niemeyer Findlay. New York: Humanities Press.

Haugeland, John. (1990) "The Intentionality All-Stars," *Philosophical Perspectives*, 4, pp. 383–427.

Lee, Edward N., and Maurice Mandelbaum, eds. (1967) *Phenomenology and Existentialism*. Baltimore: Johns Hopkins University Press.

Lycan, William G. (1994) "Functionalism." In Guttenplan, *A Companion to the Philosophy of Mind*, pp. 317–323.

McAlister, Linda L. (1976) "Chisholm and Brentano on Intentionality." In *The Philosophy of Brentano*. London: Duckworth.

Moran, Dermot. (1996) "The Inaugural Address: Brentano's Thesis," *Proceedings of the Aristotelian Society*, supplemental vol. 70, pp. 1–27.

———. (2000) *Introduction to Phenomenology*. London: Routledge.

Mulligan, Kevin, and Barry Smith. (1984) "Franz Brentano on the Ontology of Mind," *Philosophy and Phenomenological Research*, 45, pp. 627–644.

Smith, Barry. (1994) *Austrian Philosophy: The Legacy of Franz Brentano*. LaSalle, Illinois: Open Court.

Spiegelberg, Herbert. (1982) *The Phenomenological Movement*. 3rd ed. The Hague: Martinus Nijhoff.

Wolenski, Jan. (1996) "Brentano and the Reist Tradition." In Albertazzi et al., *The School of Franz Brentano*, pp. 357–374.

Chapter Three: William Fish

Addis, Laird. (1995) "The Ontology of Emotion," *The Southern Journal of Philosophy*, 33:3 (September), pp. 261–278.

Crane, Tim. (1998) "Intentionality as the Mark of the Mental." In O'Hear, *Current Issues in the Philosophy of Mind*, pp. 136–157.

de Sousa, Ronald. (1987) *The Rationality of Emotion*. Cambridge, Mass: MIT Press.

Heidegger, Martin. (1927) *Being and Time*. Translated by John Macquarrie and Edward Robinson. Oxford: Blackwell.

Kenny, Anthony. (1963) *Action, Emotion, and Will*. London: Routledge and Kegan Paul.

O'Hear, Anthony, ed. (1998) *Current Issues in the Philosophy of Mind*. Cambridge: Cambridge University Press.

Roberts, Robert Campbell. (1988) "What An Emotion Is: A Sketch," *The Philosophical Review*, 47:2 (April), pp. 183–209.

Sartre, Jean-Paul. (1939) *Sketch for a Theory of the Emotions*. Translated by Philip Mairet. London: Routledge.

Searle, John. (1983) *Intentionality: An Essay in the Philosophy of Mind*. Cambridge: Cambridge University Press.

Solomon, Robert C. (1976) *The Passions*. New York: Anchor Press.

Wilson, J. R. S. (1972) *Emotion and Object*. Cambridge: Cambridge University Press.

Chapter Four: Gábor Forrai

Acworth, Richard. (1971) "Locke's First Reply to John Norris," *The Locke Newsletter*, 2, pp. 7–11.

Ayers, Michael R. (1991) *Locke: Epistemology and Ontology*, vol. 1, 2. London and New York: Routledge.

Chappell, Vere. (1994) "Locke's Theory of Ideas." In *The Cambridge Companion to Locke*, pp. 26–55. Cambridge, England: Cambridge University Press.

Crane, Tim. (2001) *Elements of Mind: An Introduction to the Philosophy of Mind*. Oxford: Oxford University Press.

Cummins, Robert. (1989) *Meaning and Mental Representation*. Cambridge, Mass., London: MIT Press.

Gibson, James. (1918) *Locke's Theory of Knowledge and its Historical Relations*. Cambridge: Cambridge University Press.

Locke, John. (1823) *The Works of John Locke in Ten Volumes*. London.

———. (1975) *An Essay Concerning Human Understanding*. Edited by Peter Harold Nidditch. Oxford: Oxford University Press, 1975.

Smith, David Woodruff, and Ronald McIntyre. (1982) *Husserl and Intentionality: A Study of Mind, Meaning, and Language*. Dordrecht, Holland: D. Reidel.

Yolton, John W. (1984) *Perceptual Acquaintance from Descartes to Reid*. Minneapolis, Minn.: University of Minnesota Press.

Chapter Five: Jussi Haukioja

Barnes, Barry. (1982) "On the Extensions of Concepts and the Growth of Knowledge," *Sociological Review*, 30:1 (February), pp. 23–44.

Blackburn, Simon. (1984) "The Individual Strikes Back," *Synthese*, 58:3 (March), pp. 281–301.

Bloor, David. (1997) *Wittgenstein, Rules, and Institutions*. London: Routledge.

Boghossian, Paul A. (1989) "The Rule-Following Considerations," *Mind*, 98:3 (October), pp. 507–549.

Brandom, Robert B. (1994) *Making It Explicit: Reasoning, Representing, and Discursive Commitment*. Cambridge: Harvard University Press.

Byrne, Alex. (1996) "On Misinterpreting Kripke's Wittgenstein," *Philosophy and Phenomenological Research*, 56:2 (June), pp. 339–343.

Field, Hartry. (1973) "Theory Change and the Indeterminacy of Reference," *Journal of Philosophy*, 70:14 (August), pp. 462–481.

Fodor, Jerry A. (1990) *A Theory of Content and Other Essays*. Cambridge: MIT Press.

French, Peter A., Theodore Edward Uehling, Jr., and Howard K. Wettstein, eds. (1994) *Philosophical Naturalism*. Midwest Studies in Philosophy, vol. 19. South Bend, Ind.: University of Notre Dame Press.

Haukioja, Jussi. (2002) "Soames and Zalabardo on Kripke's Wittgenstein," *Grazer Philosophische Studien*, 64, pp. 157–173.

Hindrik, Frank A. (2004) "A Modest Solution to the Problem of Rule-Following," *Philosophical Studies*, 121:1 (October), pp. 65–97.

Jackson, Frank, and Philip Pettit. (2002) "Response-Dependence without Tears," *Philosophical Issues*, 12 (Realism and Relativism), pp. 97–117.

Kripke, Saul. (1982) *Wittgenstein: On Rules and Private Language*. Oxford: Basil Blackwell.

McDowell, John. (1984) "Wittgenstein on Following a Rule," *Synthese*, 58:3 (March), pp. 325–363.

Miller, Alexander. (1998a) *Philosophy of Language*. London: UCL Press.

———. (1998b) "Rule-Following, Response-Dependence, and McDowell's Debate with Anti-Realism," *European Review of Philosophy*, 3 (Response-Dependence), pp. 175–197.

————. (2003) "Objectivity of Content," *Proceedings of the Aristotelian Society*, suppl. vol. 77, pp. 73–90.

Pettit, Philip. (1990) "The Reality of Rule-Following," *Mind*, 99:1 (January), pp. 1–21.

————. (1991) "Realism and Response-Dependence," *Mind*, 100:4 (October), pp. 587–626.

————. (1999) "A Theory of Normal and Ideal Conditions," *Philosophical Studies*, 96:1 (October), pp. 21–44.

Quinton, Anthony. (1957) "Properties and Classes," *Proceedings of the Aristotelian Society*, 48, pp. 33–58.

Soames, Scott. (1998) "Skepticism about Meaning: Indeterminacy, Normativity, and the Rule-Following Paradox," *Canadian Journal of Philosophy*, suppl. vol. 23, pp. 211–249.

Wilson, George M. (1994) "Kripke on Wittgenstein and Normativity." In French et al., *Philosophical Naturalism*, pp. 366–390.

————. (1998) "Semantic Realism and Kripke's Wittgenstein," *Philosophy and Phenomenological Research*, 58:1 (March), pp. 99–122.

Wilson, Mark. (1982) "Predicate Meets Property," *Philosophical Review*, 91:4 (October), pp. 549–589.

Wright, Crispin. (1980) *Wittgenstein on the Foundations of Mathematics*. Cambridge, Mass.: Harvard University Press.

Zalabardo, José L. (1997) "Kripke's Normativity Argument," *Canadian Journal of Philosophy* 27:4 (December), pp. 467–488.

Chapter Six: Greg Jesson

Anscombe, G. E. M. (1965) "The Intentionality of Sensation: A Grammatical Feature", *Analytical Philosophy*: Second Series. Edited by Ronald Joseph Butler. Oxford: Basil Blackwell, pp. 158–180.

Aristotle. (1941) *De Anima (On the Soul)*. In McKeon, *The Basic Works of Aristotle*, pp. 533–603.

Burge, Tyler. (1979) "Sinning Against Frege," *Philosophical Review*, 88:3 (July), pp. 398–432.

————. (1996) "Frege on Knowing and the Third Realm." In Schirn, *Frege*, pp. 347–368.

Currie, Gregory. (1980) "Frege on Thoughts," *Mind*, 89:410 (April), pp. 234–248.

————. (1982) *Frege: An Introduction to His Philosophy*. Totowa: Barnes and Noble.

Dummett, Michael A. E. (1978) *Truth and Other Enigmas*. Cambridge, Mass.: Harvard University Press.

————. (1978a) "Frege's Philosophy." In *Truth and Other Enigmas*, pp. 87–115.

————. (1978b) "Frege's Distinction Between Sense and Reference." In *Truth and Other Enigmas*, pp. 116–144.

————. (1981) "Was Frege a Philosopher of Language?" In *The Interpretation of Frege's Philosophy*, pp. 36–55. Cambridge, Mass.: Harvard University Press.

————. (1991) *Frege and Other Philosophers*. Oxford: Clarendon Press.

Frege, Gottlob. (1967) *The Basic Laws of Arithmetic: Exposition of the System*. Translated and edited by Montgomery Furth. Berkeley: University of California Press.

————. (1979) *Posthumous Writings*. Edited by Hans Hermes, Friedrich Kambartel, and Friedrich Kaulbach. Translated by Peter Long and Roger White. Chicago: The University of Chicago Press.

————. (1980) "On Sense and Meaning." In Geach and Black, *Translations from the Philosophical Writings of Gottlob Frege*, pp. 56–78.

————. (1984) *Collected Papers on Mathematics, Logic, and Philosophy*. Edited by Brian McGuinness. Oxford: Basil Blackwell.

Geach, Peter T., and Max Black, eds. (1980) *Translations from the Philosophical Writings of Gottlob Frege*. Totowa, N.J.: Rowman and Littlefield.

Haaparanta, Leila. (1994) *Mind, Meaning, and Mathematics*. Dordrecht, Holland: Kluwer.

McKeon, Richard, ed. (1941) *The Basic Works of Aristotle*. New York: Random House.

Schirn, Matthias, ed. (1996) *Frege: Importance and Legacy*. Berlin: Walter de Gruyter.

Smith, Barry. (1994) "Husserl's Theory of Meaning and Reference." In Haaparanta, *Mind, Meaning and Mathematics*, pp. 163–183.

Smith, David Woodruff, and Ronald McIntyre. (1982) *Husserl and Intentionality: A Study of Mind, Meaning, and Language*. Dordrecht, Holland: D. Reidel.

Weiner, Joan. (1990) *Frege in Perspective*. Ithaca: Cornell University Press.

Willard, Dallas. (1984) *Logic and the Objectivity of Knowledge: A Study in Husserl's Early Philosophy*. Athens: Ohio University Press.

————. (1994) "The Integrity of the Mental Act: Husserlian Reflections on a Fregian Problem." In Haaparanta, *Mind, Meaning, and Mathematics*, pp. 235–262.

Chapter Seven: Howard Robinson

Ayer, A. J. (1968) *The Origins of Pragmatism*. London: Macmillan.

Ayers, Michael R. (1991) *Locke*, vol. 1: *Epistemology*. London: Routledge.

Bradley, F. H. (1930) *Appearance and Reality*. Oxford: Clarendon Press.

Brentano, Franz. (1981) *Sensory and Noetic Consciousness*. Translated by Margaret Schättle and Linda L. McAlistair. London: Routledge and Kegan Paul.

Broad, C. D. (1923) *Scientific Thought*. London: Routledge and Kegan Paul.

Chisholm, Roderick. (1957) *Perceiving: a Philosophical Study*. Ithaca, New York: Cornell University Press.

Kaplan, David. (1978) "The Logic of Demonstratives," *Journal of Philosophical Logic*, 8:1 (January), pp. 81–98.

Locke, John. (1689) *An Essay Concerning Human Understanding: In Four Books*. London: Printed by Eliz. Holt for Thomas Bassett.

McTaggart, J. M. E. (1921/1927) *The Nature of Existence*. Cambridge, England: Cambridge University Press.

Moore, G. E. (1918–1919) "Some Judgments of Perception," *Proceedings of the Aristotelian Society*, 19, pp. 1–29.

Price, Henry Habberly. (1932) *Perception*. London: Methuen.

Robinson, Howard. (1974) "The Irrelevance of Intentionality to Perception," *Philosophical Quarterly*, 24:4 (October), pp. 300–315.

————. (1994) *Perception*. London: Routledge.

Yolton, John W. (1984) *Perceptual Acquaintance from Descartes to Reid.* Oxford: Blackwell.

Chapter 8: János Tözsér

Ayer, A. J. (1979) *Perception and Identity: Essays Presented to A. J. Ayer with His Replies to Them.* Edited by Graham Macdonald. London: Macmillan.

Berkeley, George. (1965) "Three Dialogues Between Hylas and Philonus in Opposition to Sceptics and Atheists," *Berkeley's Philosophical Writings.* Edited by David Malet Armstrong. New York: Collier Books, pp. 129–226.

Bermudez, José. (1998) *The Paradox of Self-Consciousness.* Cambridge, Mass.: MIT Press.

Block, Ned. (1994a) "Inverted Earth." In Block et al., *Nature of Consciousness*, pp. 677–695.

Block, Ned, Owen Flanagan, and Güven Güzeldere, eds. (1994) *Nature of Consciousness.* Cambridge, Mass.: MIT Press

Cassam, Quassim, ed. (1994) *Self-Knowledge.* Oxford: Oxford University Press

Chisholm, Roderick. (1994) "On the Observability of the Self." In Cassam, *Self-Knowledge*, pp. 94–109.

Crane, Tim. (1992) "The Nonconceptual Content of Perception." In *The Contents of Perception*, pp. 136–157. Cambridge, England: Cambridge University Press.

———. (2001) *Elements of Mind.* Oxford: Oxford University Press.

Evans, Gareth. (1982) *The Varieties of Reference.* Oxford: Clarendon Press.

Farkas, Katalin. (2003) "What is Externalism?" *Philosophical Studies*, 113:2 (February), pp. 187–208.

Guttenplan, Samuel, ed. (1995) *A Companion to the Philosophy of Mind.* Oxford: Blackwell.

Harman, Gilbert. (1994) "The Intrinsic Quality of Experience." In Block et al., pp. 663–677. *Nature of Consciousness.*

Hume, David. (1975) *Enquiries Concerning Human Understanding,* and *Concerning the Principles of Morals.* Oxford: Clarendon Press.

Lycan, William G. (1996) *Consciousness and Experience.* Cambridge, Mass.: MIT Press.

Martin, Michael. (1995) "Perceptual Content." In Guttenplan, *A Companion to the Philosophy of Mind*, pp. 463–471.

McDowell, John. (1982) "Criteria, Defeasibility, and Knowledge," *Proceedings of the British Academy*, 68, pp. 455–479.

McGinn, Colin. (1989) *Mental Content.* Oxford: Blackwell.

Paul, George A. (1936) "Is There a Problem About Sense Data?" *Proceedings of the Aristotelian Society*, suppl. vol. 15, pp. 61–77.

Peacocke, Christopher. (1992) *A Study of Concepts.* Cambridge, Mass.: MIT Press.

———. (1994) "Sensation and the Content of Experience: A Distinction." In Block et al., *Nature of Consciousness*, pp. 341–355.

Price, Henry Habberly. (1932) *Perception.* London: Methuen.

Robinson, Howard. (1994) *Perception.* London: Routledge.

Searle, John. (1983) *Intentionality.* Cambridge: Cambridge University Press.

Shoemaker, Sydney. (1994) "The Inverted Spectrum." In Block et al., *Nature of Consciousness*, pp. 643–663.

Strawson, P. F. (1979) "Perception and Its Objects." In Ayer, *Perception and Identity*, pp. 41–60.

Tye, Michael. (1992) "Visual Qualia and Visual Content." In *Contents of Perception*, pp. 158–177. Cambridge: Cambridge University Press.

———. (1995) *Ten Problems of Consciousness*. Cambridge, Mass.: MIT Press.

Chapter 9: Shannon Vallor

Cobb-Stevens, Richard. (1990) *Husserl and Analytic Philosophy*. Dordrecht, Holland: Kluwer Academic Publishers.

Devitt, Michael, and Kim Sterelny. (1999) *Language and Reality: An Introduction to the Philosophy of Language*, 2nd ed. Cambridge, Massachusetts: MIT Press.

Frege, Gottlob. (1967) "Letter to Russell," (1902). In van Heijenoort, *From Frege to Gödel*, pp. 126–128.

———. (1984) "Review of E. G. Husserl's *Philosophie der Arithmetik I*," (1894). In *Collected Papers on Mathematics, Logic, and Philosophy*. Edited by Brian McGuinness, translated by Hans Kaal, pp. 195–209. Oxford: Basil Blackwell.

———. (1993) "On Sense and Reference." In Moore, *Meaning and Reference*, pp. 23–42. (Orig. Frege. (1892). "*Über Sinn und Bedeutung*," *Zeitschrift für Philosophie und Philosophische Kritik*, 100, pp. 25–50.)

Husserl, Edmund. (1970) *Philosophie der Arithmetik: Mit ergänzenden Texten (1890–1901)*. Edited by Lothar Eley. Hague: Nijhoff.

———. (1978) *Formal and Transcendental Logic*. Translated by Dorion Cairns. The Hague: Martinus Nijhoff.

———. (1982) *Ideas Pertaining to a Pure Phenomenology and to a Phenomenological Philosophy* (First Book). Translated by Fred Kersten. Dordrecht, Holland: Kluwer Academic Publishers.

———. (1994) "Review of Ernst Schröder's *Vorlesungen über die Algebra der Logik*." In *Early Writings in the Philosophy of Logic and Mathematics*. Edited and translated by Dallas Willard. Dordrecht, Holland: Kluwer Academic Publishers.

Kripke, Saul. (1980) *Naming and Necessity*. Cambridge, Massachusetts: Harvard University Press.

Moore, A. W., ed. (1993) *Meaning and Reference*. Oxford: Oxford University Press.

Ortiz-Hill, Claire. (1991) *Word and Object in Husserl, Frege, and Russell: The Roots of Twentieth Century Philosophy*. Athens, Ohio: Ohio University Press.

Quine, W. V. O. (1961) "Reference and Modality," *From a Logical Point of View: Logico-Philosophical Essays*. 2nd revised ed. New York: Harper & Row, pp. 139–159.

Russell, Bertrand. (1993) "Descriptions." In Moore, *Meaning and Reference*, pp. 46–55.

Salmon, Nathan. (1986) *Frege's Puzzle*. Cambridge, Massachusetts: MIT Press.

Searle, John. (1983) *Intentionality*. Cambridge, England: Cambridge University Press.

Vallor, Shannon. (2002) "Frege's Puzzle: A Phenomenological Solution," *Philosophy Today*, 46:5 (SPEP suppl.), pp. 178–185.

van Heijenoort, Jean, ed. (1967) *From Frege to Gödel: A Source Book in Mathematical Logic, 1879–1931.* Cambridge, Massachusetts: Harvard University Press.

Chapter 10: Alberto Voltolini

Almog, Joseph, John Perry, and Howard K. Wettstein, eds. (1989) *Themes from Kaplan.* Oxford: Oxford University Press.

Chisholm, Roderick. (1957) *Perceiving: A Philosophical Study.* Ithaca, N.Y.: Cornell University Press.

———. (1967a) "Intentionality." In Edwards, *Encyclopedia of Philosophy,* pp. 201–204.

———. (1972) "Sentences about Believing." In Marras, *Intentionality, Mind, and Language,* pp. 31–51.

Cornman, James W. (1972) "Intentionality and Intensionality." In Marras, *Intentionality, Mind, and Language,* pp. 52–65.

Crane, Tim. (1995) *The Mechanical Mind: A Philosophical Introduction to Minds, Machines, and Mental Representation.* London: Penguin.

———. (2001a) *Elements of Mind.* Oxford: Oxford University Press.

———. (2001b) "Intentional Objects," *Ratio,* 14:4 (December), pp. 336–349.

Crimmins, Mark. (1998) "Hesperus and Phosphorus: Sense, Pretense, and Reference," *The Philosophical Review,* 107:1 (January), pp. 1–47.

Edwards, Paul, ed. (1967) *Encyclopedia of Philosophy.* New York: Macmillan.

Evans, Gareth. (1982) *The Varieties of Reference.* Oxford: Clarendon Press.

Frege, Gottlob. (1952) *"Über Sinn und Bedeutung."* In Geach and Black, *Translations from the Philosophical Writings of Gottlob Frege,* pp. 56–78.

Geach, Peter T., and Max Black, eds. (1952) *Translations from the Philosophical Writings of Gottlob Frege.* Oxford: Blackwell.

Hintikka, Kaarlo, Julius M. E. Moravcsik, and Patrick Suppes, eds. (1973) *Approaches to Natural Language.* Dordrecht, Holland: Reidel,

Kaplan, David. (1973) "Bob and Carol and Ted and Alice." In Hintikka et al., *Approaches to Natural Language,* pp. 490–518.

———. (1989) "Afterthoughts." In Almog et al., *Themes from Kaplan,* pp. 565–614.

Kenny, Anthony. (1963) *Action, Emotion, and Will.* London: Routledge and Kegan Paul.

Kneale, William. (1968) "Intentionality and Intensionality," *Proceedings of the Aristotelian Society,* suppl. vol. 42, pp. 73–90.

Linsky, Leonard, ed. (1971) *Reference and Modality.* Oxford: Oxford University Press.

Marras, Ausonio. (1972) "Intentionality and Cognitive Sentences." In *Intentionality, Mind, and Language,* pp. 66–74.

Marras, Ausonio, ed. (1972) *Intentionality, Mind, and Language.* Urbana, Ill.: University of Illinois Press.

Martin, C. B., and K. Pfeifer. (1986) "Intentionality and the Non-Psychological," *Philosophy and Phenomenological Research,* 46, 531–554.

Place, Ullin T. (1996), "Intentionality as the Mark of the Dispositional," *Dialectica,* 50:2, pp. 91–120.

Quine, W. V. O. (1971a) "Reference and Modality." In Linsky, *Reference and Modality,* pp. 17–34.

————. (1971b) "Quantifiers and Propositional Attitudes." In Linsky, *Reference and Modality*, pp. 101–111.

Salmon, Nathan. (1982) *Reference and Essence*. Oxford: Blackwell.

Smith, David Woodruff, and Ronald McIntyre. (1982) *Husserl and Intentionality*. Dordrecht, Holland: Reidel.

Chapter Eleven: Kenneth Williford

Addis, Laird. (1989) *Natural Signs: A Theory of Intentionality*. Philadelphia, Pa.: Temple University Press.

Arvidson, P. Sven. (2000) "Transformations in Consciousness: Continuity, the Self, and Marginal Consciousness," *Journal of Consciousness Studies*, 7:3 (March), pp. 3–26.

Barwise, Jon, and Lawrence Moss. (1996) *Vicious Circles*. Stanford, Calif.: CSLI Publications.

Brentano, Franz. (1995) *Psychology from an Empirical Standpoint*. Translated by Antos C. Rancurello, D. B. Terrell, and Linda L. McAlister. London: Routledge.

Carruthers, Peter. (2000) *Phenomenal Consciousness: A Naturalistic Theory*. Cambridge, England: Cambridge University Press.

Caston, Victor. (2002) "Aristotle on Consciousness," *Mind*, 111:4 (October), pp. 751–815.

Chalmers, David, ed. (2002) *Philosophy of Mind: Classical and Contemporary Readings*. Oxford: Oxford University Press.

Clark, Austen. (1993) *Sensory Qualities*. Oxford: Oxford University Press.

Dainton, Barry. (2000) *Stream of Consciousness*. London: Routledge.

Damasio, Antonio R. (1999) *The Feeling of What Happens*. New York: Harcourt Brace.

Davies, Martin, and Glyn W. Humphreys, eds. (1993) *Consciousness: Psychological and Philosophical Essays*. Oxford: Blackwell.

Dretske, Fred. (1995) *Naturalizing the Mind*. Cambridge, Mass.: MIT Press.

Edelman, Gerald M., and Giulio Tononi. (2000) *A Universe of Consciousness*. New York: Basic Books.

Evans, Cedric Oliver. (1970) *The Subject of Consciousness*. London: Allen & Unwin.

Gennaro, Rocco J. (1996) *Consciousness and Self-Consciousness*. Amsterdam: John Benjamins.

Goldman, Alvin. (1970) *A Theory of Action*. Princeton, N.J.: Princeton University Press.

Grinbaum, Alexei. (2001) *Sur la Nécessité de la Théorie Quantique pour l'Étude de la Conscience*. DEA Thesis. Paris: CREA, Ecole Polytechnique.

Gurwitsch, Aron. (1964) *The Field of Consciousness*. Pittsburgh: Duquesne University Press.

————. (1985) *Marginal Consciousness*. Athens, Ohio: Ohio University Press.

Hofstadter, Douglas R. (1979) *Gödel, Escher, Bach*. New York: Basic Books.

Horgan, Terence, and John Tienson. (2002) "The Intentionality of Phenomenology and the Phenomenology of Intentionality." In Chalmers, *Philosophy of Mind*, pp. 520–533.

Hossack, Keith. (2002) "Self-Knowledge and Consciousness," *Proceedings of the Aristotelian Society*, 102:2 (January), pp. 163–181.

Husserl, Edmund. (1991) *On the Phenomenology of the Consciousness of Internal Time (1893–1917)*. Translated by John Barnett Brough. Dordrecht, Holland: Kluwer Academic Publishers.

Kapitan, Tomis. (1999) "The Ubiquity of Self-Awareness," *Grazer Philosophische Studien*, 57, pp. 17–43.

Kauffman, Louis H. (1987) "Self-Reference and Recursive Forms," *Journal of Social and Biological Structures*, 10:1 (January), pp. 53–72.

Khromov, Andrei G. (2001) "Logical Self-Reference as a Model for Conscious Experience," *Journal of Mathematical Psychology*, 45:5 (October), pp. 720–731.

Kriegel, Uriah. (2003) "Consciousness as Intransitive Self-Consciousness: Two Views and an Argument," *Canadian Journal of Philosophy*, 33:1 (March), pp. 103–132.

Levine, Joseph. (1983) "Materialism and Qualia: The Explanatory Gap," *Pacific Philosophical Quarterly*, 64:4 (October), pp. 354–361.

———. (1993) "On Leaving Out What It's Like." In Davies and Humphreys, *Consciousness*, pp. 121–136.

———. (2001) *Purple Haze: The Puzzle of Consciousness*. Oxford: Oxford University Press.

Lycan, William G. (1996) *Consciousness and Experience*. Cambridge, Mass.: MIT Press.

McGinn, Colin. (1989) *Mental Content*. Oxford: Blackwell.

———. (1991) *The Problem of Consciousness*. Oxford: Blackwell.

Petitot, Jean, Francisco J. Varela, Bernard Pachoud, and Jean-Michel Roy, eds. (1999) *Naturalizing Phenomenology*. Stanford: Stanford University Press.

Rosenthal, David M. (1990) *A Theory of Consciousness*, Technical Report. Bielefeld, Germany: ZiF.

Sartre, Jean-Paul. (1956) *Being and Nothingness*. Translated by Hazel E. Barnes. New York: Philosophical Library.

———. (1957) *The Transcendence of the Ego*. Translated by Forrest Williams and Robert Kirkpatrick. New York: Hill & Wang.

Searle, John. (1992) *The Rediscovery of the Mind*. Cambridge, Mass.: MIT Press.

Smith, David Woodruff. (1989) *The Circle of Acquaintance*. Dordrecht, Holland: Kluwer Academic Publishers.

Smorynski, Craig. (1985) *Self-Reference and Modal Logic*. New York: Springer-Verlag.

Smullyan, Raymond M. (1994) *Diagonalization and Self-Reference*. Oxford: Oxford University Press.

Tye, Michael. (1995) *Ten Problems of Consciousness: A Representational Theory of the Phenomenal Mind*. Cambridge, Mass.: MIT Press

Van Gulick, Robert. (1993) "Understanding the Phenomenal Mind: Are We All just Armadillos?" In Davies and Humphreys, *Consciousness*, pp. 137–154.

Varela, Francisco J. (1975) "A Calculus for Self-Reference." *International Journal of General Systems*, 2, pp. 5–24.

———. (1979) *Principles of Biological Autonomy*. New York: North Holland.

Zahavi, Dan. (1999) *Self-Awareness and Alterity*. Evanston, Ill.: Northwestern University Press.

ABOUT THE CONTRIBUTORS

LAIRD ADDIS is Emeritus Professor of Philosophy at the University of Iowa where he was on the faculty for forty-one years. He has published books and articles in metaphysics, philosophy of mind, philosophy of the social sciences, philosophy of music, and other areas. He was a Fulbright professor at Rijksuniversiteit Groningen, and has lectured in many European countries. His books include *Natural Signs: A Theory of Intentionality* (Philadephia: Temple University Press, 1989) and *Of Mind and Music* (Ithaca, N. Y.: Cornell University Press, 1999).

PHILIP J. BARTOK teaches in the Great Books program at St. John's College, Santa Fe. His primary research interests are in phenomenology, philosophical anthropology, and the philosophy of mind. He has an article on Brentano forthcoming (2005) in *Journal of the History of Philosophy*.

WILLIAM FISH is Lecturer in Philosophy at Massey University, New Zealand. He has published papers on the philosophy of mind, perception and the philosophy of language. He is currently writing a book developing a disjunctive theory of appearances.

GÁBOR FORRAI is Professor of Philosophy at the University of Miskolc, Hungary. He has published papers on philosophy of science, philosophy of language and philosophy of mind. His recent publications include *Reference, Truth and Conceptual Schemes* (Dordrecht, Boston, London: Kluwer, 2001). He is currently completing a book on Locke's epistemology.

JUSSI HAUKIOJA is a Post-Doctoral Fellow of the Academy of Finland, working at the Department of Philosophy, University of Turku. His main interests are philosophy of language and philosophy of mind. His work has been published in journals such as *Mind, Philosophical Studies*, and the *International Journal of Philosophical Studies*.

GREG JESSON is finishing his doctorate at The University of Iowa. His dissertation is entitled The Ontology of the Epistemic Act: A Defense of Husserlian Intentionality and the Foundations of Epistemic Realism. His areas of interest are Philosophy of Mind, Metaphysics, Epistemology, Phenomenology, and Formal Ontology.

HOWARD ROBINSON is Professor of Philosophy at the Central European University, Budapest. He is author of *Matter and Sense* (Cambridge, England: Cambridge University Press, 1982), and *Perception* (London: Routledge, 1994), and editor of *Objections to Physicalism* (Oxford: Clarendon, 1993). He is author of a variety of articles on the philosophy of mind and on idealism. These topics, together with general metaphysics, are his principle interests.

JÁNOS TŐZSÉR is Research Fellow at the Hungarian Academy of Sciences – Office of Supported Research (TKI). He is currently finishing his PhD thesis at Eötvös Loránd University, Budapest. He is mainly interested in the philosophy of Wittgenstein, the metaphysics of mind and perception. His publications include "Four Arguments against Physicalism," "Is There an Explanatory Gap?", and "The Disjunctive Theory of Perception."

SHANNON VALLOR is Lecturer at Santa Clara University in California. She has received her doctorate in philosophy at Boston College. Her primary philosophical interests are in the contributions of phenomenology to traditional problems in the philosophy of mind, language, and cognitive science. Published articles include "How We Think About Things: Husserl, Putnam and the Metaphysics of Reference," and "Frege's Puzzle: A Phenomenological Solution?". She is currently working on phenomenological and enactive approaches to the problem of veridical perception.

ALBERTO VOLTOLINI is Associate Professor in Philosophy of Language at University of Eastern Piedmont at Vercelli, Italy. Beyond various articles in international reviews of philosophy (*Dialectica, Erkenntnis, European Journal of Philosophy, Topoi*), his recent publications include a book on the later Wittgenstein (*Guida alla lettura delle Ricerche Filosofiche di L. Wittgenstein*, Laterza, Roma-Bari 1998) and an edited volume on fictional entities (*Do Ficta Follow Fiction? Dialectica*, 57 (2003)). Current research interests include various topics in philosophy of language (theories of reference, analysis of belief and fictional contexts), philosophy of mind (intentionality, the ontology of the mind, mental causation), as well as Wittgenstein's philosophy.

KENNETH WILLIFORD completed his PhD at The University of Iowa in 2003. He is currently Assistant Professor of Philosophy at St. Cloud State University in St. Cloud, Minnesota. His interests include the history of philosophy, phenomenology, mathematical logic, metaphysics, and the philosophy of mind. He is current research focus is on consciousness and reflexivity. He is editing a collection of essays with Uriah Kriegel, *Self-Representational Approaches to Consciousness*, forthcoming with MIT Press.

INDEX

VIBS

The **Value Inquiry Book Series** is co-sponsored by:

Titles Published

1. Noel Balzer, *The Human Being as a Logical Thinker*

2. Archie J. Bahm, *Axiology: The Science of Values*

3. H. P. P. (Hennie) Lötter, *Justice for an Unjust Society*

4. H. G. Callaway, *Context for Meaning and Analysis: A Critical Study in the Philosophy of Language*

5. Benjamin S. Llamzon, *A Humane Case for Moral Intuition*

6. James R. Watson, *Between Auschwitz and Tradition: Postmodern Reflections on the Task of Thinking*. A volume in **Holocaust and Genocide Studies**

7. Robert S. Hartman, *Freedom to Live: The Robert Hartman Story*, Edited by Arthur R. Ellis. A volume in **Hartman Institute Axiology Studies**

8. Archie J. Bahm, *Ethics: The Science of Oughtness*

9. George David Miller, *An Idiosyncratic Ethics; Or, the Lauramachean Ethics*

10. Joseph P. DeMarco, *A Coherence Theory in Ethics*

11. Frank G. Forrest, *Valuemetrics^N: The Science of Personal and Professional Ethics*. A volume in **Hartman Institute Axiology Studies**

12. William Gerber, *The Meaning of Life: Insights of the World's Great Thinkers*

13. Richard T. Hull, Editor, *A Quarter Century of Value Inquiry: Presidential Addresses of the American Society for Value Inquiry*. A volume in **Histories and Addresses of Philosophical Societies**

14. William Gerber, *Nuggets of Wisdom from Great Jewish Thinkers: From Biblical Times to the Present*

74. Malcolm D. Evans, *Whitehead and Philosophy of Education: The Seamless Coat of Learning*. A volume in **Philosophy of Education**

75. Warren E. Steinkraus, *Taking Religious Claims Seriously: A Philosophy of Religion*, Edited by Michael H. Mitias. A volume in **Universal Justice**

76. Thomas Magnell, Editor, *Values and Education*

77. Kenneth A. Bryson, *Persons and Immortality*. A volume in **Natural Law Studies**

78. Steven V. Hicks, *International Law and the Possibility of a Just World Order: An Essay on Hegel's Universalism*. A volume in **Universal Justice**

79. E. F. Kaelin, *Texts on Texts and Textuality: A Phenomenology of Literary Art*, Edited by Ellen J. Burns

80. Amihud Gilead, *Saving Possibilities: A Study in Philosophical Psychology*. A volume in Philosophy and Psychology

81. André Mineau, *The Making of the Holocaust: Ideology and Ethics in the Systems Perspective*. A volume in **Holocaust and Genocide Studies**

82. Howard P. Kainz, *Politically Incorrect Dialogues: Topics Not Discussed in Polite Circles*

83. Veikko Launis, Juhani Pietarinen, and Juha Räikkä, Editors, *Genes and Morality: New Essays*. A volume in **Nordic Value Studies**

84. Steven Schroeder, *The Metaphysics of Cooperation: A Study of F. D. Maurice*

85. Caroline Joan ("Kay") S. Picart, *Thomas Mann and Friedrich Nietzsche: Eroticism, Death, Music, and Laughter*. A volume in **Central-European Value Studies**

86. G. John M. Abbarno, Editor, *The Ethics of Homelessness: Philosophical Perspectives*

87. James Giles, Editor, *French Existentialism: Consciousness, Ethics, and Relations with Others*. A volume in **Nordic Value Studies**

88. Deane Curtin and Robert Litke, Editors, *Institutional Violence*. A volume in **Philosophy of Peace**

103. Paul van Dijk, *Anthropology in the Age of Technology: The Philosophical Contribution of Günther Anders*

104. Giambattista Vico, *Universal Right*. Translated from Latin and edited by Giorgio Pinton and Margaret Diehl. A volume in **Values in Italian Philosophy**

105. Judith Presler and Sally J. Scholz, Editors, *Peacemaking: Lessons from the Past, Visions for the Future*. A volume in **Philosophy of Peace**

106. Dennis Bonnette, *Origin of the Human Species*. A volume in **Studies in the History of Western Philosophy**

107. Phyllis Chiasson, *Peirce's Pragmatism: The Design for Thinking*. A volume in **Studies in Pragmatism and Values**

108. Dan Stone, Editor, *Theoretical Interpretations of the Hol*ocaust. A volume in **Holocaust and Genocide Studies**

109. Raymond Angelo Belliotti, *What Is the Meaning of Human Life?*

110. Lennart Nordenfelt, *Health, Science, and Ordinary Language*, with Contributions by George Khushf and K. W. M. Fulford

111. Daryl Koehn, *Local Insights, Global Ethics for Business*. A volume in **Studies in Applied Ethics**

112. Matti Häyry and Tuija Takala, Editors, *The Future of Value Inquiry*. A volume in **Nordic Value Studies**

113. Conrad P. Pritscher, *Quantum Learning: Beyond Duality*

114. Thomas M. Dicken and Rem B. Edwards, *Dialogues on Values and Centers of Value: Old Friends, New Thoughts*. A volume in **Hartman Institute Axiology Studies**

115. Rem B. Edwards, *What Caused the Big Bang?* A volume in **Philosophy and Religion**

116. Jon Mills, Editor, *A Pedagogy of Becoming*. A volume in **Philosophy of Education**

117. Robert T. Radford, *Cicero: A Study in the Origins of Republican Philosophy*. A volume in **Studies in the History of Western Philosophy**

118. Arleen L. F. Salles and María Julia Bertomeu, Editors, *Bioethics: Latin American Perspectives*. A volume in **Philosophy in Latin America**

119. Nicola Abbagnano, *The Human Project: The Year 2000*, with an Interview by Guiseppe Grieco. Translated from Italian by Bruno Martini and Nino Langiulli. Edited with an introduction by Nino Langiulli. A volume in **Studies in the History of Western Philosophy**

120. Daniel M. Haybron, Editor, *Earth's Abominations: Philosophical Studies of Evil*. A volume in **Personalist Studies**

121. Anna T. Challenger, *Philosophy and Art in Gurdjieff's* Beelzebub: *A Modern Sufi Odyssey*

122. George David Miller, *Peace, Value, and Wisdom: The Educational Philosophy of Daisaku Ikeda*. A volume in **Daisaku Ikeda Studies**

123. Haim Gordon and Rivca Gordon, *Sophistry and Twentieth-Century Art*

124. Thomas O. Buford and Harold H. Oliver, Editors *Personalism Revisited: Its Proponents and Critics*. A volume in **Histories and Addresses of Philosophical Societies**

125. Avi Sagi, *Albert Camus and the Philosophy of the Absurd*. Translated from Hebrew by Batya Stein

126. Robert S. Hartman, *The Knowledge of Good: Critique of Axiological Reason*. Expanded translation from the Spanish by Robert S. Hartman. Edited by Arthur R. Ellis and Rem B. Edwards.A volume in **Hartman Institute Axiology Studies**

127. Alison Bailey and Paula J. Smithka, Editors. *Community, Diversity, and Difference: Implications for Peace*. A volume in **Philosophy of Peace**

128. Oscar Vilarroya, *The Dissolution of Mind: A Fable of How Experience Gives Rise to Cognition*. A volume in **Cognitive Science**

129. Paul Custodio Bube and Jeffery Geller, Editors, *Conversations with Pragmatism: A Multi-Disciplinary Study*. A volume in **Studies in Pragmatism and Values**

130.   Richard Rumana, *Richard Rorty: An Annotated Bibliography of Secondary Literature*. A volume in **Studies in Pragmatism and Values**

131.   Stephen Schneck, Editor, *Max Scheler's Acting Persons: New Perspectives* A volume in **Personalist Studies**

132.   Michael Kazanjian, *Learning Values Lifelong: From Inert Ideas to Wholes*. A volume in **Philosophy of Education**

133.   Rudolph Alexander Kofi Cain, Alain Leroy Locke: *Race, Culture, and the Education of African American Adults*. A volume in **African American Philosophy**

134.   Werner Krieglstein, *Compassion: A New Philosophy of the Other*

135.   Robert N. Fisher, Daniel T. Primozic, Peter A. Day, and Joel A. Thompson, Editors, *Suffering, Death, and Identity*. A volume in **Personalist Studies**

136.   Steven Schroeder, *Touching Philosophy, Sounding Religion, Placing Education*. A volume in **Philosophy of Education**

137.   Guy DeBrock, *Process Pragmatism: Essays on a Quiet Philosophical Revolution*. A volume in **Studies in Pragmatism and Values**

138.   Lennart Nordenfelt and Per-Erik Liss, Editors, *Dimensions of Health and Health Promotion*

139.   Amihud Gilead, *Singularity and Other Possibilities: Panenmentalist Novelties*

140.   Samantha Mei-che Pang, *Nursing Ethics in Modern China: Conflicting Values and Competing Role Requirements*. A volume in **Studies in Applied Ethics**

141.   Christine M. Koggel, Allannah Furlong, and Charles Levin, Editors, *Confidential Relationships: Psychoanalytic, Ethical, and Legal Contexts*. A volume in **Philosophy and Psychology**

142.   Peter A. Redpath, Editor, *A Thomistic Tapestry: Essays in Memory of Étienne Gilson*. A volume in **Gilson Studies**

157.   Javier Muguerza, *Ethics and Perplexity: Toward a Critique of Dialogical Reason*. Translated from the Spanish by Jody L. Doran. Edited by John R. Welch. A volume in **Philosophy in Spain**

158.   Gregory F. Mellema, *The Expectations of Morality*

159.   Robert Ginsberg, *The Aesthetics of Ruins*

160.   Stan van Hooft, *Life, Death, and Subjectivity: Moral Sources in Bioethics* A volume in **Values in Bioethics**

161.   André Mineau, *Operation Barbarossa: Ideology and Ethics Against Human Dignity*

162.   Arthur Efron, *Expriencing Tess of the D'Urbervilles: A Deweyan Account.* A volume in **Studies in Pragmatism and Values**

163.   Reyes Mate, *Memory of the West: The Contemporaneity of Forgotten Jewish Thinkers*. Translated from the Spanish by Anne Day Dewey. Edited by John R. Welch. A volume in **Philosophy in Spain**

164.   Nancy Nyquist Potter, Editor, *Putting Peace into Practice: Evaluating Policy on Local and Global Levels*. A volume in **Philosophy of Peace**

165.   Matti Häyry, Tuija Takala, and Peter Herissone-Kelly, Editors, *Bioethics and Social Reality*. A volume in **Values in Bioethics**

166.   Maureen Sie, *Justifying Blame: Why Free Will Matters and Why it Does Not*. A volume in **Studies in Applied Ethics**

167.   Leszek Koczanowicz and Beth J. Singer, Editors, *Democracy and the Post-Totalitarian Experience*. A volume in **Studies in Pragmatism and Values**

168.   Michael W. Riley, *Plato's Cratylus: Argument, Form, and Structure*. A volume in **Studies in the History of Western Philosophy**

169.   Leon Pomeroy, *The New Science of Axiological Psychology*. Edited by Rem B. Edwards. A volume in **Hartman Institute Axiology Studies**

170.   Eric Wolf Fried, *Inwardness and Morality*